KHRUSHCHEV AND KHRUSHCHEVISM

KHRUSHCHEV AND KHRUSHCHEVISM

Edited by

Martin McCauley

INDIANA UNIVERSITY PRESS
Bloomington and Indianapolis

Manufactured in Great Britain

Library of Congress Cataloging-in-Publication Data

Khrushchev and Khrushchevism.
  Bibliography: p.
  Includes index.
  Contents: Khrushchev as leader/Martin McCauley—
Khrushchev and systemic development/Graeme Gill—
State and ideology/Ronald J. Hill — [etc.]
1. Soviet Union—Politics and government—1953–
2. Khrushchev, Nikita Sergeevich, 1894–1971.
I. McCauley, Martin.
DK274.3.K47 1987   947.085′2   86–33896
ISBN 0–253–33142–0
ISBN 0–253–20438–0 (pbk.)
1 2 3 4 5 91 90 89 88 87

Contents

Contents

List of Tables

Preface

Most of the papers in this volume were originally read at a conference on 21 and 22 March 1985. Some of the themes aired at the conference had already been discussed in a series of seminars which ran from January to early March 1985. These seminars threw up many points and led to more papers being commissioned in order to attempt a fuller appraisal of the many-faceted aspects of the Khrushchev era.

Cordial thanks are extended to the School of Slavonic and East European Studies, especially to its Director, Professor M. A. Branch, and Philip Robinson, for all their help and encouragement.

Warm thanks are also due to the Ford Foundation and the Nuffield Foundation, without whose generous financial aid the conference could not have taken place.

MARTIN McCAULEY

Notes on the Contributors

M. J. Berry is Lecturer in Russian for Social Scientists at the Centre for Russian and East European Studies, University of Birmingham. He has contributed to studies of *Science Policy in the USSR*, the *Technological Level of Soviet Industry* and *Innovation in Soviet Industry*.

Christoph Bluth is a postgraduate student in the Department of War Studies, King's College, London.

D. Filtzer is Honorary Research Fellow at the Centre for Russian and East European Studies, University of Birmingham, and is the author of a major study of Soviet labour during the first three Five-Year Plans 1928–41.

Graeme Gill is a Senior Lecturer in the Department of Government, University of Sydney. He is the author of *Peasants and Government in the Russian Revolution* and *The Rules of the Communist Party of the Soviet Union*, and many articles on Soviet politics.

Harry Hanak is Reader in International Relations at the School of Slavonic and East European Studies, University of London. He is the author of several books and many articles on Soviet foreign policy.

Ronald J. Hill is Professor of Political Science, Trinity College, Dublin. He is the author of many books, of which the most recent is the *Soviet Union: Politics, Economics, Society*.

Alastair McAuley is Senior Lecturer in Economics, University of Essex. He is the author of several books and many articles on Soviet economic and social affairs.

Martin McCauley is Senior Lecturer in Soviet and East European Studies, School of Slavonic and East European Studies, University of London. He is the author of many books, of which the most recent is *The German Democratic Republic since 1945*.

Notes on the Contributors

Alec Nove is Emeritus Professor of Economics, University of Glasgow. He has published many books and articles on Soviet economics, life and society.

Sir Frank Roberts is a British diplomat who retired in 1968. He was a member of the Strang Mission to the Soviet Union in 1939 and accompanied Anthony Eden to Moscow in 1941. He was British Minister (and frequently Chargé d'Affaires) in Moscow 1945–7, after attending the Yalta Conference. He was British Ambassador to Moscow between 1960 and the end of 1962.

Michael Shafir is Lecturer in Political Science at the University of Tel Aviv. He is the author of *Romania: Politics, Economics and Society*; *Political Stagnation and Simulated Change*; and of numerous articles on communist affairs.

G. A. E. Smith is Senior Lecturer in Economics, Portsmouth Polytechnic. He has published several articles on Soviet agriculture.

Introduction

MARTIN McCAULEY

The election of Mikhail Sergeevich Gorbachev as Secretary-General of the Central Committee of the Communist Party of the Soviet Union (CPSU) in March 1985 introduced expectancy, even excitement into Soviet politics. He was in many ways reminiscent of Nikita Sergeevich Khrushchev, who became First Secretary of the CPSU in September 1953. Khrushchev took office shortly after the death of Stalin – whose power and authority had remained undiminished to the end – but many pressing problems, nevertheless, had been left unresolved. Gorbachev, in 1985, was confronted with a Soviet Union which was stagnant and which had to be galvanised into confronting the scientific and technical problems of the day. The problems facing both of them on taking office were in many ways similar: a powerful bureaucracy not enamoured of change; industry capable of producing quantity but not quality and technologically behind the West; agriculture incapable of feeding the Soviet population; a military facing an adversary re-equipping with high-technology weapons and a labour force needing to be motivated to raise the unacceptably (from the state's point of view) low level of productivity. Hence there are many lessons for Gorbachev in the Khrushchev period. Khrushchev, as a dedicated Marxist–Leninist, turned his back on the market mechanism as a way out of the economic problems facing the country. Gorbachev has done the same. Khrushchev, initially, saw the Party as the main instrument of change, yet in the end he came to the conclusion that it was a barrier to progress. Will Gorbachev come to the same conclusion?

The Khrushchev period was one of hope and despair. Great enthusiasm was engendered in the early years, but eventually despair set in as the problems of modernising the Soviet Union became intractable. Perhaps Khrushchev demanded and expected too much of the population. Certainly his belief in the creative potential of the working man and woman was dented by the time he was forced to cede the political stage to his successors. If he had a fault it was his optimism which led him into hasty reforms. They in turn required more reforms to rectify their shortcomings. If it is not clear what Gorbachev should do to revitalise Soviet life, at least the lessons of the Khrushchev period are such as to make it plain what should not be done. The fact that the bureaucracy was powerful enough to frustrate Khrushchev's reforms and in the end to contribute to his removal, is a salutary warning to Gorbachev. Since the power structure has changed very little since 1964 an analysis of the Khrushchev era can provide many valuable insights into the problems facing any leader bent on changing established practices. There was little point in studying Khrushchev during the Brezhnev era, given the latter's commitment to consensus politics which in effect meant that as little as possible changed on the domestic scene. However with a reforming leader again in the Kremlin the Khrushchev era becomes alive again.

The object of this volume is to provide an overview of the Khrushchev period for the general reader. Contributors were asked to consider the legacy of the Stalin period, then to analyse the period between 1953 and 1964 and then to assess the legacy, if any, of the Khrushchev years. Was there such a thing as Khrushchevism? No claim is made that this survey covers all aspects of the period, but the variety of policy areas surveyed will give the reader the flavour of those innovative years.

When Khrushchev became First Secretary of the CPSU the Party was not acknowledged as the leading institution in the state. Georgy Malenkov, as Prime Minister, was seen as occupying the more senior position. In order to become a strong, national leader Khrushchev's task was clear: either become Prime Minister as well or establish the primacy of the Communist Party. In the end he did both, but in so doing placed the Party at the centre of power in the Soviet state, a position it has retained ever since.

His road to the top was paved with Stalinist stones. In many ways the rise of Stalin and Khrushchev was similar and they both surprised their political opponents by emerging as the dominant leader. Both were masters of coalition politics – at least this applied to Khrushchev on the way up, when at the top he forgot the political rules he had mastered. This latter weakness revealed a positive side of the man, he did not wish to emulate his mentor in everything he did. What he found objectionable, he made public at the XX Party Congress in 1956. He wanted to break the mould of Soviet politics and to narrow the gap between the leadership and the masses. De-Stalinisation was applied fitfully. How could it be wholeheartedly applied when Khrushchev, his allies and his opponents had all emerged from the Stalinist mill? It served several purposes: it permitted him to vilify his political opponents as Stalinists and replace them with his own cadres; it allowed him to advocate radically different policies; it ushered in new initiatives in foreign policy, but entailed much risk-taking; it emptied the labour camps and gave a new meaning to socialist legality and it introduced some fresh air into the world of Soviet culture. Not surprisingly his denunciation of Stalin (this only affected Stalin's behaviour after 1934) weakened his position at home and abroad. It contributed to the upheavals in Poland and Hungary in 1956 and destroyed for ever the infallibility of Soviet leadership of the communist movement.

When he departed the scene in 1964 he was more popular abroad than at home. One of his achievements was to bring the Soviet Union on to the world stage, to reduce some of the fear it engendered and to increase respect for it. His policy of peaceful coexistence – borrowed from the Stalin period, the first Sputnik and man in space added immensely to the Soviet Union's international prestige. On the other hand he was overconfident in foreign policy and imagined he could change the 'correlation of forces' on his own. One of his most egregious mistakes was the Cuban missile crisis of 1962, but even in defeat he ensured that Cuba would never again be attacked by official or unofficial US forces.

Why did Khrushchev achieve relatively little? One explanation, advanced by Martin McCauley, is to see him as an original leader, trying fundamentally to change Soviet society. The reason why he failed, according to this view, is that the bureaucracy was powerful enough to ensure that most of his reforms were not implemented. A corollary would be that despite his modest success he was good for the Soviet Union and the world.

Graeme Gill sees a 'process of institutionalisation' taking place during the Khrushchev years. De-Stalinisation discredited the model based on a single dominant leader. As a result greater emphasis was placed on the significance of the Party as an institution. How was the Party to function? The answer was to resurrect the 'Leninist norms of Party Life'. The new Party statute of 1961 offered a new basis of internal legitimacy for the Party's operations.

In analysing state and ideology under Khrushchev Ronald Hill points out that his contribution to the development of the theory and practice of the Soviet state, including that of related institutions such as the Communist Party, has turned out to be more enduring than might have been assumed during the first decade after his removal. It surprised many when the Khrushchevian concept of the 'all-people's state' was resurrected and planted in the 1977 Brezhnev Constitution. Khrushchev tried to breathe new life into the soviets and wished to develop their representative side and in so doing to train more and more citizens in the day-to-day running of local affairs. His aim was to transfer to them some of the functions of the, from his point of view, too powerful central bureaucracy. His 'going to the people' also included opening up meetings of the soviets and indeed CC plenums and congresses to non-elected members.

In introducing the concept of the 'all-people's state' he ended the period of the dictatorship of the proletariat and in so doing rejected the Stalinist view that the class struggle intensifies as socialism develops. This also permitted him to restrict the powers of the political police and to place new emphasis on socialist legality. The new Party Programme, adopted in 1961, looked forward to the building of communism. One can even argue that the glimmerings of a civil society were visible between 1962 and 1964.

Khrushchev overcame the challenge of Malenkov with the help of the heavy industry lobby. However the First Secretary's subsequent actions suggest that his own priorities were also pro-consumer, with greater relative emphasis on agriculture, writes Alec Nove. It is impossible to disentangle political from economic motives in the setting up of the councils of the national economy (*sovnarkhozy*) and the Seven-Year Plan which ran from 1958 to 1965. Given the centralising logic of a modern industrial economy of the non-market type, Nove regards the establishment of the *sovnarkhozy* as a step in the wrong direction. Since management was not decentralised, a local authority with power over the resources of a given area will direct them towards the needs of that area, in the absence of orders from the centre to do otherwise. Experience also revealed that Party secretaries, far from bearing in mind the interests of the centre, afforded priority to local needs. Nove sees the planning system itself as one of the main reasons why Khrushchev's economic goals were not realised. Khrushchev had inherited a highly centralised system, created by Stalin, to transform, as rapidly as possible, an underdeveloped country into a great military power. It was too wasteful of resources to cope adequately with the demands of modernising agriculture, building more flats and providing more consumer goods and services. Despite the setbacks, Nove evaluates Khrushchev's record positively, giving him credit for devoting much attention to sectors neglected by Stalin.

Science and technology are of cardinal importance in a modern industrial state and the Khrushchev era saw a determined effort to reduce the perceived gap with the West. Many disciplines, such as genetics, were rehabilitated. Soviet science was exposed to developments in Western science in a way reminiscent of the years before 1929. Khrushchev's main aim, according to M. J. Berry, was to discover an efficient system of continuous innovation appropriate to a planned economy. Berry judges him to have failed in this aim and quotes Kapitsa, a leading scientist, who maintained in 1965 that the gulf in science between the USSR and the USA had 'actually increased'. The *sovnarkhoz* reform of 1957 confused the issue and technical progress suffered as a result. Despite Khrushchev's confidence that the Soviet Union could win the economic race with the capitalist West, it remained difficult for Soviet scientists to visit the West and to establish personal contacts with Western scientists. The vast sums of money which were poured into science did not produce commensurate results. It merely strengthened research and development without bridging the gulf between theoretical research and the application of these findings in industry.

G. A. E. Smith regards the First Secretary's most significant contribution to agricultural policy to be his success in convincing the Party leadership that policies had to be changed radically. It was no longer possible to extract the maximum surplus from the agrarian sector. Further development of the economy depended on raising agricultural output and productivity. Party officials, however, were not suited to these new tasks. Schooled under Stalin, they lacked the skill and sympathy necessary to play a new role. However in the final analysis it was the agricultural worker who was more important, since he was the producer. Given the fact that the post-Khrushchev leadership have had no more success in resolving the contradictions of Soviet agriculture, Khrushchev, perhaps, should not be too harshly judged. His successors have attempted to solve the agrarian crisis by investing vast sums of money in agriculture. The lesson to be drawn from the spending spree of the last thirty years is that the human

factor, the farm worker, is the key variable. Until he can be motivated to raise his abysmally low level of productivity Soviet agriculture
will remain in the doldrums.

The coercive labour legislation, one of the hallmarks of the Stalin
period, was repealed under Khrushchev. Don Filtzer comes to the
conclusion that no reform of the wage and norm setting system
can genuinely succeed under Soviet conditions. Losses of worktime,
absenteeism and poor quality work remained major problems. Filtzer
argues that the Khrushchev leadership failed to provide the population with the political and economic incentives which were
necessary to achieve the gains in labour productivity desired by the
planners.

The Khrushchev period, according to Alastair McAuley, witnessed
a crucial shift in social priorities. A concentrated effort was made to
solve some of the pressing problems which had accumulated over
the previous twenty-five years. However the First Secretary did not
deviate from the traditional Soviet view that the best way to fight
poverty was to work. No non-work-related income-supplement
programmes to alleviate poverty were introduced under Khrushchev.
(The first such programme appeared in 1974.) There is still no
adequate Soviet public assistance programme. The work ethic was
emphasised under Khrushchev and anti-parasitic laws were enacted
to combat 'idlers'. Pensions were related to prior earnings. Indeed
disability pensions, sickness benefits and maternity allowances were
also calculated on the same basis. As it emerged under Khrushchev
the new socialist welfare state was committed to the value of labour.
Those who contributed to the official economy could look forward
to state support in adversity and old age. It had much less to offer
those who were incapable, either for congenital reasons or for
reasons of their own, of contributing to the state economy. No safety
net – a minimum standard of living below which no one was allowed
to fall – was provided, and has still not been provided.

Khrushchev exerted great influence on the evolution of Eastern
Europe. Involuntarily he contributed to the upheavals in Poland and
Hungary in 1956 and without the impetus given to democratic
thought by the 'all-people's state' it is difficult to conceive of the
Prague Spring occurring. In trying to draw Tito back into the socialist
fold he underlined his conviction that a Marxist–Leninist society, as
given expression in the Soviet Union, was the most advanced society
in the world. Why should Yugoslavia not welcome Soviet help and
guidance?

What would Eastern Europe look like if Khrushchev had never acquired power? Michael Shafir thinks it would resemble Alia's Albania! Khrushchev, inadvertently, set in motion a process in which reformists learnt from one another's mistakes.

Harry Hanak regards Khrushchev's foreign policy as resting on two pillars: peaceful coexistence and the unpeaceful national liberation struggle. The USA was the key country. To get to know it and the wider world Khrushchev travelled widely and thereby became the first Soviet leader to have first-hand knowledge of many countries. He changed Soviet policy towards the Third World and courted nationalist leaders. Opportunities abounded to increase Soviet influence – in Egypt, to quote but one example. His greatest foreign policy failure must remain China where he succeeded in constantly offending the Chinese. They took umbrage when he failed to consult them on his anti-Stalin speech at the XX Party Congress. Soviet failure to support Peking against the USA and the Indians added insult to injury.

In August 1953 the Soviet Union exploded a thermonuclear device. In 1957 the first Sputnik was launched, demonstrating the capacity of the Soviet Union to develop intercontinental ballistic missiles (ICBMs). By 1959 Khrushchev claimed that nuclear parity with the USA had been achieved. In 1960 the USSR, it was asserted, had the capacity to wipe any country which had the temerity to attack it off the face of the earth. In reality, however, as Christoph Bluth points out, no such capacity existed. Khrushchev could not curb his tongue when contemplating his new missiles and the emphasis placed, in 1961, on nuclear weapons in a conflict with the West frightened many abroad. The result was that a new impetus was given to arms production in the West. Much of Khrushchev's braggadocio was counter-productive. His successors condemned his style in foreign and security policy as bombastic and adventurous. His humiliating retreats were regarded as quite unacceptable and as blows to Soviet national pride. What the new leadership did not condemn was his adversarial style, rather it was the fact that he took too many risks with the resources at his command and failed.

What was Khrushchev like as a negotiator? Sir Frank Roberts, as a former British Ambassador in Moscow, gives his impressions of the ebullient Soviet leader. He found him accessible, communicative, adversarial and a human and stimulating leader with whom to do business. Khrushchev was likeable, folksy and capable of great charm. He has left an indelible mark on the Soviet Union and the world.

1 Khrushchev as Leader

MARTIN McCAULEY

INTRODUCTION

When Stalin died on 5 March 1953 he was head of the Soviet government and of the Communist Party of the Soviet Union (CPSU). His formal title as Prime Minister was Chairman of the USSR Council of Ministers but he was only a secretary of the Central Committee (CC) of the CPSU. Hence it was not clear how anyone could become head of the CPSU; there was no office which formally conferred on the incumbent that position. Should anyone, however, wish to emulate Stalin, it was clear that he needed to acquire the headship of government and Party. There were four main contenders: Georgy Malenkov, Lavrenty Beria, Vyacheslav Molotov and Nikita Khrushchev. The first division of power was dated 6 March 1953. Malenkov became Chairman, and Molotov and Beria First Deputy Chairmen of the USSR Council of Ministers. There were two other First Deputy Chairmen: Nikolai Bulganin and Lazar Kaganovich. After the distribution of government offices had been decided a CC plenum met on 7 March to elect a new Presidium (as the Politburo was called between 1952 and 1966) and Secretariat. Malenkov and all the Deputy Prime Ministers were confirmed as full members of the Presidium. However Malenkov's name was placed at the top of the list of CC secretaries. This made him *de facto* head of the Party. Khrushchev was one of ten full members of the Presidium and was placed last in the list of five CC secretaries. He, unlike his competitors, occupied no great office of state. Within two days, therefore, of Stalin's death, Malenkov had stepped into his two great offices, head of the government and of the Party. These two positions conferred considerable authority on Malenkov, but Stalin's formidable power did not devolve on him.

Malenkov's elevation only lasted a week. On 14 March 1953 he left the Secretariat but remained in the Presidium. His opponents had been strong enough to compel him to give up one great office and, given a choice, he preferred to stay on as Prime Minister. Khrushchev's name appeared at the head of the new Secretariat and thereby he became *de facto* Party leader. Since Khrushchev was the main beneficiary of the change it can be deemed that he was the main driving force in the struggle to force Malenkov to divest himself of a key office. It was fortunate for Khrushchev that Malenkov decided to retain the position of Prime Minister. Had Malenkov chosen to give up that position Beria would have been the obvious successor.

The second post-Stalin division of power lasted until about 26 June 1953 when Beria fell. Very few details are available to explain how first Khrushchev prised Malenkov out of the Party leadership and then broke the Malenkov–Beria partnership, but these moves reveal Khrushchev to have been a master of coalition politics.

With Beria out of commission Khrushchev could concentrate his energies on outmanoeuvring Malenkov. Since he had no government power base he was obliged to use his position in the Party to undermine the Prime Minister's position.

Khrushchev used a policy issue, agriculture, to exert pressure on Malenkov. It was at a CC plenum on agriculture, convened at Khrushchev's request, which began on 3 September 1953, that he became First Secretary of the CC, CPSU. This new post was created to designate the Party Leader and thereby Khrushchev became *de jure* head of the CPSU.

The skirmishes between the First Secretary and the Prime Minister, on the surface about policy preferences, continued until 8 February 1955 when the Prime Minister resigned. Defeated but not disgraced, he became Deputy Chairman of the USSR Council of Ministers. His successor, Khrushchev's nominee, was Marshal Nikolai Bulganin. He was thus rewarded for the loyal support he had extended to the Party leader since Stalin's death.

At the XX Party Congress, convened in February 1956, Khrushchev launched his attack on Stalin. Later he undermined the power of the government bureaucracy by instituting councils of the national economy, *sovnarkhozy*, and in so doing decentralised much of the economic decision-making. In a move, masterminded by Molotov, the government bureaucrats hit back but were defeated in June 1957. The vanquished group was labelled the Anti-Party Group to underline the fact that it had opposed the primacy of the Party in the state. Until then the government had been regarded as the leading political institution but Khrushchev's victory elevated the Party to that position, a place it has retained ever since.

With Malenkov, Beria and Molotov outmanoeuvred Khrushchev was the *de facto* head of Party and government, but chose to allow Bulganin to remain in office even though he had sided with Molotov. In March 1958 Khrushchev became *de jure* head of Party and government when he assumed the mantle of Chairman of the USSR Council of Ministers. He had emulated his mentor, Stalin, and he had needed five years to do so, exactly the same period of time Stalin had taken after his mentor's, Lenin's, death.

Khrushchev began as Party leader, then became a member of a collective leadership and finally emerged as a strong, national leader. The posts he held conferred on him authority, but the power he wielded depended on his skilful use of coalition politics and his ability to satisfy the aspirations of his followers. His heyday was the period between July 1957 and October 1962 when the Cuban Missile Crisis erupted. Despite his apparent defeat at the hands of the US President John F. Kennedy, one can argue that the Soviet leader achieved one of his objectives, that of ensuring that the US did not attack Cuba. The Caribbean island was to remain secure as an outpost of Marxism–Leninism. Despite this his power at home waned. He managed to antagonise practically every élite group in the Soviet Union and as a consequence he was removed as First Secretary of the Party and Prime Minister on 14 October 1964. His successors agreed that henceforth no single person should hold these two offices simultaneously.

FROM PARTY TO STRONG, NATIONAL LEADER

Patronage

As Harry Rigby has pointed out (Miller and Fehér, 1984: pp. 39–70) Khrushchev's rise to power mirrors in many ways that of Stalin. Both started as dark horses; their power base was the Party Secretariat;

through it they promoted their allies and demoted their opponents; by placing these nominees in key Party positions they built up support in the CC and in so doing put pressure on the majority of the Presidium which opposed them; they widened the arena of Party discussion by taking the average Party member into their confidence; and they formed temporary policy alliances with their main political opponents. There are many other similarities, but the above list will suffice to underline that the 'rules of the political game' (again Rigby's felicitious phrase) in the Soviet Union were, in many ways, similar in the 1920s and the 1950s. When a strong, national leader emerges he seeks to bend these rules to retain power. Stalin retained his power almost to his dying day, but Khrushchev was removed in a bloodless coup. Had Khrushchev wanted to be another Stalin he would have employed the same methods as Stalin to ensure that no one encroached on his power. First and foremost this would have meant employing the fearful efficiency of the political police, the KGB, against his political competitors. Since Khrushchev abjured the use of coercion in the higher echelons of Soviet politics the 'rules of the political game' changed under his leadership. In so doing it became more difficult for anyone to become stronger than all the other members of the Presidium combined. Khrushchev, in the end, became a victim of his own predilection for more civilised, political infighting, at the top.

What are the 'rules of the political game' in the Soviet Union and how did the fertile mind of Khrushchev apply them?

Patron–client relations are at the core of Soviet politics. At the heart of this is the *nomenklatura* system. This word has two meanings: it is a list of all the posts in the Party and the state which cannot be filled without the permission of the higher Party instance and it is also a list of the candidates qualified to fill these posts. Once in full-time Party work an official can only progress if his superiors regard him as a reliable apparatchik. One does not progress by merit alone, but also by ingratiating oneself with one's superiors. The higher an official rises the more assistants he needs to carry out the functions allocated to him. In rising he will take with him those who have served him well at the lower level. The more successful the official becomes the longer his *khvost* or tail will grow. Khrushchev, in the CC Secretariat, was in a key position to place his nominees in lower-level Party posts and also to infiltrate the government bureaucracy where he lacked influence.

There were five main types of official whom Khrushchev sought to bind to his chariot:

(i) those who had served successfully under him in previous assignments, especially in the Ukraine and Moscow;

(ii) those whose patron had lost ground in the leadership struggle. e.g. Beria's men after June 1953 and Malenkov's tail after February 1955;

(iii) those who had been Stalin's men until March 1953 and who had then lost out to the aspirations of Malenkov, Beria, Molotov and their tails;

(iv) those who had lost out in the factional infighting of the late Stalin era; e.g. in the Leningrad affair;

(v) bright, capable young officials promoted over the heads of their elders.

The group which did best in the immediate period after Khrushchev entered the Secretariat were, not surprisingly, those who had previously worked under him in the Ukraine (1938–49) and Moscow (1949–52). Many of these were promoted to first Party secretaryships at the *oblast* and *krai* levels and others joined the central Party apparatus in Moscow. The advantage of recruiting men and women from groups (iii) and (iv) was that they were resentful of Malenkov and Beria and therefore more likely to remain loyal to Khrushchev. Harry Rigby estimates that by the time of the XX Party Congress in February 1956 Khrushchev's Ukrainian and Moscow supporters and the others mentioned above had progressed so far as to constitute about a third of the full members of the CC (Miller and Féhér, 1984: p. 56). By the end of 1957, after consolidating his victory over the Anti-Party Group, Khrushchev's followers from the above categories made up the overwhelming majority of full CC members.

En route to enhancing his position in the CC of the CPSU Khrushchev had been able to do the same in the CC of the republican Communist Parties. He was able to select from all five groups mentioned above and, of course, the more successful he became the greater the reservoir of talent he could choose from became. Harry Rigby thinks that Khrushchev's range of patronage over the years 1953–7 extended beyond the Party apparatus to take in republican, *oblast* and *krai* government heads, top echelon police officers and officials of agricultural ministries. However the majority of senior posts in the central government apparatus were beyond his reach (Miller and Féhér, 1984: p. 57).

The Stalinist command economy had placed great economic power in the central government ministries. Since Khrushchev's main Presidium opponents had their power bases in precisely those ministries there was little the aspiring First Secretary could do to dislodge them if the economy continued to function along Stalinist lines. It occurred to him that if economic decision-making could be decentralised it would benefit him in two ways. It would undermine the political base of his opponents and since a socialist market economy was not envisaged, an organisation would be needed to control, co-ordinate, supervise and resolve the conflicts which were bound to arise. The Party was ideally suited to play this role and thereby became potentially more powerful than the government apparatus. This was aided by the fact that through the *nomenklatura* system his clients in the Party central committees at the republican and lower levels could influence the choice of government, especially soviet appointments. In this way Khrushchev's tail in the provinces grew and grew.

Harry Rigby gives examples of how Khrushchev gradually decentralised economic decision-making (Miller and Féhér, 1984: p. 57). In 1954–5 about 11 000 enterprises were transferred from central to republican control. In May 1955 many major planning and financial decisions, hitherto taken in Moscow, were devolved to republican governments. In May 1956 factories administered by twelve central government Ministres were placed under the jurisdiction of republican bodies. Then in May 1957 over a hundred Councils of the National Economy (*sovnarkhozy*) were set up, thereby eliminating most of the central economic ministries. The main exception to this move were the ministries involved in defence production.

Khrushchev's Presidium opponents could eye the revitalisation of the *oblast*, *krai* and republican Party apparatus with some interest, but this did not automatically undermine their position at the centre. Those representing top government posts had a clear majority in the Presidium and it was only in the wake of the *sovnarkhoz* reform that they acted to conserve their power. Khrushchev forced them to act since if they had not done so they would have retreated from power without a struggle.

Khrushchev chose agriculture as the main focus of his economic attack on Malenkov. There were several reasons for this. In 1953, as now, the problem of provisioning the population with good, wholesome food had not been solved. Malenkov had given a hostage to fortune at the XIX Party Congress in October 1952 by claiming that the grain problem, in the main, had been solved. Khrushchev believed that a new agricultural initiative was bound to redound to his benefit. He was also convinced that he had a profound knowledge of rural affairs and that this guaranteed success in the days ahead. Experience was to prove that his optimism was ill founded.

However it was the central Ministries of Agriculture and Procurement, and *Sovkhozes*, which would administer his initiatives in this sector and how was he to obtain enough control over the implementation of his ideas to ensure success? He had to establish a Party agency which could overrule agricultural organs. In September 1953 when he launched his agricultural programme – essentially it amounted to extensive agriculture, sow more, grow more, eat more – he was able to make a *raion* Party secretary and his assistants, centred in the Machine Tractor Stations (MTS), the key supervisors of the policy. Hitherto the *raion* agricultural department of the soviet had been the main agricultural agency overseeing farm production. The latter now became largely irrelevant and was subsequently abolished. The effect of this was to cut the agricultural agencies and Ministries off from their grassroots in the countryside. Those who benefited would be Party officials and the information flow which reached the CC Secretariat in Moscow would ensure that Khrushchev was the best-informed person on rural affairs. It also provided him with the ammunition to attack the central government bureaucracy. If the Party became the main agency for the implementation of central agricultural decisions Khrushchev would be in an ideal position to propagate his policies and undermine those of his opponents. The Party organisation in the MTS remained until 1958 when it was abolished along with the MTS. The Party's functions were then handed back to the *raion* executive committee of the soviet and thereby the central agricultural ministries had their grassroots links in the countryside restored. However by 1958 the *raion* first Party secretary had become the main person responsible for the implementation of central directives in the agricultural sphere. Hence the balance of power had slipped irreversibly in favour of the Party bureaucracy. Another reason why the Party organisation in the MTS could be abolished was that in 1958 Khrushchev became Prime Minister and thereby head of the government administration. This revealed that the driving force behind the 1953 change had been political, not administrative or economic.

Before looking at the way Khrushchev enhanced the role of the

Central Committee – it is worth tracing the evolution of political and economic decision-making over the years 1953–7.

In the late Stalin era the key centre of decision-making was Stalin's private Secretariat. The Party Politburo and Central Committee rarely met as their functions were appropriated by commissions of the Politburo. These commissions varied in size and covered the main policy areas. The Presidium of the USSR Council of Ministers had an imposing apparatus composed of various bureaux and departments. The workload of this apparatus was very great since between 1946 and 1955 Ministries were not permitted to consult directly with one another. If a problem arose it had to be resolved at the centre. Membership of the Party Politburo and the government Presidium overlapped, the only exception being Khrushchev, who held no government office. The government apparatus was much larger and more influential than the Party apparatus.

At Stalin's death the number of Deputy Prime Ministers was reduced from twelve to four and they were all made First Deputy Prime Ministers. The number of Ministries dropped from seventy to thirty-four. An immediate result of this was that the number of decrees promulgated by the central government fell from about seventy to forty daily. In April 1953 the rights of Ministries *vis-à-vis* the USSR Council of Ministers were extended.

In December 1953 Kosygin, Malyshev, Saburov and Pervukhin, all connected with industry, who had been dismissed as Deputy Prime Ministers in March 1953, were reinstated and simultaneously the number of Ministries rose.

After Malenkov's resignation, fundamental reforms were introduced which altered the Stalinist political and economic decision-making system. These reforms had three objectives: (i) to reduce overmanning in the apparatus of the USSR Council of Ministers; (ii) alter the power relationship between the ministries and the USSR Council of Ministers in favour of the former; (iii) strengthen the position of the Party departments at the central and local levels. The areas of policy where this was most noticeable were industry, transport and agriculture.

The apparatus of the government Presidium declined by about 50 per cent as a result and the number of government decrees dropped dramatically from about 14 000 in 1955 to 7000–8000 in 1956.

Economic planning and management were also reformed in 1955. Planning was divided into perspective planning (this remained the responsibility of Gosplan) and current policy. A new body, the State

Economic Commission of the USSR Council of Ministers, was established and given the task of managing the economy. A year later its powers were extended and in fact it became an economic cabinet. Whereas previously the only person from the USSR Council of Ministers had been its chairman, a First Deputy Prime Minister, it now contained all the Deputy Prime Ministers (except Malenkov) and the ministers responsible for agriculture.

Khrushchev, predictably, opposed the Commission, arguing that it duplicated much of Gosplan's work and managed the economy inefficiently. In 1957 it lost some of its functions to Gosplan.

Malenkov was quite right to choose to remain Prime Minister and to leave the Party Secretariat in March 1953 since the government apparatus was clearly stronger. What he failed to anticipate, however, was the great skill which Khrushchev was to deploy in promoting the Party apparatus.

Initially the Presidium of the USSR Council of Ministers consisted of Malenkov and the four First Deputy Prime Ministers. Nevertheless, Khrushchev, according to his memoirs, attended its meetings, presumably in a personal capacity (Khrushchev, 1971: p. 336). Tangible evidence of Khrushchev's influence is that, whereas the number of joint government and Party decrees in 1952 was four, this rose to seventeen in 1953 and thence to fifty-five in 1956, thus re-establishing the pre-1941 practice (van den Berg, 1984: p. 116).

Reducing the size of the government Presidium apparatus and devolving more power to the ministries strengthened Khrushchev's position, but had the Economic Commission flourished it would have taken over the running of the Soviet economy to the detriment of the Party apparatus.

Stacking the Central Committee and Upgrading its Role

Between March 1953 and June 1957 the Central Committee played a role reminiscent of that of the latter part of the 1920s. After Lenin's death Stalin had more supporters and clients in the CC than in the Politburo. Hence it was natural for him to favour the CC as a forum for policy discussions and as a court of appeal if a Politburo member opposed a Stalinist policy. In this way the CC could chastise Politburo members but the CC's power was more apparent than real. It declined after 1929 and during the last six years of Stalin's life it only convened in plenary session on two occasions. Membership of it appeared merely to confirm one's status in the Party and the state.

When Stalin died the centre of legitimacy was unclear. The government was clearly the leading organ of the state, but with Malenkov head of the government and the Party what was the exact relationship between the two? Malenkov's departure from the CC Secretariat allowed Khrushchev to become *de facto* Party leader. Since his position in the Presidium was much weaker than in the CC it can be assumed that he avidly propagated the view that all key decisions in the Party and the state should be confirmed by the CC in plenary session. Khrushchev could point out that the CC, according to the Party Rules, is the supreme Party body. The practice grew up that every major shift in power among the élite should be confirmed by a CC plenum. The first division of power after Stalin's death, Malenkov's leaving the Secretariat, Beria's arrest, Khrushchev's appointment as First Secretary and Malenkov's dismissal as Prime Minister, were all endorsed by a CC plenum.

Since Khrushchev had no government office the only way he could propagate officially his agricultural policies was to convene a CC plenum. Being head of the Secretariat made this a simple task. However some of his speeches on the rural sector were not carried by *Pravda* or *Izvestiya*. Khrushchev used various other tactics to publicise his views, such as forwarding memoranda to the Presidium. Khrushchev's use of the CC Plenum transformed it into a body which participated in the formation of policy. Great publicity attended its meetings and proceedings were later published, a major innovation. CC plenums took place in September 1953 to launch Khrushchev's agricultural policy, in February 1954 to instigate the Virgin Lands campaign, in June 1954 again on the Virgin Lands, but his major speech went unpublished until 1962, and in January 1955 to put across his views on livestock.

Khrushchev's cultivation of the CC and its expanding role in policy formation were to bear fruit in June 1957 when, with its help, he was able to overturn the challenge of the majority of the Presidium who had called on him to resign. Before examining the reasons for that victory it is worth considering the policies adopted by the First Secretary.

The Art of Coalition Politics

On Stalin's death several important problems faced the new ruling élite. With the cornerstone of the legitimacy of the Soviet system gone, some new source of political legitimacy had to be found. Food and consumer-goods output had to be raised since living standards were low. Social conflict had to be avoided at all costs in order to allow the political élite time to decide who was going to succeed Stalin. Malenkov made the running by espousing the New Course, which involved switching some heavy industry capacity to the production of consumer goods and the intensification of agriculture – grow more from the same area. Beria was also consumer-oriented and also favoured the promotion of non-Russians in ethnically non-Russian areas. Since he headed the civil and political police he was in a powerful position to launch a challenge against Malenkov. However he made the fatal mistake of not striking an alliance with the Soviet military. They were to play a key role in his arrest. Khrushchev's response to Malenkov's New Course was to stress the continued significance of heavy industry and to claim that an extensive agricultural policy was the sure route to success. The latter, he explained, would repay its modest outlay in 'two to three years', one of his favourite expressions.

Besides competing with Malenkov on the domestic front Khrushchev was also active in foreign affairs, the domain of Molotov. In September 1954 he set off at the head of a delegation to Peking to visit Mao and made many concessions in the name of the Soviet state. In May 1955 he and other top leaders went to Belgrade to try and heal the breach with Yugoslavia. Molotov, the Foreign Minister, was not a member of either delegation. Khrushchev went as head of the CPSU. Since China and Yugoslavia could be classified as socialist states, relations with them were principally Party-Party relations. Again the Party apparatus took precedence over the government apparatus.

Khrushchev's attack on Stalin at the XX Party Congress in early 1956 contributed to the upheavals in Poland and Hungary later that year and put the First Secretary under considerable pressure. Fortunately for him his agricultural initiatives had been rewarded with a record harvest in 1956 in the Virgin Lands. Industrial performance, on the other hand, left much to be desired. A compromise was reached at the December 1956 CC Plenum with the central industrial ministries being strengthened while some administrative responsibilities were passed down to the regional level (Miller and Féhér, 1984: p. 63). The compromise on industrial affairs was shattered a short time afterwards at the February 1957 CC Plenum. Khrushchev called for and got a commitment to abolish most of the central ministries in favour of *sovnarkhozy*. He explained that such a reform was necessary to move the 'centre of gravity' of public administration 'nearer production'. This was the only way to counter the functional bias inherent in the ministerial system (*Pravda*, 30 Mar. 1957). The decree on the decentralisation of industry was then promulgated by the USSR Supreme Soviet in May 1957.

It is not difficult to see why the CC should have favoured the decentralisation of industry since it greatly enhanced the role of the local Party secretary. Just why the CC Plenum in December 1956 should have voted to increase the powers of the central economic ministries while reversing totally its position in February 1957 can only remain surmise, especially since the composition of the CC was almost the same. It may have been that Khrushchev, in December 1956, under pressure because of events in Poland and Hungary, conceded victory on the industrial front to his Presidium opponents. Having weathered that storm and with a record Virgin Lands harvest under his belt, he then proposed the decentralisation of industry, knowing that it would meet with CC approval but would be opposed by Malenkov, Molotov and others.

Khrushchev was quite aware of the risks he was taking since the majority of Presidium members were from the government apparatus. Beria was the only full member dropped from the Presidium since March 1953. Khrushchev had been strong enough to advance two of his supporters, Kirichenko and Suslov, to full membership. Nevertheless he was still clearly in a minority. His decision to gamble all on a full frontal attack on the government was typical of the man. Not willing to plod along, waiting for the propitious moment to arrive, like a Stalin, he risked all to win all. Outvoted in the Presidium he was able to switch the debate to the CC, where he had a clear majority. However without the help of Marshal Zhukov and the military who ferried his supporters to the Kremlin in time, he would probably have failed. In the last resort it was not the CC which had saved him, but the Secretariat.

His victory allowed him to fill the Presidium with his own nominees, but it could not guarantee him a permanent majority. It was full of his clients, as was the CC, but he overlooked the fact that a client has to receive some satisfaction for his loyalty.

The average Party official expected a reasonable tenure of office so as to enjoy the status, power and privilege associated with the job.

After 1958 Khrushchev enforced a high turn-over of the political élite and does not appear to have been concerned about a possible political backlash. Of the thirteen supporters whom he had advanced to membership of the Party Presidium by 1958, only six remained in 1961. One of those who fell by the wayside in May 1960 was A. L. Kirichenko, removed from the Party Presidium and the CC Secretariat, who had served Khrushchev faithfully since 1955. He was simply made a scapegoat for the agricultural failures of 1959. Another Presidium member who also fell because of the poor harvest was N. I. Belyaev, first secretary of the Communist Party of Kazakhstan. The First Secretary was given to discarding old supporters like old clothes. Given his insouciance of former allies it may have been an accident that in 1960 in the Party Presidium neither the CC Secretariat nor the government Presidium held a majority.

Casualties at the local level were just as high. In early 1960 two-thirds of RSFSR *krai* and *obkom* first secretaries who had acquired office in the mid-1950s had been removed. This trend continued until Khrushchev passed from the scene.

Khrushchev made tenure of office even more insecure at the XXII Party Congress in 1961 when the new Party Programme and Statutes were adopted. Article 25 of the Statutes had alarming possibilities. One-quarter of the CC and Party Presidium was to be renewed at each regular election. Presidium members could not be elected for more than three terms. This restricted Presidium membership to twelve years. However, 'outstanding' politicians were excluded from this rule. One of the 'outstanding' politicians would inevitably be the First Secretary!

One-third of the CC of the Communist Parties of the republics and of *krai* and *obkom* first secretaries had to be renewed. One half of raion and city Party bureaux had to be changed. Whereas republican Parties elected their CC every four years the other organisations elected their leaderships every two years. Hence no one could serve as first secretary of an *obkom* or of a city Party organisation for more than six years. He or she would then have to find another post at the same level. The risk of failure here was quite high. The implications of this new rule were profound, since it meant that henceforth very few Party officials could regard the apparatus as a full-time career. The majority would serve a period and then have to find employment elsewhere.

The Congress also saw a considerable turnover in the Party Presidium and CC Secretariat. Three members lost their seats in the Presidium and only Khrushchev, M. A. Suslov and F. R. Kozlov were left in the Secretariat. Four new CC secretaries were appointed however. In November another four CC secretaries made their appearance.

In late 1962 it was decided to bifurcate the Party into industrial and agricultural wings. This could only confuse and alienate Party officials further.

Whereas until 1962 important Party and government legislation was preceded by an All-Union debate afterwards it was rushed through as if Khrushchev was unwilling to listen to advice. One of the consequences of this was that the likelihood of success of policy initiatives declined even further.

Along with the growing conviction that he knew what was best for the population – not based on any fundamental sociological research – went less and less respect for the views of his colleagues. Indeed he came to see Presidium members more as executors of his will rather than as colleagues.

Khrushchev identified many of those who had held high office under Stalin as his most potent opponents and systematically removed them from positions of political power. Those who remained and those whom the First Secretary promoted to the Party Presidium were not feared or even respected as time passed. He simply did not regard them as potentially powerful political rivals. It was as if he held Stalin's men in such awe and was so fascinated by that special breed that when they were politically emasculated he could not perceive their ever again posing a threat to his power. Those whom he promoted to 'his' Party Presidium – Khrushchev's men – were simply seen as his creatures. Even when rumours about plans to remove him reached his ears in early 1964 he merely brought the matter up with Podgorny and when the latter denied it – what other response did Khrushchev expect? – he allowed the matter to lie. This astonishing carelessness revealed the neglect of the rules of the Soviet political game. How differently Stalin would have acted! Since Khrushchev did not fear his political associates he never attempted to use coercion against them. This must be a key reason for not making use of the instruments of coercion in his own interests.

Paradoxically by exercising restraint he made it less risky to oppose him and in so doing increased opposition to himself and his policies.

In 1964 most of the *krai* and *obkom* first secretaries, chairmen of *sovnarkhozy* and state committees who were members of the CC owed their appointments to him. He had power but he neglected authority. He paid too little attention to the fact that officials, if driven too far, would turn against him. Authority is derived from charisma, the sweet smell of policy success and a general belief that the leader is good for rulers and ruled alike.

One of the reasons why Khrushchev was removed so easily in October 1964 was his false sense of security. Having experienced the war at first hand he should always have been on his guard against one enemy, surprise. When summoned to the Kremlin to face his peers he was taken completely off his guard. It is understandable that he was in a state of shock for several weeks after his removal.

Suslov delivered the indictment. Among the accusations was the claim by his colleagues that they had received abrasive and supercilious rebuffs when they had ventured to point out policy deficiencies. Khrushchev would simply not entertain suggestions which contradicted his own policy predilections.

Why did Khrushchev get into the tragic position of alienating practically all those on whom he had to rely to implement his policies? He had a vision for the Soviet Union and was driven to implement it. His vision was flawed, but on encountering opposition he became more and more determined to find the right route to cornucopia. Khrushchev was a wizard at lateral thinking, of finding several alternative administrative solutions to a problem. The conclusions he drew from the disappointing results were often inaccurate but were always based on the notion that the culprit was not the system, but those who served it. His faith in the Party as an instrument of radical change gradually diminished and he came to see it in its 1960s guise as often a barrier to progress. Whereas he had enhanced the standing of CC plenums and congresses before 1960 he put this process into reverse afterwards by inviting supporters to participate who were not entitled to attend. Party and government officials wanted to build successful careers, but Khrushchev came to see this phenomenon as inimical to the goals he set society. Career men and women would minimise risk-taking and seek compromise solutions. Khrushchev needed radicals who would tear the existing structure apart and build a new, dynamic vehicle of change. The First Secretary wanted a revolutionary attitude to work, whereas officials wanted an administrative attitude to prevail. They wanted life and work to be predictable. Not surprisingly 'Khrushchev's' CC voted to remove him since he posed a powerful threat to their well-being. Khrushchev in trying to do too much too quickly only succeeded in doing himself out of a job. It is difficult to understand why he so carelessly neglected those political skills which had taken him to the position of a strong, national leader by 1958. This was to have fatal consequences for his ideals as well as himself.

KHRUSHCHEV AS LEADER

Khrushchev's leadership style evolved over time as did his policy preferences. As Party leader his task was to revitalise that body after the depredations of the Stalin period and to recruit, train and install cadres who shared his own view of the future. As a collective leader his policy options were restricted and it was only after the summer of 1957 that he was able to give full vent to his creative thinking about the way ahead for Soviet society. Since he was also *de facto* Prime Minister from the summer of 1957 he could reform the government apparatus as he thought fit. However it would be more accurate to say that he tried to reform the government apparatus, and later the Party apparatus, according to his own predilections. He found them frustratingly difficult to mould into a new shape after forty years of Soviet rule. One's view of him as a leader depends on whether one judges him according to what he achieved or what he tried to achieve in his struggle to change the legacy bequeathed by Stalin.

There are three main ways of viewing him:

(i) as a transitory leader;
(ii) as a transitional leader;
(iii) as an original leader.

Many of the arguments which would qualify Khrushchev as a transitory leader are to be found in the *Pravda* editorial of 17 October 1964 in which his successors sought to explain why he had been dismissed. It is a fine piece of character assassination which manages to avoid mentioning him by name. He is accused of engaging in 'hare-brained schemes', in taking 'hasty decisions' and of being arbitrary and high-handed with colleagues and subordinates. So eminently forgettable was he that he was not referred to by name afterwards and hence became an unperson. How then was one to explain his success? After all he did become national leader. One would argue that he was the product of circumstances, that in 1953 the Soviet political landscape was in a state of flux and that Khrushchev's extraordinary personality permitted him, more by luck than judgement, to climb to the top. When the post-Stalin political system had taken shape, Khrushchev became an anachronism, so he had to go.

Those politically on the right and the left can adopt this position. An anti-communist can argue that Khrushchev, in suppressing the Hungarian revolution and in attempting to blackmail the USA into acquiescing in the installation of Soviet missiles in Cuba, was merely showing his Stalinist colours. What about his faith in the creativity of the people? Was he not a populist? Did he not attempt to break the power of the central bureaucracy in favour of the periphery? Did he not insist on socialist legality instead of the arbitrariness of the Stalinist period? Did he not debase Stalin? The answers to these questions would be that Khrushchev did not attack the central tenets of Marxism–Leninism: the single ruling Party and democratic centralism. He made it quite clear that as the Soviet Union approached communism the role of the CPSU would increase. He vigorously opposed the coming into being of political pluralism. Hence he was no democrat in the Western sense of the word. The main reason why he abjured terror was because he saw it as counter-productive. The only legitimate view throughout his period in office was the Party view, and in the last resort he decided what that was. In no fundamental way did he dismantle the monopoly of political and economic power at the centre built up by Lenin and Stalin. He was a little more civilised than Stalin when it came to dealing with the regime's friends, but was quite as ruthless in combatting its perceived enemies. His vicious anti-religious campaign is a case in point.

Those on the left can also come to the same conclusion. Stalin hijacked socialism, but Khrushchev did not return it to its Marxist roots. If one views the Party–government apparatus as the mechanism by which the Soviet ruling class exploits the population then Khrushchev is just a more refined version of Stalin. Indeed he is more dangerous since he was so appealing and plausible.

The view that Khrushchev is a transitional leader is held by those who see him embodying the transition from coercive, arbitrary

Stalinism to conservative, consensus-seeking Brezhnevism. The emphasis placed on socialist legality gradually whittled away the arbitrariness of Soviet bureaucratic life. The fundamentals of the system remained, with Khrushchev favouring a reversion to 'Leninist norms'. Party and state bureaucrats, after the travails of the Stalinist period, wanted to administer the country quietly and to enjoy and extend the privileges of power. Khrushchev was unwilling to allow them to run the Soviet Union in their own interests, but the advent of Brezhnev saw the dawning of consensus politics and the bureaucrats came into their own. The social radicalism of the Khrushchev period was rejected in favour of the ideological status quo. Developed socialism, the hallmark of the Brezhnev years, was an admission that communism was only visible on the distant horizon. Under Khrushchev it was promised for 1980, an embarrassment for all and sundry later. Brezhnev did not make the mistake of picking a point in time. On the other hand he stressed that developed socialism was here to stay and would stay a long time. This suited the official status quo type of thought of the Brezhnev era. In economic policy the fundamental weaknesses of the Stalin command economy were not resolved under Khrushchev. In science and technology more harm than good was occasioned by the *sovnarkhoz* reform of 1957. So many reforms were initiated in agriculture that the end result was confusion and frustration. The Soviet Union in 1964 was only a little nearer providing the population with all the food it craved than it had been in 1953. Indeed it still had not solved the problem when Brezhnev died in 1982 despite huge capital investments in the rural sector. This indicates that the weakness is systemic and hence endemic to the collective farming system. The extraordinary number of reforms launched between 1957 and 1964 bear testimony to the fact that Khrushchev had little insight into the systemic weaknesses of the Soviet Union. His failure on so many fronts was based primarily on a lack of understanding of how to motivate the Soviet population. Brezhnev learned from Khrushchev's mistakes; he introduced very few reforms.

Khrushchev is an original leader to those who believe that he tried fundamentally to change Soviet society. His understanding of the good society, communism, was derived from his interpretation of Marxism-Leninism. Since he never questioned the veracity of the founding fathers he was convinced that the Soviet Union could develop quite rapidly in that direction. The new Party Programme of

1961, with its ideological innovations which included the all-people's state, the advent of communism and with it the advent of the new Soviet man and woman was meant to inspire the Soviet population to greater efforts. These efforts, in turn, would guarantee that per capita productivity would exceed that of the USA. Socially Khrushchev was egalitarian and attempted through the educational reform of 1958 to break the near monopoly of the intelligentsia in gaining access to higher education. By insisting on manual labour between school and university he tried to restore some dignity to physical work. The decentralisation of non-defence related industry in 1957 was an attempt to balance the centre and the periphery. He genuinely favoured mass participation in decision-making, seeing this as the surest way of releasing the creative potential of the population. The devolution of more power to the local soviets, especially in the realm of sport, was the harbinger of more to come. Hence the glimmerings of a civil society were visible between 1962 and 1964. This presupposed, of course, that civil society had the same objectives as the Party, the construction of communism, again as defined by the Party. Khrushchev extended the arena of decision-making by drawing in specialists and allowing them to address CC plenums even when they were not CC members. Since Khrushchev came to see the Party and state bureaucracy as potential barriers to rapid expansion, he proposed a quick turnover of cadres, from the bottom to the top.

Why then did he fail? Why did his innovations produce such confusion and engender such resentment? The key reason was that he was systematically dismantling the system on which the privileges and power of the bureaucracy rested. He was forced to adopt reform after reform because his original solution had been blocked. His zigzagging is testimony to the strength of the bureaucratic opposition, but also to his refusal to concede defeat. Like Stolypin he needed time to change the habits of generations, but like Stolypin he was denied the time he needed. The rapidity with which the old centralised system was put back into place after his removal testifies to this. The *sovnarkhozy* were abolished, the bifurcation of the Party ended, the enforced turnover of Party cadres was quietly forgotten, the educational reform ran into the sand and reform became a word to avoid. Given time he could have fundamentally changed the Soviet system but by the time he was removed his innovations had still such delicate roots that they could be extirpated. Since his goal was not the accumulation of personal power he put his own position at risk on many occasions in a desperate attempt to remould Soviet society.

He employed Stalinist tactics to become national leader, but his opponents used the same tactics to unseat him. The Stalinist legacy was much more durable than he ever imagined and proved itself to be a viable way of ruling the Soviet Union.

Is there such a phenomenon as Khrushchevism? This would imply a distinctive leadership style and mode of operation. It can be argued that each of the approaches adopted above can be categorised as Khrushchevism. If he is seen as a transitory leader Khrushchevism amounts to very unskilled guidance of the country, of producing reform after reform, like rabbits out of a hat, in a vain attempt to solve basic problems. The reason why so many initiatives were necessary was because Khrushchev could not grasp the root causes of the deficiencies he was attempting to eliminate. Since his conceptual grasp was faulty his solutions were also flawed. His wilfulness led him to reject advice which conflicted with his own analysis and this even extended to science where on one occasion he berated A. I. Baraev, an eminent soil scientist, for advising him to expand the area under fallow. As it turned out Baraev was right and Khrushchev wrong. Called by some a populist he nevertheless gradually cut himself off more and more from the organs of the people. His bifurcation of the Party apparatus could only make that institution less efficient and the *sovnarkhozy* did nothing to solve the travails of Soviet industry. Indeed they hindered the emergence of solutions in science and technology. Hence this version sees him as having a butterfly mind and being a scatterbrain. Since his legacy is largely negative he deserves to be forgotten.

The transitional view accords Khrushchev a more positive position. He should be praised for rehabilitating millions of Stalin's victims and reintegrating them into Soviet life. He was humane and well-meaning, but he did not come up with any lasting solutions to the basic problems of the Soviet economy. His concern for the have nots of Soviet society, his emphasis on pensions and his desire to reduce differentials in economic rewards are all positive aspects of his rule.

Highest marks are given by those who see him as an original leader. Here Khrushchevism signifies heroic failure. A noble vision was eventually brought to nought, not because of its shortcomings, but because of the greed and concern for position of those in authority. Those who share his view of the future Soviet society hope that another Khrushchev will eventually emerge and do battle with the entrenched power of the bureaucrats.

Khrushchevism can be understood in a totally different sense. According to the Communist Party of China Khrushchevism is a 'coherent and systematic position, incompatible with and antagonistic to Marxism-Leninism' (Young and Woodward in Miller and Féhér, 1984: p. 169). They equate Khrushchevism with 'modern revisionism'.

Khrushchev's legacy is not entirely negative since some of the changes he introduced had a lasting impact on the Soviet Union. Was the USSR a better place to live in in 1964 than in 1953? If one's answer is yes then the main credit for this state of affairs rests with Nikita Sergeevich Khrushchev.

2 Khrushchev and Systemic Development

GRAEME GILL

Western scholarship on the Khrushchev period, like that on the Soviet Union generally, has tended to focus overwhelmingly on the person of the Party leader. Such a focus is understandable. The prominent role played by Lenin both in the founding of the regime and in its early years and the dominating position of Stalin encouraged a view of Soviet politics that was leader-centred. The greyness of much of the institutional arena reinforced this focus, while Khrushchev's own personality, his idiosyncratic operating style and many of the policies he espoused provided a colourful figure which could sustain the continued salience of this tradition. Such a focus clearly has much to recommend it. Individual leaders have played a major part in shaping the contours of the Soviet system and any analysis which sought to deny this would need to be treated with some caution. But at the same time over-emphasis upon a leading figure, no matter how important, risks ignoring the context within which the political actor must play out his role. An important aspect of this context in regard to Khrushchev was the existence of strong pressures for institutionalisation in the structure of the Soviet system. Particularly important here was the Party, but such pressures were also at work in the other leading bureaucratic structures of the system.

Institutionalisation is a process which all structures must undergo if they are to function effectively internally and to complete the tasks accorded to them in a satisfactory fashion. A process of institutionalisation involves the construction of a framework within which 'a particular set of political interactions can be maintained' or 'stable, valued, recurring patterns of behaviour' can develop (Calvert, 1969, p. 505; Huntington, 1968, p. 12). Institutionalisation means the regularisation of operating procedures, the development of patterns of action which are accepted as the norm and through which the institution functions. A process of institutionalisation may take place along the lines of the formal regulations which seek to structure an organisation's operation. It may take place on the basis of informal conventions which, although not codified in the form of statutes or regulations, are very significant in structuring the patterns of interaction or the flow of authority within a particular structure. Or, more usually, it may take place on the basis of a combination of these formal and informal rules (Gill, 1985). Institutionalisation is strong where activity is constrained within established procedural norms; it is weak where actors can act with little regard for the content of such norms. When formal rules are reinforced by conventions the likelihood of political activity being structured effectively and of individual idiosyncrasy being constrained is increased. If formal rules and conventions are inconsistent the process of institutionalisation will be more uncertain and the capacity of these to structure an individual's behaviour will be lower; personal conduct may be justified on the basis of either formal or informal rules, and therefore predictability and certainty will be reduced. The efficient operation of a bureaucracy requires such predictability and certainty, the regularised performance of functions according to norms and rules which are known, accepted and adhered to by all. It requires the development of institutional integrity and coherence, but these are precisely what have been lacking in the Soviet political system.

The development of strong, independent institutions got off to a bad start under Lenin. The difficulties of state- and institution-building, substantial at the best of times, were exacerbated enormously by the situation of civil war and economic ruin in which the Bolsheviks found themselves. Forced to react quickly to crises, ad hoc-ishness was often the order of the day, not only in policy matters, but in those of institutional development as well. The effect of this was reinforced by the established Bolshevik disregard for constitutional forms and by Lenin's desire to retain a degree of fluidity in institutional relations at the apex because this maximised the room for manoeuvre available to him. This unpromising start did not mean that the development of strong and independent institutions was impossible in the Soviet system, but it did make such a development less likely. What sealed the fate of this, at least in the short term, was the sort of dominance Stalin was able to achieve. A number of aspects of what has been called the mature Stalinist system were instrumental in blocking the development of strong, independent institutions (Bialer, 1980: ch. 1).

One of the most important factors preventing the development of regularised institutional norms was the system of all-pervasive mass terror which is the keystone of Stalinism. The effect of this terror was a very high level of uncertainty and unpredictability among all ranks of the population, including the élite. The uncertainty stemmed from the arbitrariness of the terror. The purges of the 1930s had shown that no one was exempt from the direction of 'administrative measures' against them, and although terror of the 1930s type was not unleashed after the war, events like the Leningrad affair and the so-called doctors' plot and the continued high profile of Beria's police were sufficient to sustain this uncertainty up until Stalin's death. The continuing high level of uncertainty clearly undermined pressures for institutional coherence, regularity and integrity. It discouraged personal initiative on the part of those working in the institutions of Soviet society, disrupted bureaucratic procedures of operation and cut away the basis upon which trust in both colleagues and procedures could rest. Terror and uncertainty resulted in institutional stasis and decay, not vigorous institutional growth.

The effect of this was reinforced by the personal dominance exercised by Stalin. While Stalin personally did not decide all issues of importance, he did make the decisions on those issues which he chose to decide. Once Stalin had made his views known debate on a question ceased and those views became accepted as orthodoxy; before he made his views known others were often reluctant to stake out a personal position in case it conflicted with that of Stalin, thereby at times leading to a sense of drift and indecisiveness. One of the problems was that Stalin's involvement in issues was idiosyncratic and arbitrary. While all major questions were likely to be resolved through Stalin's involvement, a range of minor, even trivial, issues also became the subject of the leader's attention. Under such circumstances institutional regularity, coherence and integrity could not develop. Decisions which, in a bureaucratic sense, should have been the province of a particular Party organ or government department could immediately be transformed by Stalin's intervention. Institutions were thus subject to arbitrary intervention from outside, with the result that both formal rules and informal conventions which defined their areas of responsibility and structured their efforts to meet those responsibilities took on a contingent character: their operation was always contingent on the absence of Stalinist intervention. The best example of this is the atrophy of the leading Party organs. The infrequent meetings of those bodies at the apex of the Party structure (see Bialer, 1980: pp. 32–3) reflects the fact that not only was their ability to consider matters subject to Stalin's whim, but their very existence depended overwhelmingly on the disposition of the *vozhd*. Problems of institutional integrity and coherence were here combined with the issue of institutional existence.

The uncertainties in the jurisdictions of individual institutions resulting from the nature of Stalinist intervention discussed above was paralleled by a similar uncertainty in relations with other institutions. Bureaucracies and political structures under mature Stalinism did not possess clearly discrete spheres of responsibility, but overlapped, often substantially, at the edges with neighbouring structures. The result in particular instances could be confusion of responsibility and powers, while in general it resulted in parallelism, duplication, competition, checking and mutual distrust and surveillance which not only reduced the overall efficiency of the system, but also eroded particular institutions' corporate norms and patterns. With institutional relations so fluid the development of institutional borders was impossible, and thereby also the growth of institutional coherence.

Underlying this system was an overriding emphasis upon a personalised basis of legitimacy. The ideological matrix of the regime was dominated by the figure of Stalin as projected through the cult, with the result that the legitimacy of both political action and the regime as a whole was focused in the person of Stalin. This was a peculiarly personalised and non-bureaucratic form of legitimation because his words were presented as the source of guidance and inspiration which emanated from Stalin the personal leader, not Stalin the office-holder. Such a source of legitimation clearly cut right across institutional boundaries and prerogatives; directions were accepted because of their personalised source, not because of their conformity with bureaucratic rules or their consistency with bureaucratic structures or procedures. Thus the formal rules of the regime also took on a contingent character as the ultimate source of authority lay outside the bureaucratic sphere.

The final aspect of the mature Stalinist system which should be mentioned in this regard is the mobilisational model of social and economic development. This had its root in the first five-year plan period and consisted principally of attempts to mobilise all efforts to achieve particular tasks at hand. It found its most striking expression in 'storming' in the economy, but was also present in the manifold efforts to structure social life around the achievement of goals deemed desirable. As a result all aspects of life were politicised as citizens were called upon to direct all of their energies into the achievement of these goals. The effect, in institutional terms, was to render institutions as coherent bodies largely irrelevant to the achievement of those goals. Institutional boundaries, responsibilities, prerogatives and powers were less important than the achievement of the specified goals and the process of mass mobilisation through which they were to be attained. Institutions could play a positive part in helping to mobilise the population in this way, but they were essentially acting as transmission belts between leader and followers. Under such a model, institutional integrity and independence were impossible to attain.

While those characteristics of mature Stalinism sketched above depict a political system in which strong and stable institutions could not develop, this does not mean that some degree of institutionalisation did not occur within these structures. Formal rules and informal conventions did emerge to structure the operation of these bodies. Indeed, they could not have functioned at all unless there was some form of rules regulating their operation, structuring the way in which they worked and handled their responsibilities. At the bare minimum such bodies clearly needed administrative regulations and procedural instructions determining the division of responsibility and power in the organisation, the flow of paper-work and modes of decision-making. But such a regulative milieu was always subject to the sorts of influences and constraints stemming from the characteristics of Stalinism discussed above. At the heart of this was the arbitrary, interventionist leader figure of Stalin whose role in the system, supported by the terror and justified by the personalised basis of legitimacy, was the chief factor in the contingent nature of this regulative milieu. The amorphousness of institutional relations at the top reflects the fact that the inheritance bequeathed from the Stalinist period was one in which the exigencies of personalised power bulked much larger than did those of a bureaucratic, rule-based system.

The death of Stalin created crisis in this system. It removed the linch pin which had been the sole rationalisation for the system as it existed in the post-war years. The bureaucratic confusion, the amorphousness of institutional and policy arrangements had been overcome by the existence of a single, directing centre which could cut through the institutional uncertainties to ensure the flow of policy. Without such a centre the inefficiencies inherent in the ill-defined bureaucratic structure promised to become overwhelming and lead to an inflexibility and stasis within the system as a whole unless steps were taken to prevent this. In principle two types of solution were possible. The first involved the replacement of Stalin by another directing centre which could give the guidance and direction which could not spontaneously emerge from the policy-making structure bequeathed by the dead leader. In effect this involved a continuation of the tradition of a supreme leader. The second was, in the Soviet context, a more radical alternative. This involved the rejection of the principle of a directing centre of the Stalin type and its replacement by a system in which the various bureaucratic structures and hierarchies were able in a regularised way to formulate and implement the necessary policies themselves. This implied an institutionalisation of the system along bureaucratic and institutional lines rather than a system resting on the personalised basis of the Stalin period. The high level of ambiguity and confusion which had characterised institutional relations would need to be dissipated as the individual institutions worked out more discrete areas of responsibility whereby they could co-ordinate their efforts more effectively. Institutions would have to develop a greater sense of integrity and coherence, working as bodies according to their own formal regulations and conventions without fear of arbitrary intervention from outside. In sum this second alternative was one in which the formal bureaucratic structures played a part as relatively autonomous entities in the political sphere, with policy-making becoming much more a function of interaction between institutions than it had been at any time in the past. Personalities would be far less important in this type of system than in the continuation of a system based on Stalinist lines.

In the aftermath of Stalin's death there were considerable pressures favouring the latter of these two alternatives. Oppositions to the emergence of another dictator in the Stalin mould was widespread. While for many support for the principle of leadership collectivism may have been significant it is clear that concern for personal safety based upon the Stalin experience was a powerful factor in the generation of pressures against the emergence of another *vozhd*. Similarly, recognition of the debilitating effects on society harmonised with personal interests to lead to the elimination of terror as a central aspect of the system's operation.

Such negative responses to the Stalin experience were reinforced by more positive pressures. From within the bureaucratic structures themselves pressures emerged favouring institutional consolidation and strengthening. The disappearance of Stalin and the absence of a dominant leader figure for the first few years following Stalin's death, removed the principal source of external intervention into the workings of the bureaucratic structures. This created scope for the rules and conventions which had always operated in these institutions to expand and embrace those institutions far more completely than they had been able to do before. As a result a kind of bureaucratic inertia came into play which served to strengthen the institutional integrity and coherence of these bodies in the absence of an active, interventionist leader. This was reflected in the field of practical politics by the struggles between bureaucrats to strengthen their own particular institutions by expanding or defining more clearly the discrete scope of their institution's concern or by seeking more resources for their area of responsibility. Their own personal position, power and future was seen to be bound up with the growth in importance of the institution in which they worked, and indirectly with the institutionalisation of the whole system. Such forces for institutional consolidation were reinforced by concerns about efficiency in decision-making. Institutional domination of top-level policy-making was supported not only on the grounds of institutional and personal self-interest, but also because of concern about the quality of the decision-making process and of the decisions which emerged from it. The argument that specialised and technical knowledge was necessary for satisfactory decision-making was as difficult to resist in high Soviet circles as it was in the West. All of these forces came together to support a higher level of institutionalisation of the system along bureaucratic lines.

But such pressures were not unchallenged. Personal ambition could also be a source of pressures favouring a system in which individual leadership was a central component. Indeed, although Stalin's death had removed the supreme leader at the national level, most of those 'little Stalins' at lower levels of the hierarchy remained in place and, presumably, were eager to carry on their leading roles even in the absence of the personalised apex of the system. Furthermore the system of centralised personnel management, the *nomenklatura*, which had been so important for Stalin's rise and was central to the dominance of these individuals at lower levels, remained intact and thereby constituted a ready weapon which aspiring leaders could hope to use to consolidate their position. But as well as considerations of self-interest there was another important factor favouring the continuation of a personalised system: the limits of the experience of the members of the Soviet hierarchy. Their political lives had been spent in and shaped by a highly personalised system. This was the only type of system with which they were familiar; they knew the rules and conventions whereby this system operated, and their own positions were dependent upon their ability to manipulate those rules. Consequently any move toward a less personalised system was a move into the unknown and therefore one which potentially held dangers of the sort which might not be immediately apparent. Such a sentiment was clearly a counsel of caution in any move toward a more institutionally based structure.

In the clash between these pressures for a more highly institutionalised structure and a more personalised command style the odds were loaded heavily in favour of the former by the early decision to eliminate terror as a central operating principle of the system. By doing away with terror – reflected by the removal of Beria – the subordination of the police apparatus to the Party and the opening of some of the camps, the leadership eliminated one of the major weapons which had enabled Stalin to intervene in all areas of society at will. Without personal control over a centralised terror machine like that which had existed under Stalin, a leader had now to rely upon more traditional methods of exerting influence, most importantly through personnel manipulation. His power to coerce was significantly weakened, and although this may have been hidden in the early years of Khrushchev's rule it had become readily apparent by the end. Furthermore the elimination of terror had a marked effect on the contours of élite politics (see Hodnett in Bialer, 1981: p. 89). It removed both the dominance of one man and the climate of uncertainty which had been so important in preventing open conflict in the élite. With death no longer the penalty for failure, organisation against a leader became much more attractive as a realistic course of action than it had been at any time since the 1920s. This meant that élite relations had now to be managed in a way that was alien to the Stalinist heritage. Rules and conventions governing these relations had now to be generated.

In a number of respects Khrushchev leant his weight to the process of institutionalisation. Perhaps more importantly, by championing de-Stalinisation, Khrushchev openly discredited the model based upon a single predominant leader. In doing so he reaffirmed the importance of the Party as an institution and called for a restoration of its integrity and coherence, a return to the situation whereby it functioned according to its own rules and procedures. This is reflected in the frequent appeals to 'the Leninist norms of Party life'. He stimulated this process by sponsoring the new Party statute introduced in 1961, a document which seemed to break with the Stalinist past and to offer a new basis of internal legality for the Party's operations. Khrushchev also publicly sponsored the introduction of a new state constitution, a project left uncompleted at the time of his fall, the re-enlivening of the soviets and a new emphasis upon law. On a more practical level, under his leadership Party and state organs met with a much higher degree of regularity than under his predecessor, a development essential to any hopes of increased institutionalisation within the system.

But while Khrushchev contributed to the move toward a higher level of institutionalisation of institutional procedures the effect of many of his actions was to undermine such pressures and to fuel those making for a more personalised system. Perhaps the most fundamental challenge to the pressures for institutionalisation was Khrushchev's attempt to increase mass participation in political life, and in particular to expand the boundaries of decision-making (see Breslauer in Cohen, Rabinowitch and Sharlet, 1980: pp. 50–70). Khrushchev fostered a relationship between political system and society that was, in symbolic terms, non-adversarial and which involved full participation by the populace in political life. This is reflected in the change in name of Party and state from bodies representing the dictatorship of one class to bodies that, in type, were designated 'all-people's'. It is also reflected in attempts sponsored by Khrushchev to open up decision-making procedures to popular scrutiny and participation, the most important of which was probably the attempt to devolve many state functions to public or volunteer bodies, a process hailed as reflecting the withering away of the state.

Although the encouragement of popular participation in the forms Khrushchev espoused may have brought the system closer to some of its ideological roots, its immediate political impact was to call into question the role and position of office-holders at all levels of the system. There were a number of aspects of this. By opening issues up to public scrutiny, Khrushchev automatically exposed decision-makers at all levels to the same scrutiny. If previously decisions had emanated from the anonymity of closed committee meetings the opening of those meetings eliminated any possibility of such anonymity being retained. Furthermore public scrutiny could lead to public accountability, and therefore to a much more uncertain and perhaps even dangerous environment for functionaries to operate in. Indeed, the emphasis upon public participation even called into question the special status of office-holders; if they were to share decision-making power with the populace generally, which meant that they no longer possessed the qualities which made them uniquely suited to exercise decision-making power, why should they have a special standing in society? Their rights and privileges were thereby called into question. Furthermore this applied at the institutional level as well. If communist self-administration was to be the order of the day, the state machine would appear superfluous and the Party's position would be more difficult to justify. Thus Khrushchev's emphasis upon mass participation challenged not only the institutional coherence of the major structures of the society, Party and state, but also their very existence.

Khrushchev's policies challenged the pressures for institutionalisation in other ways as well (Roy and Zhores Medvedev, 1976; Roy Medvedev, 1982). The establishment of the *sovnarkhozy* in 1957 and the associated abolition of the central industrial ministries overturned traditional patterns of administration and cut right across the institutional interests of these traditionally powerful structures. Similarly his bifurcation of the Party apparatus into industrial and agricultural wings flew in the face of established practice and of those pressures for the consolidation of the Party along established territorial lines. Such changes not only caused administrative confusion in the short term, but established new lines of organisation which, if successful, threatened the entire existing structure of Party and state. Lack of concern for institutional properties is evident too in his championing of an increased Party role in the economic sphere and in his post-1958 occupancy of the leading positions in both Party and state.

As well as challenging the institutionalisation of Party and state structures in these ways, Khrushchev's operating style also called into question the institutional coherence and integrity of various constituent organs of these structures. When confronted by opposition in the Party Presidium Khrushchev sought to circumvent this by ignoring this body and appealing directly to the CC, as in the case of the anti-Party group of 1957, or by announcing a decision in public in an attempt to lock the Presidium in behind him, as in his proposal for the establishment of a CC Bureau for Central Asia in late 1962. The ability of the CC to act as a coherent organ was undermined by Khrushchev's practice of swamping its meetings with 'technical experts', many of whom were not only not members of the CC, but may not even have been members of the Party. Conventions about committee membership were ignored as Khrushchev introduced compulsory minimum turn-over levels and maximum periods of tenure for committees at all levels. The frequent membership changes of executive organs encouraged by such measures undermined any collective ethos these organs sought to develop. And, finally, his reliance upon a coterie of personal advisers and cronies supplanted the formal sources of advice based in the Party and state structures. In all of these ways Khrushchev espoused policies which subverted the main thrust of the pressures for institutionalisation and reflected a model of the system much more like that of the personalised leadership system reminiscent of Stalin, albeit without the terror.

Why was Khrushchev able to pursue such policies? The powers he was able to exercise over personnel disposition enabled him to promote supporters in such a way as to consolidate his personal power base. As such he used the same technique which had been used with such effect by Stalin. Khrushchev skilfully projected policy positions which gained him the support of major power centres in the system. But also important was the contradictory mood within the system as a whole, the tension between pressures for bureaucratic institutionalisation and the tradition of a more personalised dominant-leader system. This tension was reflected in the widespread recognition of the need for change accompanied by an uncertainty about both the speed and extent which could characterise such measures. This sort of uncertainty left the way clear for anyone who was in Khrushchev's position and was willing to act to push through measures which he believed to be necessary. The effect of this uncertainty was reinforced by another sort of ambiguity at the élite level. Stalin had so dominated the leadership that his disappearance, plus the removal of the terror, created a completely new environment of élite relations, but it was one which was characterised by an extraordinary weakness of formal rules and conventions governing élite behaviour. As a result, despite public avowals of the importance of the collective principle, there were no rules of either the formal or conventional type which were sufficiently well-established and sufficiently strong to contain a First Secretary who wished to breach that principle. Thus when Khrushchev had used his manipulative skills to consolidate his power base, he could make use of the contradictions in the political mood to push through many of his ideas unconstrained by a highly institutionalised leadership structure.

But ultimately Khrushchev was removed. The absence of terror was instrumental in his fall because it meant that, unlike Stalin, Khrushchev had been unable to get rid of his rivals permanently and to cow potential opposition. This meant that Khrushchev had to rely on support that had to be earned from people for whom the First Secretary's disfavour no longer had the dire consequence it had had previously. But this is where Khrushchev was defeated by those pressures for a higher level of institutionalisation of the structure as a whole. In the absence of a truly dominant leader, the pursuit of the goals of communist construction could not be sustained efficiently without a higher level of institutionalisation, and it was certainly inconsistent with the institutional tampering of which Khrushchev was so fond. Considerations of efficiency and good management therefore clearly counselled against the type of system which many of Khrushchev's actions suggested. Furthermore such considerations meshed nicely with understandable concern for self-interest on the part of those in the organisations which Khrushchev's policies threatened. Anxieties about personal security were easily combined with concern for institutional coherence and integrity. Khrushchev's alienation of virtually all élite groups in society led to their coup against him, an act which clearly asserted the primacy of pressures for institutionalisation over the tradition of a single dominant leader. Just as the weak institutionalisation of the leadership structure had enabled Khrushchev to play the role of activist leader, so when his basis of support had crumbled no institutional buffers existed which might sustain him against the ire of his foes.

The clash between pressures for institutionalisation and for the dominant leader model constituted the major dynamic of the Khrushchev period. Recognition of this enables some reconciliation of the two major types of interpretation of the Khrushchev period that have dominated Western literature on this subject. The focus of both interpretations is the attempt to explain the zigzags of Soviet policy under Khrushchev. The first type of interpretation is that of the so-called conflict school (Tatu, 1968; Linden, 1966). This sees Khrushchev as a consistent reformer who is constantly opposed by conservative diehards who seek to frustrate his efforts at reform. While Khrushchev is seen as the single most powerful individual in the leadership after 1957, he is not powerful enough to override the opposition, with the result that conservative aspects of policy are seen as defeats for Khrushchev or as attempts by him to pre-empt or ward-off conservative attacks upon him. The fall of Khrushchev is seen as a result of his loss of direct control over personnel to conservative forces in the form of Frol Kozlov in 1960. The second type of interpretation sees Khrushchev as essentially a 'transitional' leader (Fainsod, 1965b). Khrushchev is depicted as the type of leader who recognised the need to depart from established practice and policy, but, having spent all of his life within those established mores, was uncertain about how to make those departures or the sorts of limits to change which were viable. Khrushchev thus appears not as a consistent reformer, but as someone torn between recognition of the need for change yet fearful of the potential consequences. This interpretation sees Khrushchev as supreme from 1957 in the sense that he could not be defeated by his colleagues in policy debate. The zigzags thus reflect the ambiguities in the nature of Khrushchev himself rather than defeats by colleagues or tactical retreats. Khrushchev's fall is attributed to his neglect of the political arts which carried him to the top.

Both interpretations have a good deal of merit, but their focus on the leadership level is unnecessarily restrictive. If the sort of ambiguity attributed to Khrushchev in the second interpretation is accepted as being applicable generally throughout the system, as argued earlier in this paper, the power position at the apex of the system becomes much more fluid than either interpretation suggests. The conservative and reformist coalitions of the first interpretation become much less solid and diametrically opposed, while the supremacy attributed to Khrushchev in the second interpretation becomes much less stable because of fluctuations in reformist-conservative sentiments within the ranks of Khrushchev's supporters. Such an interpretation sees policy zigzags as reflective of the instability of mood throughout the system as a whole, an instability which characterised Khrushchev as well as the remainder of the élite. Thus while Khrushchev's personal role was clearly of central importance and while he was faced with considerable opposition at different times (and an opposition which increased in force as the period wore on) the central dynamic for the politics of the period was the tension between pressures for institutionalisation along bureaucratic lines and those for the maintenance of a dominant-leader system.

With strong pressures for institutionalisation central to Khrushchev's fall, it should come as no surprise that those pressures emerged as the dominant force in the Soviet political arena under the

Brezhnev leadership. Many of Khrushchev's initiatives which had run counter to such pressures were revoked. In November 1964 the division of the Party apparatus into industrial and agricultural wings was ended, in September 1965 the *sovnarkhozy* were abolished and the central industrial ministries restored, and a 1966 amendment to the Party Rules abolished compulsory turn-over levels in Party organs. These measures helped to restore some of the institutional integrity which had been stripped from these bodies under Khrushchev. In addition various measures were introduced in an attempt to bring about a higher level of institutionalisation of the leadership. A CC decision of October 1964 forbade a First Secretary simultaneously to be Chairman of the USSR Council of Ministers. Another 1966 amendment to the Party Rules provided for the election of the General Secretary by the CC, thereby formally establishing the mode of filling this office. A compact was made between the leaders which sought to prevent one individual from swamping his colleagues with his supporters by providing for a form of balanced appointments to leading positions, and an understanding seems to have been reached governing the overlap of leading organs (Rigby, 1970). These measures at the apex of the system were aimed at increasing the level of institutionalisation of the leadership through the introduction of formal rules and conventional injunctions designed to strengthen collective leadership and to impose serious constraints upon the ability of a Party leader to escape from the bounds of the collective. They reflect both a dissatisfaction with Khrushchev's style of leadership and the continuing strength of pressures for institutionalisation.

The strength of such pressures is also evident in the policy introduced under Brezhnev entitled 'stability of cadres'. Khrushchev's policies had involved a high level of unpredictability in personnel matters; frequent turnover and the corollary of short-term tenure in office made career planning and prospects uncertain for office-holders at all levels. There was, therefore, considerable opposition to Khrushchev's policy, resulting after his fall in the 'stability of cadres' policy. This guaranteed to office-holders a more certain long-term tenure of positions and therefore a much higher degree of personal job security than had been present under Khrushchev. One important effect of this policy has been a strengthening of the coherence of individual institutions because, as a general rule, when positions have fallen vacant, they have tended to be filled by promotion from within the organisation rather than through transfer from outside. Career structures could thus develop within institutions in a way that was much more isolated from external influences than had been possible before, and with this development went a greater sense of institutional identification and loyalty on the part of individual workers. Such a development facilitated the growth of institutional coherence and integrity.

This sort of strengthening of institutional identity fitted well with the type of decision-making procedures which emerged under Brezhnev. The emphasis upon collectivism at the top of the political structure was reflected in a decision-making style which emphasised consensus and a lowest common denominator approach in the Politburo. Such an approach has also been evident more generally in the leading levels of the system. Access to the policy-making arena was opened up on a regularised basis to a range of institutional actors which had not previously enjoyed such opportunities for involvement in leading councils. While Khrushchev had sought the advice of various institutions and groups on specific policy matters, this was done on an *ad hoc* basis. Under Brezhnev such advice became far more institutionalised, principally through the convention of consulting all interested organisations and institutions about proposed measures (Valenta, 1979; Gustafson, 1981). Although this created a decision-making procedure which was ponderous and slow to react, it was perfectly designed to enable institutional interests to defend their concerns in the policy-making arena and to feed into that arena the technical expertise upon which their access formally rested. Thus the arbitrariness of decision-making under Khrushchev gave way to a much more regularised procedure as the whole process of policy-making became more institutionalised.

From this perspective, Khrushchev's role in Soviet history as essentially a transitional figure is clear. Like his colleagues he was subject to the diverse pressures for a higher level of institutionalisation along bureaucratic lines and for the maintenance of a leader-dominant system. Like most of his colleagues he oscillated between these two positions, although tending toward the latter. However, ultimately it was the strength of the former sort of pressure, resting upon considerations of rationality and efficiency in government and of institutional and personal interest, which carried the day and led to the rejection of Khrushchev and the activist style of leadership with which many of his actions were associated. In the period which followed his fall those pressures for institutionalisation have dominated the field. However the permanency of those pressures should not be over-estimated. The formal rules and informal conventions which structure political life have, for the most part, been operative for a comparatively short period of time and it is not yet clear that they have attained the normative authority necessary to embed the process of institutionalisation so firmly within the firmament as to be able once for all to banish the *single*-leader tradition as an acceptable model of leadership structure in the eyes of potential Soviet leaders.

3   State and Ideology

RONALD J. HILL

Khrushchev's contribution to the development of the Soviet state, ideology and the political system generally is significant not only for his bold denunciation of Stalin and his attempts to induce the system's evolution away from the rigidities of orthodoxy that had prevailed for the previous quarter of a century or more. He had views about the broad direction in which he wished to see the system and society develop, and, although his successors denigrated his personal style and reversed some of his ill-advised institutional restructurings, some of his innovations have had a lasting impact. Indeed, his contribution to the development of both the theory and the practice of the Soviet state, together with associated institutions including the Party, has proved more enduring than might have been assumed in the first decade after his removal from office: it was a surprise to many observers that the 'Brezhnev' constitution of 1977 revived the Khrushchev concept of the all-people's state (or state of the whole people: *vsenarodnoe gosudarstvo*), and identified it as a characteristic feature of the phase of 'developed socialism' (see Hill, 1984).

Khrushchev's interest in developing the Soviet state and political system, and the ideological explication of it, stemmed from several considerations. First, the state and its nature is an important element in the Marxist-Leninist theoretical heritage. Second, the development of the state had become a symbolic feature of Soviet society which Lenin and Stalin (particularly Stalin) had used in order to demonstrate the progressive vitality of the USSR under their personal tutelage: Khrushchev likewise needed to use the state in such a fashion. Third, the needs of the day demanded certain kinds of pragmatic development in the state's functioning, as Stalin's harsh methods of rule were dispensed with in favour of a more persuasive, conciliatory approach to the population, and as the complexity of Soviet society grew.

The state organisation inherited by Khrushchev from Stalin was one in which the *administrative* organs (the ministries and state committees) had burgeoned, while the soviets of toilers' deputies, referred to in the 1936 constitution as 'organs of state power', had never been allowed to develop their potential as *representative* bodies. Indeed, while Stalin used the powerful ministries as the main instrument for governing the USSR, the soviets were filled with hand-picked deputies, selected not for their political skills or flair as representatives but as a reward for their prowess as workers (many in the early 1950s were identified as Stakhanovites) and their willingness to raise their right arm in consistently voting for the policy proposed by the centre. As representatives of their constituents' interests their role scarcely existed. The Communist Party likewise had been severely downgraded in the Stalinist system: its institutions met irregularly, congresses were rarely convened, even the Politburo was divided into groups of Stalin's cronies of various degrees of intimacy, and membership came to be used as a means of imposing discipline on important sectors of society and of securing the regime's acceptance by patriotic citizens, particularly during the Second World War.

This factual situation stood in marked contrast to the aims and assumptions of communist leaders from Marx on. He had seen bureaucracy as the central element in the modern state apparatus, while Lenin had been particularly concerned – in *The State and Revolution* and elsewhere – to destroy the old bureaucratic machine and replace it with a different kind of administrative apparatus that would permit the eventual abolition of all bureaucracy (Lenin, *CW*, vol. 25: p. 462). During the transitional period administration would be simplified to such an extent that 'any cook' could participate in what would amount to a bookkeeping exercise; society would be run 'on the lines of the postal service', and eventually 'communist self-administration' by ordinary citizens would replace professional bureaucracy as a second element in the 'withering away' of the state.

Under Stalin, there was no development in that direction: quite the reverse, justified perhaps by the vastness of the task of directing a grand-scale economic and social transformation of society. Khrushchev, as a kind of populist (Breslauer, 1976: pp. 19–20), resolved to bring the 'organs of state power' closer to the people, and to put the overgrown state administration firmly in its place. His memoirs reveal a dismissive view of the 'bulky administrative apparatus' that justifies its existence by 'grinding out telegrams, dispatching inspectors . . ., quoting cable references back and forth, keeping track of the ministry's own expenses, and issuing proclamations which often came down to platitudes like "one should drink only boiled water" ' (Khrushchev, 1974. p. 115); elsewhere he referred to the need to 'tear down the bureaucratic obstacles which are impeding our economy' (1974: p. 138). Moreover, in retirement he unrepentantly saw the apparatus as the main obstacle to progress: 'In my old age, I find myself worrying more than ever about the future. I would hate to see the Soviet Union impeded in its progress by its own bureaucracy. If we can keep ourselves from getting bogged down, there's no limit to what we can accomplish.' (Khrushchev, 1974: p. 147). In attacking the apparatus in this way in the 1950s, however, Khrushchev most likely also had another, more directly political, purpose in mind: in the process of undermining the position of the state bureaucracy as such he could downgrade the apparatus on which his main rival, the former prime minister, Georgy Malenkov, had based his power.

In the wake of the XX CPSU Congress, which began in earnest the process of de-Stalinisation, the year 1957 saw Khrushchev act on both of these fronts. On 22 January, the Central Committee issued a statement 'On Improving the Activity of the Soviets of Toilers' Deputies and Strengthening their Links with the Masses', which has been seen as '[marking] the beginning of organised attempts to reform local government and revive its participatory elements' (Friedgut, 1979: p. 52). After presenting a glowing image of the soviets and their work, the statement listed serious weaknesses: the soviets' failure to use their legal rights and to examine important areas of administration, and their tendency to discuss petty and ephemeral matters in irregular sessions that simply gave ceremonial approval to draft decisions; the executive committees did not report back to the soviets, deputies' proposals remained unacted upon and decisions were so vague as to be valueless. The statement suggested measures to rectify the situation, including the selection of more worker and peasant deputies, the reactivation of the standing commissions, and the elimination of red tape, bureaucracy, rudeness and other well-known ills among Soviet officials (text in *KPSS v rez.*, vol. 7, 1971: pp. 237–48). This statement testified to the largely ceremonial nature of the soviets in the 1950s, and the low level from which Khrushchev intended to raise them; it also bore witness to the appalling calibre of state administrators.

Shortly thereafter came the crisis of the anti-Party Group, a challenge to Khrushchev's leadership over the issue of economic management (see Pethybridge, 1962; Linden, 1966: ch. 3). In an attempt to destroy the power of the state administration Khrushchev proposed to abolish the central economic ministries and replace them by some 100 regional economic councils, against the protests of his political opponents including Malenkov and his allies, whose position he wished to undermine. Khrushchev's victory over the group led to the implementation of the policy, and the councils ran the economy until after his removal from power. In a linked measure he also favoured a scheme for completely abolishing the local soviets' administrative departments and transferring their functions to the standing commissions: in some places this was attempted experimentally, but not widely adopted (Hill, 1980: pp. 79–80). This was but one episode in a period of rule described as 'one of great ferment and experiment in numerous social and scientific fields' (Friedgut, 1979: p. 63).

A further measure, introduced in November 1962, was the splitting of the administrative apparatus into agricultural and industrial sections, associated with a similar splitting of the party apparatus 'according to the production principle', and aimed at eliminating 'the tendency to govern by making declarations [*deklarativnost*] and a campaigning style' in economic management (see *KPSS v rez.*, vol. 8: p. 388; for Western accounts of this reorganisation, see Churchward, 1965; Chotiner, 1982).

These moves together constituted a broad attack on the state: the bureaucracy's coherence was severely undermined, and attempts to develop the soviets could be seen as paving the way for popular administration by giving a broader range of citizens a chance to learn the appropriate skills, and to do so following approved channels. Developing the *representative* side of the state thus paved the way for the withering of the *administrative* side.

Khrushchev introduced yet other measures aimed at reducing the administration's grip and attempting to 'return power to the people'. Their impact, however, can at best be described as mixed, if not contradictory. These included the custom of opening up sessions of the soviets to large numbers of invited 'guests', not deputies, but frequently local dignitaries of one kind or another. In some cases their presence could be justified by reference to the topic under discussion, since they possessed especially relevant expertise or responsibilities. However, in many cases they simply duplicated the experience of the deputies, whose opportunities for involvement in the work of the sessions were significantly undermined by the presence and active involvement of these 'outsiders' (for documentation of the case in the Moldavian city of Tiraspol see Hill, 1977: ch. 5). While it may perhaps have diluted the dominance of the professional state administration in the sessions of the Soviets this practice also prevented the development of these institutions as bodies consisting of genuinely representative and responsive deputies.

Khrushchev made further attempts to induce the state's withering away. First, he deliberately transferred certain functions to 'non-state' public organisations such as the trade unions, a move that is significant only if the fiction of independence for such bodies is accepted. In his memoirs he also expressed a regret at not going further in decentralising decision-making in the economy, particularly in agriculture, by abolishing many of the bureaucratic controls over the state and collective farms (Khrushchev, 1974: pp. 135, 138).

A further series of measures related to the administration of the legal system, with the expansion of the system of comrades' courts, a degree of popularisation in the criminal courts, the involvement of citizens in maintaining law and order and changes in the mechanisms for checking on administrative efficiency. Comrades' courts, in which justice is administered by formally elected members of the public rather than trained lawyers, have a history which goes back to the early years of the regime, and were seen as a social (rather than judicial) agency for the purpose of involving citizens in the functions of social regulation; a major function was to educate in the spirit of communist principles, including 'the observance of the rules of socialist community life', and they applied social pressure, rather than formal punishment, against offenders of the behavioural code. Under Khrushchev greater formality was introduced into these bodies and a wider range of petty criminal offences was brought within their purview (Butler 1983: pp. 128–9). In a parallel development non-professional 'lay assessors' were added to the regular courts of justice, again seen as part of the move towards 'communist self-administration'. These measures were supplemented by a system of *druzhiny*, or vigilantes (volunteer citizen police units), which became established in the early 1960s, and played a role – frequently resented both by citizens and by those who were enlisted through the Komsomol and similar 'public' organisations) – in patrolling the streets of Soviet cities and maintaining social discipline (Butler, 1983: p. 131; also Juviler, 1976: ch. 4).

It should, of course, be borne in mind that these measures were accompanied by an enhancement of the Party's guiding role over these institutions. In any case, taking the whole of Khrushchev's period of rule, contradictory tendencies were to be observed, for, as Juviler (1976: p. 82) records, his 'enthusiasm for popularising justice soon gave way to anger about disorder and to pressures for a harder line'. The late 1950s and early 1960s witnessed a somewhat vicious campaign against 'economic crimes' (with sharply anti-semitic over-tones), and the introduction of harsh legislation against 'parasitism': these, together with an anti-religious drive in which thousands of churches were closed and their congregations dispersed, and his philistine approach to the arts (notoriously, abstract painting), are, as Hough reminds us (1977: pp. 25–7; Hough and Fainsod, 1979: pp. 232–3) an important element that upsets the reputation of 'good old Khrushchev' as a reformer.

Nevertheless the image of Khrushchev as a populariser of public administration is not inaccurate, and a particularly significant development, with profound ideological overtones, was his elaboration of the concept of 'all-people's state', with its throwback allusion to the class nature of the state.

Much of the political dimension of the Marxian ideological heritage concerned the nature of the state and its relation to the individual and society. The state was seen as 'essentially a machine for keeping down the oppressed, exploited class' (Engels in MEW, vol. 21: p. 167), and political power as 'merely the organised power of one class for oppressing another' (Marx and Engels in MEW, vol. 4: p. 482). In other words the state was a repressive apparatus used in the war between classes. Perfectly logically, therefore, when under communism classes would themselves disappear (a definitional point in Marxist theory), the instrument of class rule would likewise become irrelevant, and the state would 'wither away'. This analysis and projection is so central to the ideology that no Soviet leader could be seen to ignore it. After all, it provided the long-term goal towards which the whole system was ostensibly striving: building the classless society of communism was the ultimate justification for the revolution and all that had followed. It also provided a yardstick against which Soviet leaders could measure their success in attaining the goals established in the ideology.

Previous leaders had already argued that the state had changed its

nature as a result of developments in Soviet society. Lenin had
come to see the Soviet state – based on the soviets of deputies and
incorporating the Council of People's Commissars as the executive
and the People's Commissariats as the administrative arm – as the
instrument through which the proletariat exercised its revolutionary
dictatorship. Hence, under Lenin, the former 'exploiting classes'
were debarred from participation, and the peasants too were
represented on a reduced franchise compared with the industrial
workers: this was logical, given the Bolsheviks' ideological view.
From the late 1920s, however, Stalin demonstrated that the state –
in Marxist terms, part of the superstructure – did not simply reflect
society's economic base, but could indeed profoundly influence that
base. The five-year plans for industrial development and the
campaign to collectivise agriculture together created a new social
structure. In the official analysis it comprised a state-employed
working class and a 'socialist' collective farm peasantry, plus a 'non-
class stratum' of specialists, managerial and other white-collar
employees, who lived by their brain power ('mental labour') and
enjoyed no special relationship to the means of production. The
former exploiting classes were destroyed, as were the *kulaks* (rich
peasants) and, to a great extent, self-employed craftsmen; the newly
created classes were supposedly characterised by socialist relations
and class antagonisms were abolished. The Constitution of 5
December 1936 (Article 1) declared the USSR to be 'a socialist
state of workers and peasants' – already a stage beyond the basic
'dictatorship of the proletariat' introduced by Lenin, and one that
permitted the introduction of equal political rights to all groups,
symbolised, for example, by granting the vote on an equal basis to
all adult citizens. The dictatorship of the proletariat was now said to
have become 'more flexible', its base 'widened', its basis 'more firm'
(Chkhikvadze 1984: p. 69, quoting the resolution of the
February–March 1937 CC Plenum).

Stalin therefore claimed to have eliminated class antagonisms, an
ideologically impressive attainment on the way towards a classless
society. (However, in justification of the heavy-handed security
organs, he also asserted that the class struggle intensifies under
socialism as remnants of 'the class enemy' resort to ever more
desperate acts of resistance.) In order to demonstrate further
progress, Khrushchev needed to make a similar claim. The elaboration of 'the state of the whole people' served his purpose, and was
accompanied by the assertion that a new phase on the road to

communism had been entered: the 'unfolding [or full-scale, or rapid] building of communism'. This was proclaimed in the 1961 third CPSU Programme, which ended with the stirring promise: 'The party solemnly proclaims: the present generation of Soviet people shall live in communism!'

The assertion that the country was now in the phase of 'the rapid building of communism' and that the state was now 'of the whole people' undermined the Stalin dogma that the class struggle intensifies as socialism develops (Linden, 1966: p. 85). This ideological development effectively confirmed that the stage of 'the dictatorship of the proletariat' had now given way to a new phase (something that was not claimed in the Stalin formulation of the abolition of class *antagonisms*, although such an inference might have been drawn), and it led to conflict over how soon the state could be expected to 'wither away' (Linden, 1966: p. 109), with Khrushchev, as noted above, taking positive steps to induce this, and the 1961 Programme also stating that 'the state as an organisation of the entire people will survive until the complete victory of communism', and would be used to organise communist construction:

> Expressing the will of the people, it must organise the building up of the material and technical base of communism, and the transformation of socialist relations into communist relations, and exercise control over the measure of work and the measure of consumption, promote the people's welfare, protect the rights and freedoms of Soviet citizens, socialist law and order and socialist property, instil in the people conscious discipline and a communist attitude to labour, guarantee the defence and security of the country, promote fraternal co-operation with the socialist countries, uphold world peace, and maintain normal relations with all countries. (Russian text in *KPSS v rez.*, vol. 8: pp. 196–305; this passage on p. 273; translation from Schapiro, 1963: p. 297).

This assertion of progress to a further stage on the road to communism also led Khrushchev to emulate his predecessors in symbolising the development by the adoption of a new constitution. As was noted above, Lenin had founded the regime, and the 1918 Constitution, followed by its 1924 successor, had been seen as establishing the appropriate ground-rules for a multinational society in the era of the 'dictatorship of the proletariat'; having established the basis of a socialist society, Stalin introduced a new constitution in 1936 to mark the changed class relations that had developed by modifying the constitutional conventions to treat all social classes equally before the state. In a similar vein, Khrushchev declared that the state now belonged to the whole people, and wished to introduce certain modifications to its structures and practices to mark the transition to the new stage. Accordingly, at the 1961 Party Congress Khrushchev referred to 'the new Constitution of the USSR, which we are beginning to draft', and rationalised the move on the grounds that a completely new constitution (rather than substantial amendments to the previous fundamental law) was required in view of the broad-ranging changes that had taken place since 1936. The congress went on to authorise the establishment of a Constitutional Commission, chaired by Khrushchev, to draft the new document; the Commission was formally appointed in April 1962. Gilison (1972: pp. 70–1) argues that this move was an integral part of Khrushchev's de-Stalinisation process and an important weapon against his enemies, whom he accused of exploiting for their own nefarious ends the manifest arbitrariness and other weaknesses in the country's legal system. In addition its presentation – in terms of protecting the Soviet public from the illegal behaviour of individuals who relied on the extra-legal activity of agencies such as the secret police – was totally consonant with the populism of Khrushchev's approach.

The various ideologically loaded statements made under Khrushchev's leadership raised broader issues about the nature of the political system than perhaps the First Secretary entirely understood. One of the implications, for example, of the notion of 'withering away' was that the law-making functions of the state, and indeed law itself, could also 'wither away'. There was certainly a need to get rid of some of the exceptionally repressive legislation of the Stalin era if society were to function more smoothly, in a somewhat more collaborative atmosphere than in the past. But it was by no means clear that Soviet society was yet ready to be guided by internalised principles of 'communist morality', with no mechanisms for enforcing duly adopted formal regulations. In fact, it could be argued (as it was in the post-Khrushchev period) that there was rather a need to establish a framework of legal controls over the bureaucracy, and to eliminate the secrecy surrounding legislation in some areas. Khrushchev, it might be argued, in attempting to eliminate the bureaucracy rather than effectively controlling it by prescribing strict legal limits to its functioning, failed to appreciate the role of administration in a modern society.

The Party Programme, which one commentator referred to as 'Khrushchev's *Mein Kampf*' (Salisbury, 1961; it was replaced by a new version at the XXVII CPSU Congress in February–March 1986), remained until the post-war generation of Soviet leaders, in the person of Mikhail Gorbachev, took over the reins of power in 1985. It put forward a number of proposals for improving the work of the soviets and the state administration and bringing the administration under democratic control, including insisting on a turn-over level of one-third among the deputies at each election, and restricting the service of officers of the executive committees normally to three terms, together with enthusiastic references to raising the role of the standing commissions by transferring decisions to them from the administrative departments, and developing the democratic principles of the electoral system (*KPSS v rez.*, vol. 8. pp. 274–5). Scholarly monographs dealing with such matters appeared frequently in the early 1960s (see Hill, 1980, *passim*).

Khrushchev's enthusiasm for reorganising and popularising administration was not confined to the organs of the Soviet state: the Communist Party itself was not immune. In the early post-Stalin years measures were introduced to popularise its administration by bringing more workers and peasants into the work of Party committees, particularly at the primary organisation level (see Breslauer, 1982: p. 127). In addition a number of the structural changes that affected the state were paralleled in the Party. As already noted, the apparatus was split into agricultural and industrial sections (that is, in Soviet terminology, 'according to the production principle') in November 1962, with the aim of 'providing more concrete leadership of industrial and agricultural production' (*KPSS v rez.*, vol. 8: p. 391). A further effect – which may also have been an intention – was to cut down the power of Party officials by reducing the range of their responsibilities, and to disrupt their careers through redeployment of the Party's officer corps. The practice of extending the sessions of the soviets to participation by non-members also applied to the plenums of Party committees at all levels (see Hill, 1969; 1977: 98–9), and the First Secretary allowed himself to undermine the authority of Central Committee members and of the plenary sessions which they attended by crudely interrupting speakers and pushing his own ideas (see Churchward, 1975: pp. 214–15, for an example of this). New rules to restrict the influence of Party officials, by requiring specific levels of turnover among Party committee members, were enshrined in the 1961 Party Programme and incorporated into rule 25 of the new rules adopted by the XXII Congress (*KPSS v rez.*, vol. 8: pp. 302–3, 313). Most significantly Khrushchev's popularisation of goverment was reflected in his opening up

the ranks of the Party to the broad masses, in a recruitment drive
that might have changed the whole nature of the Party. Between
1954 and 1964 the membership rose from 6.9 million to 11.0 million
(*Partiinaya zhizn*, 21/1977: p. 21), an increase of 59.4 per cent in a
decade. Such a rate of expansion, as Miller (1982: p. 6) has noted,
would have led to a Party of 28 million members (some 15 per cent
of the adult population) if it had continued to the late 1970s – with
profound implications for its nature and role in society (on 1 January
1984 total membership stood at 18.4 million). Moreover, as well as
identifying the establishment of the 'state of the whole people', the
1961 Programme likewise referred to the CPSU as a Party 'of the
whole people', whose role as 'the leading and guiding force of Soviet
society' would be enhanced and would require 'a new, higher stage
in the development of the Party itself' (*KPSS v rez.*, vol. 8: p. 301).
This confirmed the leading position of the Party, so assiduously re-
established in the early part of Khrushchev's period in office.

It may be seen that Khrushchev, in his approach to government
as in other specific policy areas, was acting in contradictory ways,
perhaps without appreciating the complexity of the tasks involved.
Some would argue that he was perpetuating a myth about the separation of Party and state institutions, which led him and the regime
into ideological hot water from which his successors have not been
able to extricate themselves. For many purposes it is in fact
misleading to see the Party and state as separate, since the two sets
of institutions constitute a single apparatus, linked by personnel
appointed according to the principle of *nomenklatura*, governed by
'democratic centralism', and jointly performing the functions of
policy-formulation, rule-making and rule-application: jointly
governing, in other words. But if the 'state' should wither away,
what implications would that have for the Party's 'leading and
guiding' role? And if the role were to continue, how would it be
performed? Khrushchev's '*Mein Kampf*' is reticent on this point, and
the classics of Marxism-Leninism were singularly unhelpful: certainly
Marx and Engels, and most probably Lenin too, did not envisage
that the Communist Party would be the organ through which the
Soviet working class would rule for approaching half a century – the
Party as an instrument of long-term rule was not predicted by the
founding fathers. In fact, in ruling after Stalin's death through the
position of Prime Minister, it was Malenkov rather than Khrushchev
who could claim to be following in Lenin's footsteps: the founder of
the Soviet regime had held the post of Chairman of the Council of

People's Commissars, while the position of General Secretary, seen as relatively trivial at the time, was held by Stalin, clearly Lenin's subordinate.

In other ways, too, Khrushchev seems not to have understood the real needs of a country emerging from Stalinism. He was of course correct in identifying the bureaucracy as a 'problem', but he was incorrect in believing that it could be eliminated by transferring functions to amateurs under Party guidance. Nor was he correct in attempting to solve the problem by constant structural reform, since, at the very least, he was depending still on the very individuals who had benefited from the previous arrangements. Their interests were likely to be harmed if the basis of their power were taken away, and they would therefore most likely resist and frustrate his efforts.

In any case, as has been recognised under Khrushchev's successors, an important dimension of administration is style or culture. The thousands of individuals engaged in the multiple tasks of administering the Soviet Union when Khrushchev came to power had been chosen less for their sophistication, or their administrative flair or skills, than for their loyalty to Stalin and the system he created. Their training for the task had been rudimentary, and their personal qualities included a willingness to be tough in imposing discipline if the occasion demanded it – as it was frequently deemed to do. This approach to the task had been reinforced by the tangible successes recorded: the 1930s had witnessed an unprecedented transformation of an economy and a society; the early 1940s had been crowned with the honour of capturing Berlin following the greatest war the world had ever known, much of the heaviest fighting taking place on Soviet soil; and the years to Stalin's death had seen a successful drive at reconstruction that had brought the country to aspire to equality with the leading world powers. In the wake of these successes, to which they felt their insistence on discipline had been an important contributory factor, individual careers had prospered. The system of which they felt themselves to be key parts appeared to work well: it was, indeed, deemed to be socialism, which was by now being emulated in other countries within the Soviet sphere of influence.

It is therefore not surprising if the personnel on whom Khrushchev relied in running the country were suspicious of his attempts to divert the route into uncharted areas, using untested methods of guidance; his institutional reorganisations, which grossly interfered with their inbred and tested style of doing things, not surprisingly led to chaos, since they were unplanned and the officials responsible for implementing them were not prepared (in any sense of the world) to function in the appropriate fashion. Mere administrative changes are insufficient to alter the way a country is run. New institutions will function according to the perceptions of the individuals whose roles constitute those institutions: without the appropriate training, skills, attitudes and values, they will operate differently from the ways envisaged by the designer of the system. Khrushchev failed to appreciate this: he sought a panacea in reform after reform (Hough and Fainsod, 1979: p. 223), tried to force them on an unwilling and obstinate bureaucracy and ultimately paid the political price. He was replaced by a team of less flamboyant leaders whose dull and plodding political style evidently found the favour of a country tired of inconsistency and unpredictability and anxious for a period of stability.

How much of Khrushchev's legacy in this area has survived? Perhaps surprisingly, rather a lot. The ministries were re-established by his successors within months, and the creation of the economic councils and other administrative reorganisations dismissed as one of his 'hare-brained schemes'. But the measures to revitalise the Soviets were continued, with the authorisation of a broad programme of study by social scientists and legal specialists that has culminated over the past generation in the introduction of a wave of new legislation, and the recruitment of more sophisticated deputies, who are in addition now given training to assist their better functioning. The role of the representative bodies is still ambiguous, given the overwhelming power of the Party and the remaining power of the administration; but there are signs that they are being required to perform their limited role more effectively.

On the ideological plane the argument has been preserved that the modern Soviet state is not a state in the 'classical' sense: it is not an instrument of class rule, but an instrument used by the entire Soviet people in directing the construction of a communist society. The political rhetoric of the Khrushchev era – notably the reference to the 'unfolding building of communism, but also to 'the all-people's state' – was immediately dropped by the Brezhnev administration. The 'unfolding building' was replaced by the far more euphonious 'developed [or mature] socialism' (although the former phrase still occasionally appears in textbooks (Barabashev and Kutafin, 1977: p. 19). This relieved the post-Khrushchev leadership of the rash promise that communism is just around the corner, implied in the notion of the 'unfolding building of communism' (and expressly stated in the concluding phrase of the 1961 Party Programme). With the 'state of the whole people' apparently no longer applicable, the Constitutional Commission under Brezhnev's chairmanship apparently went into suspension during 1967. To the surprise of many observers, when the Commission was reactivated and produced its draft a decade later, the 'state of the whole people' was revived and incorporated into the 1977 Constitution, which declares (Article 1) that 'The Union of Soviet Socialist Republics is a socialist state of the whole people, expressing the will and interests of the workers, peasants and intelligentsia, the working people of all the nations and nationalities of the country'.

Indeed the theoretical elaboration of the state under Khrushchev's successors has largely built on Khrushchev's basis, now with added stress on the *multinational* dimension of the state, already enshrined in the 1977 Constitution (as quoted above), but given fresh urgency by the evident shifts in the nationality balance of the population. A recent monograph by a senior Soviet lawyer refers to 'the development of the Soviet multinational state', stressing the involvement of the minority nationalities in the work of the state (Chkhikvadze, 1984: p. 134).

Khrushchev's impatience to witness the state's withering away, however, has been abandoned. The gradual transfer of functions to 'non-state' organisations has not been continued, and indeed the literature has contained numerous warnings that the pace of the withering away cannot be forced (for example, Stepanyan and Frish, 1979: p. 174). The various populist measures aimed at bringing to Party and soviets alike an image of greater democracy – principles such as the limitation on officials' terms of office – were likewise abandoned by his successors. The practice of extending meetings to participation by outsiders was briefly interrupted (but later resumed). Moreover not only the representative organs but the organs of administration too have been 'strengthened' by the addition of greater sophistication in administration, including computers in the planning system and so-called 'automated systems of management' in economic administration. Khrushchev's calls for greater responsiveness and courtesy on the part of officials has been taken further under Brezhnev and his successors, with the professionalisation of the state administration. Not only have there been attempts to recruit officials with a greater sense of responsibility, but more generally, greater competence has been stressed as the complexity of the tasks facing government has expanded with the growing sophistication of the society. This development, although not Brezhnev's response to it, was foreseen in the 1961 Programme's reference to 'the growing scope and complexity of the tasks of communist construction, which call for a higher level of political and organisational leadership' (*KPSS v rez.*, vol. 8: p. 301). And his attempts to raise the sense of public responsibility, in reaction to the widespread abuse of the legal system under Stalin's regime, have also been continued, partly, it is true, by bringing the law into closer conformity with established Soviet practice, but also to some extent by improving the provision of legal services, expanding the provision of mass legal education, and insisting more closely on sticking to the letter of the law – even by such shady bodies as the KGB.

Khrushchev dreamt of creating abundance within twenty years and training a competent citizenry to whom the state's administrative functions would gradually – but in historical terms fairly swiftly – be transferred. The Utopianism and naïvety in that vision have subsequently been recognised, in the face of the complex and difficult reality. While Khrushchev has been consigned to not even a footnote in the current Soviet history books, his successors have taken and pursued some of the populist elements in his outlook, but have firmly rejected his – and Lenin's – idea of administration by the masses, at least as far ahead as anyone cares these days to look.

4 Industry

ALEC NOVE

1 THE SITUATION AT STALIN'S DEATH AND THE MALENKOV INTERREGNUM

Stalin spoke to an 'election' meeting in Moscow on 9 February 1946. The country had been exhausted by war, conditions were exceedingly tough, and industrial output in 1946 was inevitably adversely affected by reconversion to peacetime industry and by the need to repair war damage, as well as by shortage of food. So when Stalin set out some targets, to be achieved in three quinquennia, i.e. by 1960, they must have seemed overambitious. And yet . . .

TABLE 4.1 *Plan Targets*

	1945	1960 *(Stalin target)*	1960 *(actual)*
Steel (millions of tonnes)	12.25	60	65
Coal (millions of tonnes)	149.3	500	513
Oil (millions of tonnes)	19.4	60	148

Source: Narodnoe Khozyaistvo SSSR, various years.

By 1950, even allowing for statistical exaggeration, the 1940 level had been substantially exceeded, especially for the priority producers' good sectors. While neither cotton cloth nor footwear had reached target (or 1940 levels), the output of coal, steel, oil, tractors, was above expectations. The great Dnieper dam, blown up in the retreat of 1941, was operational again as early as the spring of 1947. So when the XIX Party Congress met in 1952, and Malenkov (in Stalin's presence) made the keynote speech, presenting (two years late) the five-year plan for 1951–5, there seemed to be some very solid achievement to boast of, and on which to build future growth. However, the high growth rates of these years were partly the consequence of post-war recovery, as was also achieved in West Germany and Italy in these years. Agriculture remained in the doldrums. Industry's recovery was not accompanied by technological advance, ouside of such sectors as nuclear weapons and military aircraft. This was a time of cold war, when Soviet science was purposefully isolated from contact with Western science; we were told that everything Soviet was best, that Russians had invented everything from the radio to the steam engine. Traditional methods and patterns of production were retained: steam locomotives were favoured, while natural gas was neglected and the chemical industry languished.

Centralisation of industrial planning was strengthened, and new ideas in economic theory, whether on capitalist countries (Varga) or economic rationality at home (e.g. Novozhilov) were suppressed. No one dared mention input–output techniques. Kantorovich's ideas, originally devised in 1939, were also ignored, their author having to 'retire' into pure mathematics. The energetic and talented chief planner, Voznesensky, was arrested and executed. Finally, Stalin himself, in his last work, *The Economic Problems of Socialism in the USSR* (1952), warned economists not to interfere: 'The rational organisation of the productive forces, economic planning, etc., are not problems of political economy, but of the economic policy of the directing bodies.'

Economic policy and performance in Stalin's last years were doubt-less affected by the re-switch of resources into armaments, and a sharp rise in numbers in the armed forces (the published military budget in 1952 was 45 per cent above the level of 1950). There is evidence that war was regarded as a serious possibility on both sides of the 'Iron Curtain'.

Soon after Stalin died, Malenkov was edged out of the top position in the Party, retaining the post of Prime Minister. Khrushchev was at this point only the senior of several Party secretaries, but lost no time in consolidating his position (acquiring in September 1953 the title of First Secretary). He must therefore have had an influence –

though not yet decisive – on policy also in the period that can be called the Malenkov interregnum.

The new leadership speedily took steps to de-compress the atmosphere: agriculture, consumer goods industries, housing, were given higher priority. In October 1953 an accelerated programme of consumer goods production was announced, cutting back on investment, while also cutting prices. This proved to be unsound economically, in that all this could not be done at once without causing shortages and overstrain. When, in February 1955, Malenkov finally fell, this was accompanied by criticism of his pro-consumer-goods policy; some so-called 'woebegone economists' (*gore-ekonomisty*) were charged with having fallen for the heresy that consumer goods output could rise faster than that of producers' goods. It therefore appears that Khrushchev rode to power with the help of the heavy industry lobby. However, his subsequent actions suggest that his own priorities were also pro-consumer, though with greater relative emphasis on agriculture.

THE ABORTIVE SIXTH FIVE-YEAR PLAN AND THE POLITICAL CRISIS OF 1956–7

The fifth plan fulfilment record was a fairly successful one, even if one allows for a degree of 'inflation' in the global indices (the 'Malenkov' accelerated programme is ignored in Table 4.2). It is on this basis that the XX Party Congress adopted the Sixth Plan, of which the principal targets are given in Table 4.2.

In the process of drafting the new plan, stress was laid on the need to study foreign techniques (Khrushchev remarked acidly that some Soviet 'inventions' reproduced rather imperfectly what had been long ago introduced in the West), and a State Committee on New Techniques was created in 1955. A number of measures were also adopted to streamline and co-ordinate the planning process and to enlarge the role of management, to combat bureaucracy and so on.

Yet this plan was still-born. At a plenum of the Central Committee held in December 1956 it was decided that the investment plan was out of line with available resources, that the plan was over-taut. It was to be revised. At the same time Pervukhin was made more or less economic overlord. In fact the plan was never revised. It was abandoned. Evidently the 'Anti-Party group' (to use the label Khrushchev subsequently attached to it) was in the business of reducing

TABLE 4.2 *Plan and Fulfilment*

	1950	1955 plan	1955 actual	1960 plan
National income (1950 = 100)	100	160	171	160*
Gross industrial production	100	170	185	165*
Producers' goods	100	180	191	170*
Consumer goods	100	165	175	160*
Coal (million tonnes)	261.1	373.4	389.9	592
Oil (million tonnes)	37.9	70.9	70.8	135
Electricity (milliard kwh)	91.2	164.2	170.2	320
Pig iron (million tonnes)	19.2	33.8	33.3	53
Steel (million tonnes)	27.3	44.2	45.3	68.3
Tractors (15-h.p. units)	246.1	292.9	314.0	–
Mineral fertiliser (million tonnes)	5.5	10.3	9.7	120
Cement (million tonnes)	10.2	22.4	22.5	55
Commercial timber (million cubic metres)	161.0	251.2	212.1	301
Cotton fabrics (million metres)	3899	6277	5905	–
Wool fabrics (million metres)	155.2	239.0	252.3	–
Leather footwear (million pairs)	203	315	271	–
Sugar (thousand tonnes)	2523	4491	3419	–
Fish (thousand tonnes)	1755	2773	2737	–

*1955 = 100

Sources: *Narkhoz.*, 1965: pp. 130–9, 557; *Promyshlennost SSSR* (1957): p. 43; *Direktivy XIX Sezda Partii po pyatlitnemu planu razvitiya SSSR na 1951–5 gody* (1952): pp. 3–4; 25; *Direktivy XX Sezda KPSS po Shestomu pyatlitnemu planu razvitiya norodnogo khozyaistva SSSR na 1956–60 gg.*; *XX Sezda KPSS stenotchet*, vol. ɪɪ (1956).

Note: I am aware that, since 70 per cent of industrial output consisted of producers' goods, the 1960 Plan indices for gross industrial production are inconsistent. But that is how they appeared in the Plan.

the economic powers of the First Secretary. Khrushchev's counter-attack eventually succeeded in getting rid of his opponents, which at that moment were in a majority in the Party Presidium. In the process he pushed through the drastic remedy of abolishing virtually all the industrial Ministries, substituting regional councils (*sovnarkhozy*), which were to be co-ordinated by Gosplan.

THE *SOVNARKHOZY* AND THE SEVEN-YEAR PLAN

It is hard to disentangle the political from the economic motives for this reform. There certainly was (and still is) a tendency for Ministries to form self-contained, self-supplying 'empires', with the result of needless duplication of component production, wasteful crosshauls, waste of by-products, plus all the familiar problems of departmental boundary-lines (*Vedomstvennye baryery*). At the same time, Khrushchev may well have been influenced by his desire to attack the Ministries for political reasons, as part of his counter-attack on what came to be known (after its final defeat) as the 'Anti-Party group'. The effect of basing industrial planning on *regional* economic councils, almost all of which coincided with the boundaries of *oblasti* or republics, represented a transfer of power towards local and republican *Party* organs, since these were dominant *vis-à-vis* any state institutions operating within 'their' territories. At this stage in his career Khrushchev was apparently relying on the Party machine – though this changed a few years later, as we shall see.

However, given the centralising logic of a modern industrial economy of a non-market type, the *sovnarkhozy* (105 initially) represented a step in the wrong direction. While decentralisation to management, already being proposed by reform-minded economists in 1955-6, might have represented a viable alternative to the 'traditional' system, *sovnarkhozy* were inevitably subject to the disease known as *mestnichestvo*, or 'localism'. An authority with power over the resources of a given area is bound to direct them to the needs of the area, which is its area of knowledge and responsibility, unless prevented from doing so by orders from some superior authority. (See Nove, *Problems of Communism*, Nov–Dec 1957). Precisely this began to happen, as was attested by numerous complaints in the press. Also it is an evident weakness of regionalisation that the common problems of each industry became no one's central responsibility, except the overworked Gosplan, which, in this scheme, emerged as the supreme co-ordinator. If Khrushchev thought that the local Party secretaries would ensure the priority of central as against local needs, he was sadly mistaken, as can be seen from the wording of a decree of 4 August 1958, denouncing *mestnichestvo*.

An exception had to be made at once for the armaments industry, which quite plainly required a central 'overlord'. This was followed by the creation of numerous State Committees, which replaced some

of the functions of the Ministries, but without the power to issue
orders.

So the stage was set for recentralisation, but still without the
resurrection of the economic Ministries (these did not return until
after Khrushchev's fall). There was also a bewildering series of
changes affecting the power of Gosplan, which was split and
relabelled (thus *Gosekonomsovet* was set up in 1960, with the task
of perspective planning, and in 1962 there came into being the
Sovnarkhoz of the USSR, with the function of implementing plans
drafted by Gosplan). But this is running ahead. Suffice it to say that
there was much administrative confusion and crossed wires. Formally
speaking the enterprises' immediate superior was 'their' *sovnarkhoz*.
In practice production tasks and material allocation were progress-
ively recentralised, which in fact meant that enterprises were subject
to many masters, none of whom had direct responsibility for the
totality of the enterprises' functioning. *Sovnarkhozy* lost what power
they had: in 1962 the head of the Estonian *sovnarkhoz* complained
that it controlled only 0.2 per cent of that republic's output (*Ekonom-
icheskaya gazeta*, 10 Nov. 1962).

But let us return to the actual drafting of plans. The years 1957
and 1958 could be described as 'orphan' years, in that no long-term
plan covered them after the abandonment of the 1956–60 Plan. A
Seven-Year Plan was drafted in 1957–8, and Table 4.3 gives details
of this plan and also its fulfilment (the period ended in the year
following Khrushchev's fall).

The usual caveat concerning aggregate growth indices is needed,
but performance was reasonably good in physical terms too, even
though the rapidly expanding chemical and gas industries were well
below targets, as was also the case with textiles. Khrushchev was
well aware of the backwardness of the chemical industry (especially
in providing synthetics, and also mineral fertiliser), and pressed for
extremely ambitious projects to overcome this backwardness,
quicker than was strictly feasible. Similarly, he correctly observed
the overdependence of the USSR on solid fuels, with natural gas
neglected, and once again the plans outstripped practical possibilities. He also demanded (and obtained) a very big increase in
cement, which he believed to be superior to bricks as a building
material. Subsequent criticism rightly pointed to the tendency to
overdo things. A favourite phrase of Khrushchev's was that 'in the
next two to three years' various ambitious targets were to be reached
in industry and in agriculture. The effort to do so was not seldom

TABLE 4.3   *The Seven-Year Plan, drafted 1957–8*

	1958	1965 Plan	1965 actual
National income	100	162–5	158
Gross industrial output (index)	100	180	184
Producers' goods	100	185–8	196
Consumers' goods	100	162–5	160
Iron ore (million tonnes)	88.8	150–60	153.4
Pig iron (million tonnes)	39.6	65–70	66.2
Steel (million tonnes)	54.9	86–91	91.0
Coal (million tonnes)	493	600–12	578
Oil (million tonnes)	113	230–40	242.9
Gas (milliard cubic metres)	29.9	150	129.3
Electricity (milliard kWh)	235	500–20	507
Mineral fertiliser (million tonnes)	12	35	31.6
Synthetic fibres (thousand tonnes)	166	666	407
Machine tools (thousands)	138	190–200	185
Tractors (thousands)	220	–	355
Commercial timber (million cubic metres)	251	275–80	273
Cement (million tonnes)	33.3	75–81	72.4
Cotton fabrics (million square metres)	5.79	7.7–8.0	7.08
Wool fabrics (million square metres)	303	485	365
Leather footwear (million pairs)	356.4	515	486

Sources: *Narkhoz.*, 1960: pp. 210–12; *Narkhoz.*, 1965: pp. 136–9, 262, 557, 609; *Seven-Year Plan, 1959–65*.

disorganising in its effects. Thus 'campaigning' to produce more cement and natural gas had as one consequence shortages of coal and bricks (for evidence see, for instance, A. Birman in *Novyi mir*, no. 1, 1967). Similarly, his attack on so-called 'steel-eaters', who use and plan for too much steel, contributed to a shortage of metal – since no effective measures to stimulate economy were taken.

The years 1958–9 could be said to mark the high point of Khrushchev's confidence and relative political and economic success. The successful launch of the world' first Sputnik, followed by Gagarin's flight into space, highlighted what seemed to be the USSR's technological achievement. Growth rates were impressive. Khrushchev's travels in Third-World countries, and Soviet aid, seemed to promise substantial political dividends. The Western book markets soon saw many works on 'Soviet economic warfare'. This feeling of confidence was widely shared among the citizenry (though foreign aid was and is unpopular): living standards were rising, consumer durables of many kinds became widely available, housing improved (from very low levels, to be sure), there were significant social reforms (pensions, maternity leave, minimum wages, for example, were increased in 1956–7) and optimism seemed justified. It is on this basis that Khrushchev began confidently to forecast the date at which the USSR would overtake the USA in per-capita production, and he also announced that the first steps towards 'communism' – the provision of some goods and services free – would be taken by the early 1980s. Needless to say these things are not now spoken of. There have been disappointments. But we should not forget that the future seemed much brighter, to Khrushchev as well as to ordinary people, when the Seven-Year plan was launched.

DECLINE AND FALL: WHAT WENT WRONG?

Some of the reasons for Khrushchev's fall relate to matters uncon-nected with industry (e.g. agricultural failures, the Cuban missile crisis). However, industrial problems certainly made their contri-bution. One cause has already been touched upon: too many reor-ganisations, leading to disorganisation. In 1962–3 a series of changes affected the role of local Party officials and their relationship with industrial management (and agriculture too). The Party was split into industrial and agricultural parts, an unprecedented and shocking decision. Furthermore the number of *sovnarkhozy* was sharply reduced, from over 100 to 47, so that they no longer corresponded to the boundaries of *obkom* Party secretaries' powers. This was a puzzling set of measures: on the one hand the division of the Party seemed to be aimed at strengthening its controlling and supervising functions; on the other, the lack of correspondence between the boundaries of the *oblasti* and those of the enlarged *sovnarkhozy* made such supervision difficult, plainly reduced the powers of the local secretaries. Since something similar was being done on rural areas it seems that Khrushchev was dissatisfied with the Party officials' 'localist' deviations and meant to cut down their functions. Apart from any practical consequence of such measures they had the political effect of uniting the local Party secretariats against him and so contributed very directly to his overthrow – after which all these measures were speedily reversed.

The last years of his reign saw a notable slowdown in growth throughout the economy. It is by no means easy to explain the reasons, or to give adequate weight to each. The reasons were overwhelmingly internal: foreign trade was expanding (it expanded much faster after Khrushchev's fall), and so industry's troubles cannot be explained by external factors.

One reason could well have been the impact of the *sovnarkhozy* and the confused *ad hoc* recentralisation of these years. But a deeper-lying one concerned the nature of the planning system itself. Khrushchev inherited a highly centralised system, created under Stalin to transform an underdeveloped society into a great military power quickly. New problems were bound to arise, not only because of greater complexity, but also through what could be called the 'dilution of priorities': under Stalin's successors great efforts were made to modernise agriculture, to build more houses, to increase the supply and assortment of consumers' goods and services. No longer was it possible to give top priority to heavy industry and let all errors and shortages be absorbed by the rest of the civilian economy. The Soviet press, and economic literature, began to express numerous criticisms, highlighting the often wasteful inefficiency of the system. Liberman's articles attracted attention, as did the ideas of Kantorovich, Novozhilov, Nemchinov and many others. Leontief wrote a piece on 'The fall and rise of Soviet economics'; this was the period which saw a notable rise.

Khrushchev and his comrades became aware that something was amiss; resolutions were adopted to encourage managerial initiative, to cut down the number of compulsory plan indicators. The largely abortive *sovnarkhoz* reform was also an attempt to cope with over-centralisation. But the basic problem remained: the essence of the Soviet economic model was (and still is) the issuance of administrative orders (compulsory plans) as to whom should produce what, with resources allocated by the planning agencies; 'commodity-money relations' and the profit motive play a secondary role. Since prices do not, either in theory or practice, reflect relative scarcity or supply-and-demand relationships this is hardly surprising. Under Khrushchev there were many organisational changes, but the basic principles remained unaltered, and indeed have remained unaltered under his successors.

A further source of strain was the arms programme. The official arms expenditure figure, which must be seen as only a very partial reflection of reality, showed a sharp rise in the budget of 1961. The crushing superiority of the USA in nuclear weaponry emerged clearly in the Cuban missile crisis. So Khrushchev – and even more his successors – increased military spending, a direct competitor for resources needed for industrial investment.

A sharp fall in the rate of increase of investment was a feature of the period: increases of 16 per cent and 13 per cent were recorded in 1958 and 1959 respectively. In 1961–3 the increases ranged from 4 per cent to 5 per cent. In these years, due no doubt to shortage of material means, there was a cutback in decentralised investment and also in private house-building.

He was removed in October 1964. An ungrateful public seems to have forgotten him. In retrospect one can see him not only as a reorganiser-disorganiser, but also one under whom supplies of food-stuffs and consumer durables increased impressively; life became more tolerable for ordinary citizens. And if he was unable fully to comprehend, let alone solve, the problems which stood in the way of industrial efficiency, the same can be said of those who followed him.

An economic or political historian in the next century is, in my view, bound to evaluate Khrushchev's record positively, but would distinguish the period of his rise, 1953–8, as the most fruitful. After Stalin's grim remoteness, his much more approachable, human, folksy style was a welcome contrast (except for those of his fellow countrymen who believed that rulers should be remote and digni-fied). He did devote much attention to sectors neglected under Stalin, and he has a good record on social welfare. His first years saw not only high growth rates, but also better harvests, and much greater freedom of discussion, including discussion of economic short-comings, as well as the publication of a wide range of previously secret statistics. But he was a child of the Stalin era, he was incon-sistent, he blustered; after getting rid of his enemies he became more unpredictable, given to 'hare-brained schemes' and campaign methods, reorganisation and exhortation. He thought he could correct defects through the Party machine, and then correct the Party machine itself, but that was a fatal error: the machine was able to get rid of him.

5 Science, Technology and Innovation

M. J. BERRY

INTRODUCTION

The development of science, technology and innovation in the Khrushchev period has been dealt with in a number of Western studies. The most detailed account of developments in the period is to be found in the OECD study *Science Policy in the USSR* (Zaleski *et al.*, 1969) and a number of recent studies examine the changes in the USSR Academy of Sciences in this period (Lowenhardt, 1982: pp. 127–94; Vucinich, 1984) and the relationship between politics and technology (Parrott 1983: pp. 127–79). We are also fortunate in having Zhores Medvedev's accounts of this period from within the Soviet scientific community (Medvedev, 1975 and 1979).

The period 1953 to 1964 was one of great activity, when a wide variety of decrees and other measures poured out, dealing with almost every aspect of scientific and technical progress. It was a period of rapid expansion of manpower and financial inputs into science and technology and of dramatic Soviet successes in space, but at the end of the period many of the problems which had caused concern at the beginning of the period still remained.

THE EVOLUTION OF POLICY IN THE KHRUSHCHEV PERIOD

Continuity and Change

Even without the death of Stalin it is clear that in the early 1950s the Soviet Union was facing a difficult transitional period – a change

71

from industrialisation to what later became known as the 'scientific and technical revolution'. In practice there was considerable continuity between the pre-1953 and post-1953 periods, although, clearly in certain areas important changes took place.

The main features of the Stalinist legacy were: first, there were the negative features of the Stalinist system itself – the fear and insecurity, the isolation from foreign science, the all-pervading secrecy and the imprisonment experienced by many scientists; second, there was the dominant role played by the military priority areas which absorbed enormous amounts of resources for the development of atomic weapons, rockets and jet aircraft; and, third, there were some elements of a basic organisational structure for the administration and planning of technical progress in the Soviet economy.

The last years of Stalin saw considerable successes in the priority fields, but outside these areas problems were building up. The Soviet Union had made heroic efforts to catch up the advanced capitalist countries in the 1930s and in the post-war period had overcome the enormous problems caused by the war. Despite these achievements it had not managed to develop a system for making innovation a continuous and integrated part of its economic development. In the view of one Soviet economist, 'At the start of the 1950s a problem arose which exists to this day – the economy divided into two parts – there was production and there was new technology which had to be introduced into it' (*Problemy*, 1975: p. 9).

Khrushchev and his colleagues clearly intended from the beginning to rule in a different way from Stalin and began to modify some of the worst aspects of Stalinism. Thus the charges in the 'Doctors' Plot' and the associated campaign against Jewish scientists were soon dismissed and many scientists began to be released from prison research institutes and the camps and were rehabilitated (Medvedev, 1979: p. 57).

The new leadership soon turned its attention to other major questions of technical progress, and its views were first expressed by the 1955 conference on industry (*CDSP*, vol. VII, no. 20: pp. 3–6) and the decree of 28 May 1955 (*KPSS o kulture*, 1963: pp. 471–5), the July 1955 Party Plenum (Bulganin, 1955) and its decree (*Postanovleniya*, 1956) and the XX Party Congress in February–March 1956 (*XX sezd*, 1956). Initially the leading role at these meetings was taken by Bulganin, but already by the XX Party Congress Khrushchev was beginning to take a more active interest in questions of technical progress. These meetings and the associated measures provided the basis for many of the changes in this period.

Perhaps one of the most difficult problems which Stalin had left behind was how to change the psychological climate which had grown up during the years of Stalinism. The atmosphere of fear, uncertainty and arbitrariness which formed the background to Soviet life affected science no less than other areas of society. In addition in the post-war period science had become enmeshed in a cloak of secrecy which permeated many aspects of both military and non-military research and development (R and D), cutting off institutes from one another and even raising barriers within institutes. This was accompanied by the almost complete isolation of Soviet science from world science in the post-war period which cut off scientists from much information on the latest developments and from any contact with foreign colleagues. This was the time, as Khrushchev commented later, 'when the idea was intensively propagandised that everything that was ours was unconditionally ideal and everything foreign was unconditionally bad' (*Plenum (1963)* 1964: p. 29). As a result developments in foreign science were little-known and often underestimated while the achievements of Soviet science were exaggerated. This situation was accompanied by a strong campaign for ideological purity in science which had as its main targets 'cosmopolitanism, idealism and objectivism' (Vucinich, 1984: p. 255).

The pyschological climate which Khrushchev inherited had two main components. The first of these was a fear of taking risks and an avoidance of taking responsibility for decisions. This attitude was a natural response to the Stalinist period, but it was also reinforced by the fragmented nature of the R and D network and the centralised planning and decision-making processes which removed from the lower-level organisations any real responsibility for their actions.

The second component was a generally optimistic attitude to problems of technical progress in the Soviet economy. This view was based on a combination of real achievements, propaganda and isolation from foreign science. The Soviet Union had won the war against enormous odds and had developed the atomic and hydrogen bombs at record speed and was developing new jet aircraft and rockets. Many factories were producing much more sophisticated products than they had done in the past and found it difficult to accept that they were not at the forefront of technical progress (see Amann and Cooper, 1982: pp. 54–5).

These problems were discussed by the new leadership, but it is clear that they paid more attention to the second problem. This is because the first point was inextricably linked with the whole bureaucratic administrative and planning system. Initially it was hoped that it could be solved by criticism and exhortation. Thus Bulganin at the 1955 industry conference spoke of the loss by industrial managers of 'any sense of responsibility to the state for the tasks entrusted to them' (see *CDSP*, vol. VII, no. 20: p. 3). He also stressed the need for more criticism and self-criticism in research institutes and an end to unnecessary secrecy, which often protected people from criticism (*XX sezd*, 1956, 2: pp. 32–3). Factory managers too were criticised for their attitude, which made them unwilling to bother about new ideas. The motto of one of the managers in Granin's novel on this period *Iskateli* 'never be the first to try the new or the last to abandon the old' (Granin, 1969: p. 129) was probably shared by many managers. Khrushchev vividly described such managers in his speech at the XX Party Congress: one 'sits and thinks, why should I get involved in this? There's a lot of fuss and what's the good, you can get a lot of unpleasantness. Is it worth worrying about? Let them do the thinking at the top, let the bosses do it. If there is a directive about it, then we'll see. Another, even after receiving a directive, applies his energy to avoiding any real action' (*XX sezd*, 1956, *I*: pp. 45–6). The Ministries too came under attack for their inertia and stagnation and a number of branches were said to be 'doomed to backwardness, which inflicts considerable damage on the state'. In such Ministries there was no struggle against conservatism and tolerance of people who cling to the old and obsolete' (*KPSS o kulture*, 1963: p. 472). The May 1955 decree called for the strengthening of the control of R and D within the Ministries and the appointment of a Deputy Minister with responsibility for innovation. It also stressed that industrial management from the Minister down to the factory department heads bore personal responsibility for prompt innovation (*KPSS o kulture*, 1963: pp. 474–5).

It was much easier to introduce considerable changes in official policy towards foreign science and technology. As Vucinich points out, 'Destalinisation in science concentrated on two main activities: 1) rehabilitating theories and disciplines banned by the Stalinists on ideological grounds and 2) opening the doors of Soviet science to current revolutionary developments in Western science even when orthodox philosophers attacked them as contaminated by ideological impurities.' (Vucinich, 1984: p. 258). The ending of isolation was quickly and easily accomplished and promised considerable benefits. Scientific contacts were rapidly expanded – in 1952 the USSR Academy of Sciences was working in only three international organisations, but by 1957 this had risen to 69 (Belyaev, 1982: p. 84). The All-Union Institute for Scientific Information, which had been set up in 1952 rapidly expanded its work and by 1957, was covering over 17 000 foreign periodicals (*Survey*, Autumn 1971: p. 36). There was also a substantial increase in the number of Soviet scientists going abroad, from 175 in 1954 to over 2000 in 1958 although after this the increase slowed down considerably (*Survey*, Autumn 1971: p. 43). It still remained extremely difficult to make a visit abroad and many obstacles were put in the way of Soviet scientists who wanted to establish contacts with foreign scientists (Medvedev, 1975).

The more difficult problem was to alter people's attitudes towards Soviet achievements. Bulganin at the July 1955 Plenum attacked people who considered that it was not worth studying foreign experience. Such people, he commented, hide their own ignorance behind conceited phrases (Bulganin, 1955: p. 25). He stressed that 'we cannot, we do not have the right to forget that technology in capitalist countries does not stand still, but, under the influence of the arms race, competition and the capitalists' pursuit of maximum profits, it has moved ahead in a number of fields' (Bulganin, 1955: p. 23). He also called for greater study of foreign achievements, the expansion of links with research establishments and progressive scientists abroad, the increased purchase of foreign technical literature and its publication in the USSR (Bulganin, 1955: p. 25; see also *XX sezd*, 1956, 2: p. 33). These advances in the West meant that the Soviet Union could save time and effort by borrowing existing ideas. In Medvedev's view 'Khrushchev's initial steps were simple and logical. His plan was to assimilate the modern methods of American and West European industry, to repeat the advances made by foreign technology and to duplicate "creatively" their technological and scientific work' (Medvedev, 1979: p. 62.) This was accompanied by a considerable increase in purchases of foreign technology particularly in the engineering industry and after 1958 in the chemical industry.

It was relatively easy to remove the feeling of complacency about the technological level of Soviet civilian industry, but the problem of inertia and lack of initiative was much more difficult to deal with. The problem was made worse by the fragmented nature of the innovation process, since there was no overall goal equally meaningful for all participants. As a result each organisation involved in the process strove to maximise its own benefit. The factory as the last organisation in the process was faced with two problems – it was expected to fulfil its production plan and introduce new products, which usually had come from outside and brought the factory nothing but problems. Given the clear economic benefits which came from fulfilling the production plan it is not surprising that this took precedence over innovation. At the Ministry level too the obsession with the fulfilment of the production plan dominated everything. Since emphasis on technical progress was not accompanied by clear penalties for failure and clear rewards for success it was accorded a low-priority.

The 1955–6 meetings and decrees raised a number of other points concerning technical progress and these can be summarised as follows:

(a) Research and Development

There were said to be serious defects in the work of research institutes which were working on many trivial and abstract projects and producing poor results. The fragmentation of research between the USSR Academy of Sciences, the ministerial system and the higher education sector was criticised. There was a lack of a clear division of responsibilities, which led to duplication and parallelism in their work, and was exacerbated by poor co-ordination. The higher-education sector was not making a sufficiently large contribution to the R and D effort. There was an excessive concentration of R and D organisations in Moscow and Leningrad, which often meant that they were long distances from the industries they served. Generally the links between R and D organisations and industry were poor. The experimental facilities of research institutes and their level of equipment were in need of improvement. The rights of directors of research institutes should be expanded.

(b) Innovation

The poor provision of resources both material and financial for this stage was criticised. Many factories were unwilling to bother with innovation because of all the problems involved. In the view of scientists it was easier to invent a new machine than to introduce it (*CDSP*, vol. VII, no. 20: p. 4). In the view of Nesmeyanov, the President of the USSR Academy of Sciences, the key problem was 'the planned economy meeting an unplanned innovation' (*XX sezd*, 1956, 1: p. 371).

(c) Ministries

These were criticised for poor management of their R and D organisations and of innovation. There was no attempt to concentrate resources on major projects.

(c) Manpower

Considerable concern was expressed about the manpower situation. Many R and D personnel had produced no results for many years. Manpower should be increased, but it was important to improve its quality and to get rid of unsatisfactory workers. Too many young graduates were going straight into R and D work without any industrial experience. There was also a tendency for Ministries to ask for more and more engineers rather than technicians, which meant that there were not enough technicians per engineer to ensure their efficient work.

The situation was also complicated by a number of other factors which were emerging in this period and changing the conditions in which Soviet science and technology were operating. First, the Soviet stress on specialisation and large production runs meant that it was becoming increasingly expensive to change models, which tended to inhibit innovation. Hitherto innovation in Soviet industry had usually taken the form of periodic major changes often associated with the construction of new factories and little attention had been paid to incremental innovation. Second, in the rest of the world the rate of technical progress was accelerating. This meant that it was increasingly difficult for the Soviet Union to catch up quickly once it had fallen behind. The long lead times in Soviet industry meant that machines were sometimes obsolete before they went into production. Third, many new machines involved qualitative changes in production – it was no longer enough to turn out large numbers of relatively simple machines. The new machines were much more sophisticated and thus much more difficult to manufacture. They required a completely different approach which did not fit easily into the existing system of planning indicators. Finally, many of the new developments in science and technology were emerging at the meeting-points of established sciences and industries and were difficult to accommodate in the rigid, compartmentalised system of Soviet R and D and the industrial Ministries.

Throughout the period there was considerable discussion of the problems of Soviet R and D and innovation, but it was a discussion of symptoms rather than the underlying causes. This was not really surprising since the study of science of science – *naukovedenie* – was still in its embryonic stage in the USSR. Khrushchev had very little in the way of academic studies or reliable data to guide him in his policies.

The problems of technical progress were discussed at the XXI and XXII Party Congresses, the Party Plenums of 1958, 1959, 1960, 1962 and 1963 and the 1961 conference of scientists and other meetings and in articles in the press by politicians and administrators, practising scientists, factory managers and so on, each with their own point of view to put across. Criticism flowed in abundance, covering every aspect of Soviet R and D and innovation performance. For Khrushchev, however, it was very much a question of trying to find practical solutions which would help to improve the system he had inherited. He supported some interest groups whose ideas seemed to fit in with his own and looked for advice to leading scientists, particularly those working in the defence sector, such as Kurchatov, with whom he was on good terms (Khrushchev, 1977: pp. 92–4) though he did make mistakes as in the case of Lysenko. In addition he clearly had some ideas of his own. He was hampered in his efforts by the fact that he was largely operating in uncharted waters. He could only do the things which seemed to him sensible and operate by trial and error. The trouble was that in this field many changes needed a long time to take effect and Khrushchev wanted quick results.

In addition issuing a decree did not necessarily mean that the intended aim was achieved. The Soviet system was adept at absorbing decrees and changing nothing and many good intentions were lost in a sea of bureaucracy.

The measures which he subsequently took followed a number of main aims: (1) to create an efficient, centralised system for managing and planning technical progress while encouraging initiative and the voluntary participation of scientists in administration; (2) to rationalise the R and D network; (3) to improve the economic efficiency of the R and D process and to use economic levers to encourage technical progress; and (4) to increase the inputs into R and D as a means of increasing the results obtained.

The administration of R and D.

There were some attempts under Stalin to develop a system of administration and planning for R and D and innovation, but these had not progressed very far by the time of his death. The next eleven years saw considerable developments in this area as Khrushchev tried various methods to improve the central administration and planning of technical progress. The first steps in these policies were taken in 1955–6, but this whole area was considerably affected by the 1957 reorganisation of industrial administration. This reorganisation was not directly concerned with R and D, but by changing the whole basis of industrial administration could not but have a profound effect on it.

The 1957 reorganisation was Khrushchev's great gamble. If it had worked it promised to solve several of the key problems of Soviet industry. From the point of view of industry as a whole it had the laudable aim of revitalising industry by giving more power to the regions to develop and rationalise their own industry and to break the power of the central Ministries, which had built for themselves industrial 'empires', the power and prestige of which they guarded jealously. It was also intended to help overcome the power of the bureaucracy and encourage initiative.

The reorganisation had its greatest impact on R and D in the area of its administration and threw it into confusion for the rest of the Khrushchev period. Khrushchev had originally planned to transfer all the R and D organisations to the local economic councils (*sovnarkhozy*), but later modified this after criticism. (Parrott, 1983: p. 173). Instead the main R and D organisations of the abolished Ministries remained at the centre under the control of a new department of Gosplan, *Glavniiproekt*. At the beginning of 1959 there were 76 research institutes under this body (Belyaev and Pyshkova 1979: pp. 135–6), as well as a number of project institutes (Jackson, 1967: p. 67). This was a curious period in the development of the Soviet R and D system with research institutes placed under the direct control of the central planning body. This should have meant that the planning of R and D became easier, but this does not seem to have been the case and seems to have been only an *ad hoc* temporary measure. These major research institutes were designated 'head' research institutes and were given the task of co-ordinating the R and D organisations working in their fields and checking their plans to avoid duplication.

The problems of implementing a unified technical policy in these conditions soon became clear and gradually from 1959 onwards State Committees were set up to control specific branches of industries, rather like the old Ministries but without factories under their control. These bodies were responsible for R and D and to them were transferred not only the head research institutes from *Glavniiproekt*, but also some of the more important R and D organisations which had been placed under the *sovnarkhozy*.

Co-ordination and Planning

A central body with responsibility for innovation had existed between 1949 and 1951. Not unexpectedly one of the first steps of the new leadership was to reestablish a very similar body. A decree of May 1955 established the State Committee for New Technology (*Gostekhnika*) with a wide range of responsibilities for the encouragement and development of innovation (*KPSS o kulture*, 1963: pp. 472–3). The State Committee existed in that form for only two years and in the 1957 reorganisation was changed into the State Scientific and Technical Committee with its duties modified to take into account the new regional structure of industrial administration (Zaleski *et al.*, 1969: p. 55). The establishment of an effective central body was far from easy. In effect it had to take over responsibilities from existing organisations such as the USSR Academy of Sciences, Gosplan, the Ministries and the higher education sector. The situation became even more complicated after the 1957 reform. The first two bodies were criticised for their bureaucratic approach to planning at the 1961 conference of scientists (*Vsesoyuznoe soveshchanie*, 1961: p. 223). *Gostekhnika* had tried to co-ordinate projects both large and small and had not achieved the desired results while the State Scientific and Technical Committee could not fulfil its role of co-ordination since it did not finance projects (*Vsesoyuznoe soveshchanie*, 1961: p. 151). In recognition of the co-ordination problem the

Committee was reorganised in 1961 as the State Committee for Co-ordination of Research and given more powers (Maevskii, 1962: p. 10), and as its name implies, specific duties to co-ordinate R and D. By this time its work had become easier because of the rationalisation of planning whereby responsibility was more clearly divided between the USSR Academy of Sciences – fundamental research, the State Committee – applied research, and Gosplan – innovation (Zaleski *et al.*, 1969: p. 578).

Co-ordination had become an important issue, particularly after the 1957 reform with the proliferation of bodies controlling R and D organisations. It was carried out at the lower levels by the head institutes which were responsible for examining all the research plans of the organisations working in their fields and checking them for duplication (Zaleski *et al.*, 1969: pp. 447–8). In addition to the head institutes there were also a number of Science Councils under the USSR Academy of Sciences and the State Committee for the Co-ordination of Research which were responsible for co-ordinating work on major problems. Such Councils had existed in the pre-war period, but the system was reorganised and formalised in 1961 (Zaleski *et al.*, 1969: pp. 227–31, 446). They were part of Khrush-chev's initiative to expand the voluntary component in the adminis-tration of science and to encourage scientists to play an active role in this (*XXI sezd*, 1959, 2: p. 210). Co-ordination was a rather unclear and undeveloped legal concept at this time and difficult to implement in practice (Maevskii, 1962: pp. 6–7). What it largely came down to in practice was correcting the mistakes or omissions of the planning system. The bodies concerned lacked any financial muscle to ensure their instructions were carried out and depended on the co-operation of the bodies being co-ordinated. As Blagonravov pointed out at the 1961 Conference, co-ordination was little more than the compilation of common work plans and discussion of their prospects; it involved little real co-ordination on schedules and did not eliminate parallel work and waste (*Vsesoyuznoe soveshchanie*, 1961: pp. 178–9).

Although science had been planned for many years in the Soviet Union, in practice the level of planning was fairly primitive and it was only in the post-war period that the first steps towards an inte-grated system of plans began. In the early 1950s the plan was little more than an annual list of projects and was not integrated with research programmes or provided with equipment, investment or manpower (Noulting, 1978: p. 7).

The Khrushchev period saw the gradual expansion of the coverage of the planning of technical progress to include finance, manpower and supplies. At the same time major projects were singled out and the importance of inter-branch problems was recognised (Zaleski *et al.*, 1969: 75–7). Attempts were also made to ensure that the plan for the introduction of new technology was prepared ahead of the production plans (Zaleski *et al.*, 1969: pp. 82–3).

Despite these measures planning still remained unsatisfactory and the annual plans introduced an artificial break into research projects which often lasted for longer periods. In practice too the central plans were often simple aggregations of the plans of the R and D organisations and consisted of hundreds of pages and thousands of projects (Zaleski *et al.*, 1969: pp. 89 and 271). In such circumstances it is not surprising that Academician Semenov at the December 1963 Plenum denounced 'bureaucratic paper planning' of science (*Plenum 1963*, 1964, p. 309). Fulfilment of these plans was far from good (Zaleski *et al.* 1969: p. 89). In the case of the innovation plan this was largely due to the low status of this plan in comparison with the production plan for enterprises. As one speaker pointed out at the 1959 Party Plenum, Gosplan tried to allocate the least possible amount of materials and most often allocates nothing for its fulfilment (*Plenum 1959*, 1960: p. 359). Some attempt to deal with the problem of continuity was made by the introduction of the planning of research projects from the start of research to innovation as was called for by Kosygin at the 1961 Conference (*Vsesoyuznoe soveshchanie*, 1961: p. 42), but little was achieved in practice.

Planning did develop in this period, but remained a very complicated, slow and bureaucratic process and faced many problems. In particular it lacked an objective system for the selection of projects and this often depended on the push of organisations or individuals rather than the quality of the projects (Jackson, 1967: p. 286). In addition it failed to find a method of integrating Nesmeyanov's 'unplanned innovation' into the planned economy.

The R and D Network

At the start of the Khrushchev period the R and D network fell into three main groups: the USSR Academy of Sciences and its related bodies, the Ministerial R and D network and the higher education sector which played a markedly inferior role. As Bulganin pointed out, this network had grown up in a haphazard way over the years and had never been examined as a whole and rationalised (*XX sezd*, 1956, 2: p. 34).

(a) The USSR Academy of Sciences

The USSR Academy of Sciences was the most important single body in Soviet science at the start of the Khrushchev period. Before the October Revolution its predecessor was concerned only with fundamental research, but in the 1930s it was called on to play a larger role in helping the economic development of the USSR. The post-war period had seen a rapid increase in the number of research institutes in the Academy's division of technical sciences. Medvedev explains this by the fact that it was partly an artificial development caused by the system of categorisation of research institutes which had been instituted in 1951. As a result of this it was easier for an Academy institute to recruit good scientists than the Ministerial sector (Medvedev, 1979: pp. 70–1). This trend was a cause of concern for two main reasons. First, it led to some duplication of effort between the Academy and the Ministerial system. Second, it was viewed with suspicion by some of the leading fundamental scientists in the Academy who saw their position of dominance threatened. The explanation of subsequent developments and the reforms of 1961 and 1963 given by Lowenhardt seem the most plausible (Lowenhardt, 1982: pp. 127–94). He argues that they were largely the result of pressure from the pure scientists of the Academy, who managed to get Khrushchev's support for their view rather than something which was forced on them by Khrushchev. Thus Nesmeyanov in 1954–7 argued that pure research in the USSR needed a significant boost in order to end the dependence of Soviet applied research on Western research (Lowenhardt, 1982: p. 135). Similarly Kapitsa had argued in 1956 that the Academy needed to clarify its role and that in this 'everything which can be transferred to industry should be removed from the Academy' (Kapitsa, 1981: pp. 178–9). Not unexpectedly the main opposition to this move came from members of the technical division. (Lowenhardt 1982: pp. 155–65). Eventually the technical institutes were removed from the USSR Academy and the republican Academies in two stages in 1961 and 1963. This change was reflected in the new 1963 charter of the Academy where the main role of the Academy was given as 'the development of leading directions of the natural and social sciences' (*Ustavy*, 1974: p. 166).

This change in the role of the Academy also fitted in with Khrushchev's ideas for the rationalisation of science and this was probably why Nesmeyanov gained his support. Instead of competing central bodies for the administration of science what emerged was a clear division of responsibility among the three bodies concerned. The Academy was responsible for fundamental research, the State Committee for Co-ordination of Research dealt with applied research; innovation at the enterprise was the responsibility of Gosplan (Zaleski *et al.*, 1969: p. 63).

There was one other major development in the USSR Academy of Sciences in this period – the creation of the Siberian division and of Akademgorodok near Novosibirsk. This was not really part of the overall policy of the Academy, but rather the result of the initiative of a small number of far-sighted individual scientists who saw its value and who were fortunate that it fitted in very closely with Khrushchev's own ideas about the need to develop science away from Moscow.

The enormous area of Siberia with its huge natural resources was starved of scientific manpower and Lavrentev's bold scheme promised considerable benefits for the development of the region. It was a project which appealed particularly to young scientists who saw an oppportunity to get on faster in Novosibirsk, where there would be more opportunities for showing initiative than in the conservative institutes in Moscow. At the same time Lavrentev was able to attract a sufficiently large number of established scientists to ensure high standards of research.

(c) The Industrial R and D Network

The industrial R and D network under the Ministries and later under the State Committees and the *sovnarkhozy* consisted of a number of different components: the research institutes, the design bureaux, experimental factories or other experimental facilities and lastly factory-based R and D. The continued stress on the priority areas meant that the independent R and D organisations were strengthened while factory science was downgraded. Initially in the Khrushchev period some attempt was made to increase the role of factory science. Thus the decree of the 1955 Plenum called for the expansion of factory laboratories and the improvement of their equipment (*Postanovleniya*, 1956: p. 10), but little seems to have been done, despite support for the idea from Nesmeyanov at the XX Party Congress (*XX sezd*, 1956, I: p. 380). Instead the development of research institutes and particularly the independent design bureaux continued. Many factory-design bureaux were turned into independent organisations and removed from the control of factory directors. Although a number of good reasons were advanced for the creation of independent design bureaux in practice the disadvantages were much more important (Amann and Cooper, 1982: p. 94). The design bureaux were subject to little economic control, so that it did not matter whether their work was good or bad. In addition, because of the higher wages and easier life in these organisations, there was a brain drain from the factories to such organisations. The *sovnarkhozy* saw their R and D organisations as something of a status symbol and set up new organisations for purely prestige purposes (Belyaev and Pyshkova, 1979: p. 136). In the words of one writer, in the period 1959–61 new design organisations grew up like mushrooms after rain (quoted in Jackson, 1967: p. 81). The third link in the chain, the experimental bases, were not expanded, as they needed to be despite some call for action in this field. Thus overall the first two stages of the R and D process were strengthened in this period while the last two were weakened.

Khrushchev's changes in this area did little to alter the existing pattern. He retained and expanded the fragmented R and D network which had grown up under Stalin and made little attempt to integrate it and to eliminate the breaks between the different stages of the innovation process. As a result the factories became even more isolated from the R and D organisations and even less interested in acting on their own initiative.

(c) The Higher-education Sector

The third element of the R and D network, the higher-education sector, was very much the poor relation. The universities and institutes had largely been devoted to training specialists for the economy and had little time or resources for research. At the same time they did contain a large proportion of the nation's qualified scientific manpower and considerable attention was paid throughout this period to improving the quality of training, raising the research output of this sector and increasing its links with industry. Major decrees and other measures were passed in 1954, 1956, 1957, 1960 and 1964. Some major universities possessed research institutes and the number of these was expanded and from 1958 and 1959 onwards 'problem' and 'branch-of-industry' research laboratories were set up at many higher-educational establishments mainly to carry out work for industry (Zaleski *et al.*, 1969: pp. 319–24). Contract research carried out by the higher-education sector for industry and research institutes expanded considerably from 1957 onwards (Zaleski *et al.*, 1969: p. 367). Conditions for research remained far from good in higher-educational establishments and, as the R and D network continued to expand, they lost some of their best workers to the Academy institutes (*Vsesoyuznoe soveshchanie*, 1961: p. 62).

The Expansion of R and D

One of the crucial background factors to the developments in this period is the fact that the Khrushchev years saw an unprecedented expansion of manpower and financial inputs into science. It was hoped that this rapid growth of inputs would lead to a similar increase in scientific output in terms of new discoveries and products. As Medvedev points out, it was the easiest period to start up new projects and institutes – the only reason needed was the absence of a particular line of research in the USSR (Medvedev, 1979; p. 64).

This money was largely used to finance a rapid increase in manpower. This had a considerable impact on the economy, particularly industry, since it meant that large numbers of engineers and other skilled manpower were drawn into the R and D network. Thus of a 500 000 increase in engineers working in the economy in the five years up to 1962 42.4 per cent went into project design and research organisations while only 30.6 per cent went into industry (*Plenum 1962*, 1963: p. 420). This growth involved not only new graduates, but there was also a brain drain from factories into industrial R and D and from higher education into the Academy sector. Science became a prestige profession as a result of the considerable publicity it received particularly in the wake of the successes of the space programme. Some young people were encouraged in this by ambitious parents and others saw science as a relatively easy life without the continual pressure for plan fulfilment which occurred in industry.

There were, however, a number of features about this expansion which were far from satisfactory. In particular the rapid expansion meant that young people were going straight into R and D without any experience of industry, and as a result they did not really understand its problems. This issue had been raised by Bulganin in 1955 (Bulganin, 1955: p. 54), but persisted throughout the period. In addition because of the stress on highly trained manpower by the Ministries there was an imbalance between engineers and technicians and other support staff. As a result there were in 1955 less than two technicians per engineer (Bulganin, 1955: p. 54). Despite some improvement by 1964 this shortage, particularly of auxiliary manpower, continued to be a problem. The levels of pay generally made the situation worse, as the pay of technicians and other auxiliary staff was low. The pay for junior research staff was also low, but could be increased significantly by the award of a candidate degree. As a result many young scientists saw as their first priority the completion of their work for this degree and were often allowed to do this by the research institutes even though the research topic might not have much value for the economy. At the 1961 conference of scientists Kosygin stressed the need to judge people by the benefit they brought the economy and not by degrees and academic titles (*Vsesoyuznoe soveshchanie*, 1961: p. 44). A common theme throughout the period as manpower expanded was the importance of better selection and also the need to weed out poor workers (*Vsesoyuznoe soveshchanie*, 1961; p. 44).

In general pay scales were not geared to increasing efficiency and achieving set goals. One speaker at the 1961 conference pointed out that the system of categories of research institutes meant that it was far more profitable to work at a first category institute in Moscow than to work at a third category one in regions a long way from the capital. As a result there was no incentive to go and work there whereas in the past young scientists had gone out of Moscow to improve their prospects (*Vsesoyuznoe soveshchanie*, 1961: p. 237).

Overall the rapid expansion of manpower only tended to magnify the existing problems. Khrushchev was well aware of this problem and in his memoirs wrote: 'I saw with my own eyes that many government research institutes were sorely inadequate. The state funded these organisations and paid the researchers the same salary whether they did their work poorly or well. The institutes tended to be overstaffed which led to an atmosphere of irresponsibility.' (Khrushchev, 1971, pp. 153–4.)

Economic Measures

Although Khrushchev concentrated on improving the administration and planning of technical progress some attempts were made to extend the use of economic methods and in particular of economic incentives to increase efficiency. In the past economic factors had been little used in R and D since it was felt that satisfactory results could be achieved without them. As the Khrushchev period progressed their importance began to be increasingly recognised and attempts were made to make wider use of them. The measures followed three main aims: first, to improve links between organisations by introducing economic relations between them; second, by the greater use of incentives to encourage better performance; and, third, to use economic calculation as the main guide to decision-making about R and D. The first aim was met by the introduction of a decree in 1961 which introduced contracts as the major basis of relations between R and D organisations and industry instead of the prevailing system whereby R and D was mainly budget financed. At the same time the R and D organisations were transferred to the system of economic accounting (*khozraschet*) and had to provide a major part of their income from contract research (Zaleski *et al.*, 1969: pp. 465–9). The system had begun to develop by 1964, but it was clear that it contained a number of drawbacks which reduced its impact. In particular contracts were often for minor topics for which enterprises could see immediate benefit. At the same time the sum which the R and D organisation received was not linked to the economic return from the project and was not linked with the time taken for its use as this was the responsibility of the customer. Some small use had been made of incentives in the pre-Khrushchev period, but their use was extended considerably in the period in question. A major decree of 1960 introduced a system of bonuses for innovation for the workforce of factories based on the economic return of projects introduced (Zaleski *et al.*, 1969: pp. 482–5). As a rule, however, these were very small in relation to the incentives for the production plan and did not play a major role. Incentives for R and D staff were also introduced, but here a major problem was that it was often not clear for many years whether a project was successful or not. So in practice many bonuses were paid out on projects which turned out to be worthless. In an attempt to influence the attitude of the factory to innovation a special fund was set up in 1960 called the 'fund for the assimilation of new technology', which was meant to encourage the factory to innovate by covering some of the costs of the early stages of innovation (Zaleski *et al.*, 1969: pp. 478–9). It did not cover all the costs of innovation and some writers have argued that its real purpose was to mop up excess profit from established products to redistribute it among innovating factories (Amann and Cooper, 1982: p. 61). The third element in the scheme of economic measures was the introduction of a code for measuring the economic return of new technology (Zaleski *et al.*, 1969: pp. 458–64). This was to be used as the basis of the bonus payments mentioned above. In practice, however, the scheme could produce a multitude of answers in any given circumstance, which rather reduced its value (Zaleski *et al.*, 1969: p. 461).

These measures were not as successful as was hoped. One very important reason for this was the price system. There had been a price reform in 1955, but thereafter despite the considerable innovation in this period there was no major price reform until 1967. As a result of the rapid changes in products in this period the price-fixing authorities became overwhelmed. Because of this many new products were simply given temporary prices based on costs and instead of being reassessed later many of these temporary prices were simply made permanent. This had the effect of giving producers considerable profits and acted as a disincentive to innovation because it would lead to a considerable decline in the factory's economic indicators. One other result of the system of temporary prices was that new machinery was often much more expensive than the old machines it replaced, but this difference was not reflected in increased productivity. This in turn led factories to introduce small changes in products so that a new price could be fixed so that even when statistics showed innovation was taking place this was often pseudo-innovation. Where producer goods were concerned this often had a secondary effect in new factories and shops since the increased prices of new machinery meant a decline in the capital output ratio. These measures did have the effect of making the intervention of economic methods acceptable and innovation and technical progress became an integral part of the discussion of economic reform which followed the publication of Liberman's article in 1962 (*Pravda*, 9 Sep 1962).

The Results of Khrushchev's Measures and their Subsequent Fate

The main aim of Khrushchev's measures was a search for an efficient system of continuous innovation appropriate for a planned economy. Overall, however, it must be said that he failed in this aim. All the improvements in the administration, planning and co-ordination of R and D, the changes in the R and D network, the massive expansion of manpower and financial inputs and the introduction of economic measures to encourage technical progress and make it more efficient failed to bring about the desired result. Indeed Kapitsa pointed out in 1965, with his characteristic frankness, that 'we should not be afraid to say that in the past few years the gulf in science between our country and the USA has not only stopped declining but has increased' (Kapitsa, 1966: p. 14). How did this come about? The answer lies partly in what Khrushchev did and perhaps more in what he omitted to do. Many of Khrushchev's measures were sensible, but often affected only part of the system, while in other areas weak links and bottlenecks undid much of his work.

If one looks back at the Khrushchev period one is immediately struck by the confused nature of the organisational changes which occurred largely as a consequence of the 1957 reform. This clearly had some positive aspects, but was carried out in a hasty manner which led to many problems. In trying to sort out these problems Khrushchev wasted a great deal of effort evolving ever more complex administrative structures. The reform's aim of generating initiative in the regions and weakening the power of the Ministries was laudable. The problem was that the *sovnarkhozy* had nearly as many faults as the Ministries and *mestnichestvo* proved even more damaging than the 'empire-building' of the Ministries as far as innovation was concerned. The *sovnarkhoz* system taxed the resources of the Soviet planning system to the limit, and technical progress in particular suffered as a result. The difficulties faced by the State Committees in trying to implement a unified technical policy while not controlling the factories were stressed in the 1965 decree which abolished the *sovnarkhozy* (*Resheniya*, 1968, 5: pp. 647–8). The industrial Ministries were not removed for long enough so that when they were resurrected after eight years they were virtually unchanged, with many of the same people in charge and most of the old bad habits. On balance in view of the reform's short life it would have been better had it not taken place, since this would have meant that the problems of technical progress would have been tackled in a more stable administrative environment. If Khrushchev had tried to reform the Ministerial system instead of abolishing it the results might have been more successful.

The problem with some of the other measures was that they did not go far enough. Thus Khrushchev's expansion of foreign contacts was very limited and Soviet scientists remained underrepresented at international conferences. As Kapitsa pointed out shortly after Khrushchev's removal: 'An important factor of moral influence [on scientists] is our participation in foreign scientific life – at conferences and other such meetings. We as yet take very little part in them. Our delegations are 4–5 times smaller than the delegations of the USA and other countries and our delegates are selected by bureaucratic methods without the strict observance of the criteria of scientific qualification and interest (Kapitsa, 1966: p. 25). Medvedev has documented the enormous difficulties faced by Soviet scientists trying to make trips abroad and in making even the most simple contacts with foreign colleagues (Medvedev, 1975). Similarly the Soviet Union's trade in licences and its activity in the field of patenting has remained small despite its accession to the Paris convention in 1965. The economic measures to encourage innovation were parsimonious in the extreme and gave very small rewards compared with the bonuses for the fulfilment of production plans.

Even the attempt to solve the problems of science by massive inputs of money and manpower failed. As we have seen above the rapid expansion of manpower produced many negative consequences and the 'Khrushchev generation' of researchers still form a sizeable and ageing component of Soviet scientific manpower. At the 1961 conference of scientists two of the most frequent complaints were concerned with the inefficient wage structure for scientists and the shortage of scientific instruments and other equipment (*Vsesoyuznoe soveshchanie*, 1961, *passim*).

The other consequence of this expansion is that it strengthened pure and applied R and D without a comparable increase in the capacity of the experimental facilities for the construction of prototypes. As a result many research projects took years to get through their final stages. In the words of one speaker at the 1961 conference, there was an enormous backlog 'rotting and getting old in the archives because of the lack of experimental bases' (*Vsesoyuznoe soveshchanie*, 1961: p. 95). Similarly Khrushchev's measures did not do enough to increase innovation at the factory level, where the interests of production remained dominant.

The key problem in the whole R and D process lay in the fragmentation of the system and the lack of an overall goal equally meaningful to all participants. In the absence of such a goal each component in the process strove to maximise its own advantage. The failure to understand this was at the root of many of the problems which arose. With this is related a second issue which coloured the development of Soviet science. This was concerned with the view taken of science in this period. The 1961 Party Programme science proclaimed that science was becoming 'a direct productive force'. Although this was intended to indicate the development of a closer link between science and production in practice this represented a view that confused science and technology. Science was looked on as a straight-line process running from pure research to innovation with little necessity for feedback from the end user – industry. As a result there was a tendency to look at the first stages of this process – pure science, applied science, development – as a separate area from production. This meant that there was a lack of effective economic control over the applied R and D stage. (See *Nash sovremennik*, 9/1976: pp. 158–61, for a discussion of this view of science.) This view of science as something separate from production became entrenched in the Soviet economy, reinforced by the attitudes of many of the new scientists who came into R and D in this period for whom production was something alien, into which innovations had to be introduced as into a hostile environment.

Despite all these problems it is clear that there were successes in this period for two main reasons. First, it is clear that the priority areas remained successful. As Semenov pointed out at the 1963 Plenum: 'We do have a great number of examples of real planning and co-ordination where the advantages of the socialist system have shown up so brightly that they have astonished the world. These include, for example, work on high-speed aircraft, space rockets and long-range rockets and on controlling atomic energy (*Plenum 1963*, 1964: p. 309). Second, there was the drive of individual scientists. As one institute director explained at the 1961 conference, success in introducing projects 'is determined not so much by the industrial value of the proposal as the personal initiative, character and even professional contacts of the workers of the institute responsible for the introduction (*Vsesoyuznoe soveshchanie*, 1961: p. 280). In the view of an Academician 'where there is initiative, persistence, great interest and a healthy relationship between research and economic organisations or direct instructions from the Party and government, experimental work and introduction are carried out successfully and quickly. Where these favourable conditions are absent or not fully provided a link in the chain is missing and introduction lasts for many years. (*Vsesoyuznoe soveshchanie*, 1961: p. 223). The problem with the first method is that even the Soviet Union lacks the resources to treat all areas of science and technology as priority areas, and with the second that it is impossible to plan it.

The Soviet space programme was the great success story of the Khrushchev era. This was an enormous stroke of luck for Khrushchev, which he exploited to the full. The dramatic impact of these achievements, particularly of the first Sputniks and Gagarin's flight, cannot be overstressed. It gave the world the impression that the USSR was ahead in science, much to the consternation of the USA (*Winning*, 1965: pp. 881–914). This enabled Khrushchev to talk about the successes of Soviet science while at the same time exposing the backwardness of much of Soviet technology at the Party plenums and congresses from 1958 onwards.

Many of Khrushchev's organisational structures were swept away after he was deposed in 1964, but many of his innovations in planning and incentives were continued and expanded by his successors. The USSR Academy of Sciences soon became involved again in applied research and this was recognised in its constitution (*Vestnik akademii nauk*, 6/1977: p. 69).

CONCLUSION

In general it can be said that Khrushchev's actions, though not always his words, seem to have been based on a number of misconceptions about the problems of technical progress:

(1) that it was sufficient to multiply inputs to increase outputs;
(2) that a fragmented specialised system was more efficient than an integrated system;
(3) that technical progress could be achieved by good administration and planning alone;
(4) that initiative and voluntary bodies could overcome the problems of bureaucracy which controlled resources;
(5) that flexibility could not be allowed to limit the power of central planning;
(6) that science and technology were the same thing;

(7) that industry could cope with innovation in the conditions of taut
     planning, and that it could be persuaded to do this by very small
     rewards.

Khrushchev's mistakes led to a better understanding of the
complexity of the problems involved in technical progress. His policy
of de-Stalinisation made it easier to solve them.

It must be said, however, that in the field of technical progress
Khrushchev's successors were not much more successful than he was.
Another General Secretary some twenty years after Khrushchev's
fall and thirty years after Bulganin's speech at the 1955 Plenum could
still say, that 'the main weakness of industrial science lies in its
isolation from production', and go on to point out that 'we have
been going round these problems for many years now. . . . Today
we are coming up against essentially the same problems as arose
decades ago, but now they have become more acute. . . . The
obstacle, apparently is a dread of blundering, of going for resolute
action and at times patent conservatism as well', he stressed (*SWB*,
13 June 1985: pp. c12–13). At least Khrushchev could be acquitted
on this charge. . . . For this reason Gorbachev can perhaps be seen
as Khrushchev's heir rather than Brezhnev's. He seems to be bringing
a more intelligent approach to the problems which defeated Khrushchev, but he needs to show the same resourcefulness and drive.

6 Agriculture

G. A. E. SMITH

THE STALINIST LEGACY AND THE PRESSURE FOR REFORM

In the Stalin era the primary objective of agricultural policy was to ensure an adequate supply of food and agricultural products to allow rapid industrialisation at the lowest possible cost in terms of resources allocated to the agricultural sector. This was achieved by means of a centralised administrative system which stifled and distorted local initiative and which was based on compulsory procurement quotas paid for at very low prices. These quotas were established centrally and were based, not on what the farms produced, but on the sown area which was controlled by production plans specifying in great detail and in a very arbitrary way what each farm had to do. The procurement quotas were augmented by heavy payments-in-kind for services provided by Machine Tractor Stations (MTS) which carried out mechanised work on the farms. The system was designed to ensure that the flow of agricultural produce to the state was not significantly affected by poor harvests, whether due to bad weather or to bad farming practices. A considerable proportion of agricultural investment was funded out of the very low revenue of the farms in such a way that investment requirements had priority over payments for labour. Although effective in extracting the resources required the system alienated the agricultural workers with serious effects on output. As a result the proportion of output delivered to the state or used for investment was relatively high so that the farms were unable to pay their workers a subsistence income.

This had two consequences. It led to a very large migration of agricultural workers to the towns and it forced the state to tolerate private plots to permit the survival and reproduction of agricultural labour. This private sector existed in a symbiotic relationship with the centrally controlled public sector in which the survival of the public sector depended upon, but was held back by, the existence of the private sector (Wädekin, 1973: ch. 7). Central to this relationship was the supply of grain from the public sector to peasant households, which, because of restrictions on the size of plots, were unable to grow enough grain on them to feed themselves and, at the same time, grow potatoes, vegetables and fodder for private livestock. Grain supplied from the public sector in the form of payments-in-kind for work performed represented an essential element of peasant subsistence. However, this necessary supply of grain to peasant households, together with low yields and heavy procurement quotas for grain, severely restricted the availability of fodder in the public sector and thus its ability to meet the urban demand for livestock products. This created a demand for the produce from private plots that was surplus to peasant households' basic requirements and which was sold to the urban population on free markets, supplementing the inadequate supplies of these products (mainly livestock products, vegetables and fruit) from the public sector. The relatively high prices paid on the free markets, not only provided an essential source of cash income for peasant households, but also compelled low-income families in the towns to produce their own livestock products and vegetables on small urban allotments (Wädekin, 1973: p. 93).

During the 1930s and 1940s this sytem was successful in providing the industrial sector with the labour it required and with sufficient food to sustain industrial workers at a basic level of subsistence, but only at the cost of stagnating agricultural output and enormous human suffering. The system depended on maintaining a private sector which, by drawing away labour and other resources, especially fodder, constantly undermined it. In 1953 grain output per capita was approximately a quarter less than in 1913 and the livestock herd was smaller than it had been before the 1917 revolution. More seriously, from the point of view of the leadership, the growing imbalance between industry and agriculture was threatening to impede the process of economic growth because of agriculture's growing inability to feed the non-agricultural population and provide a source of exports, and to serve as a source of labour and raw materials for expanding industries. Further industrial development increasingly depended on raising levels of output and productivity in agriculture rather than extracting the largest possible 'surplus' from backward farms producing a relatively low output using large

amounts of labour which mainly subsisted on what peasant households produced on small private plots. Khrushchev's most significant
contribution to the development of agricultural policy was to
persuade the Party leadership that the policy of starving agriculture
of resources undermined the development of the economy as a
whole.

BARRIERS TO THE DEVELOPMENT OF SOVIET AGRICULTURE

One of the main barriers to the development of Soviet agriculture
is climate. In most regions the long, severe winters and the relatively
short growing season mean that agricultural tasks (ploughing,
sowing, harvesting, etc.) must be carried out at precisely the right
time and that, if this is not done, yields can be very significantly
reduced (Smith, 1981: p. 42). Thus, to an even greater extent than
in regions with more favourable climatic conditions, time is of the
essence for successful farming in the Soviet Union and, under such
conditions, mechanisation has a double effect on productivity. It not
only releases labour but also, by making possible the more timely
performance of basic tasks, substantially increases yields (Karcz,
1979c: p. 237). However, the successful mechanisation of agriculture
depends, to a much greater extent than in most sectors of industry
on the unsupervised initiative of agricultural workers. Because
successful farming depends so critically on carrying out basic tasks
in a way and at a time which varies depending on natural conditions,
the effects of mechanisation on agriculture and on industry have
been fundamentally different (Laird, 1964: pp. 281–4, Laird, 1967:
pp. 44–7). The mechanisation of industry has revolutionised not only
the means of production but also the sequence of productive operations, allowing greater control over the work process. By contrast,
the mechanisation of agriculture has not (except in the case of inten-
sive poultry and livestock production) affected the sequential nature
of operations but has merely involved 'a spectacular change in the
gadgets with which operations are performed' (Laird, 1967: p. 44).
Consequently, the problem of effectively controlling the work
process is much greater in agriculture than in industry (Bradley and
Clark, 1972: pp. 465–73; Clark, 1977: pp. 2–6). Because agricultural
processes typically extend over several months with significant lags
between stages (ploughing, sowing, harvesting) workers must repeat-

edly change tasks and must adapt the way in which tasks are performed depending on specific and changing circumstances. The sequential nature of production also makes it very difficult to evaluate the quality of work done: poor quality or inappropriate work only shows itself months later in the form of low yields which can be attributed to many different causes, including bad weather. Supervision and control is further limited by the fact that work is dispersed over a wide area (and, in the Soviet Union, by the lack of roads and communications in rural areas) so that control of workers is hampered by lack of knowledge of what is happening, and of what should be happening which varies widely and unpredictably depending on local variations in soil conditions, weather and in the incidence of pests and diseases. It is therefore essential that, especially where agriculture is highly mechanised, farm workers exercise unsupervised initiative, following through series of operations and adapting to particular conditions, so rendering industrial forms of incentives ineffective or perverse. It is also essential that the inputs used in agriculture are of the right specification and quality and are available at the right time to meet particular circumstances so that, with mechanisation, an effective system of transporting and distributing industrial inputs to the farms is of critical importance.

The system of control developed in the Stalin era alienated the agricultural workers and failed to supply the inputs required and, as a result, was highly contradictory. The system was over-centralised in the sense that it was necessary, but impossible, for central and regional planning agencies to take into account the specific and changing conditions on every farm and issue unambiguous directives to cover every contingency. As a consequence the system was over-decentralised in that, in the absence of effective control from above, farm managers and local administrators, faced with pressure from above to fulfil targets and by alienated and apathetic workers whose co-operation was essential to achieve 'success', sought to protect themselves by forming 'family groups' to simulate successful performance and cover up failures without regard to the wider objectives and requirements of the system as a whole, forcing higher agencies continually to intervene. Thus, because they were unable to control effectively the activities of farm managers and local administrators, central and regional agencies were forced to exercise 'petty tutelage' over local administrators with perverse and irrational consequences (Smith, 1981: pp. 51–3). This, combined with consistent under-investment, had a disastrous effect on the efficiency and performance of the agricultural sector, so that the burden of procurements imposed to meet the state's requirements left farms with insufficient supplies to meet the needs of agricultural workers and of livestock. It was essential to reduce the burden of procurements, but this could only be done if output was substantially raised. Khrushchev sought to resolve this problem by substantially increasing inputs of land and capital and by attempting to impose more effective control over farms through administrative reforms.

ADMINISTRATIVE REFORMS IN THE PERIOD 1953–8

Khrushchev recognised the need for increased investment in agriculture and, despite opposition from powerful vested interests in the defence and heavy industry sectors, successfully argued that agriculture be given greater priority. In the period 1953–8 productive investment in agriculture doubled, mainly due to a rapid increase in state investment, particularly in the period 1953–5 (Selkhoz, 1960: p. 387; Narkhoz, 1964: p. 517). As a result the capital stock in agriculture increased at an average annual rate of 11.3 per cent in the period 1953–8 (Karcz, 1979b: p. 193) and the share of agriculture in total investment rose from 13.7 per cent in 1952 to 17.6 per cent in 1956, falling to 15.8 per cent in 1958 (Narkhoz, 1964: p. 517). There was therefore a clear change of priorities favouring agriculture and rough calculations indicate that, despite the greatly increased demand for machinery created by the Virgin Lands project (see below), the number of tractors and grain combines available per unit of sown area increased in established agricultural regions (Karcz, 1979a: p. 134). If, however, this substantial investment was to yield the necessary increases in output, it was essential that it be used in ways appropriate to specific local conditions.

Khrushchev recognised that effective decisions could not be made and implemented by regional and central agencies and necessarily had to be made at farm and raion level. He was highly critical of the large number of agricultural specialists who were employed in administration and out of touch with what was happening on the farms and so unable to control them effectively (Strauss, 1969: p. 211). He fully appreciated that, because important decisions must inevitably be taken at local level, it was necessary to ensure that these local decisions were taken by technically competent officials who were informed about, and capable of influencing, policy decisions. This was exemplified by his campaigning approach in which he toured the country directly, speaking (and listening himself) to local managers and officials whom he recognised as being of crucial importance to the success of his policies.

Khrushchev's proposals for reforming the administration of agriculture were profoundly influenced by the fact that, as First Secretary, his power base lay within the Party apparatus. He believed that more effective control over the farms could be achieved by strengthening Party supervision. In September 1953 supervision of *kolkhozy* became the responsibility of the MTS, and the *raion* agencies of the Ministry of Agriculture were closed down. A Party secretary, accountable to the *raikom*, was appointed to supervise the MTS, assisted by a group of Party instructors, each responsible for one or two *kolkhozy*. In March 1955 the powers of the Ministry over *kolkhozy* were further reduced to setting delivery quotas and payments-in-kind for MTS services. Within these limits the *kolkhozy*, under the supervision of the Party-controlled MTS, were nominally free to plan their own production. However, the purpose and effect of this reform was not to give *kolkhoz* management any more decision-making power than they effectively already had. The constraints imposed by procurement quotas were in practice as restrictive as those previously imposed by production targets, and the *kolkhoz* production plans not only had to be supervised by the MTS, but also had to be approved by local authorities, who often made arbitrary changes or simply imposed their own targets. Nor did the reform substantially increase the powers of *raion* Party officials. The relationship between these officials and superior (*oblast*) authorities was not substantially changed. Indeed the latter's direct control over *kolkhozy* had been increased in March 1954 when approval of the appointment of *kolkhoz* chairmen was transferred from the raikom to the *obkom nomenklatura* (Swearer, 1964: p. 33). Giving farm managers and local Party officials a greater formal role in plan formulation did not give them any more powers than, in practice, they already had but it might allow local conditions to be more effectively taken into account. The March 1955 reform was a recognition of this fact and was an attempt to make Party supervision of decisions made by farm managers more effective.

Another important aspect of this policy was the amalgamation of *kolkhozy* and the transfer of over 20 000 technical specialists and Party members from the cities to the MTS and farms (Laird, 1967: p. 33). In 1953 many *kolkhozy* had no primary Party organisation and most *kolkhoz* chairmen were not Party members. Between 1953 and 1958 the number of *kolkhozy* was reduced from 91 200 to 67 700, and continued to decline rapidly thereafter (Strauss, 1969: pp. 79–81). As a result of this and the transfer of Party members to the farms by 1958 more than 90 per cent of *kolkhoz* chairmen were Party members and the average *kolkhoz* had a primary Party organisation of about twenty members (Laird, 1967: p. 33). In this way the Party organisation was extended into the *kolkhozy* and the administrative reforms of this period depended upon and reflected this development.

The reforms of 1953 and 1955 established the MTS as the focal point of control over the *kolkhozy*. But merging *kolkhozy* into larger units capable of making efficient use of power-driven machinery, and strengthening the *kolkhoz* Party organisation logically pointed towards concentrating activity on the farms and eliminating the MTS. Morever, the improved financial position of *kolkhozy* put many in a position where they were able to purchase equipment out of their own funds which would not only reduce the burden on the state budget at a time when demands on it were rising, but also create the conditions for the more effective use of machinery by giving *kolkhoz* management direct control over it. The economic case for eliminating the MTS was reinforced by the political consequences of strengthening *kolkhoz* Party organisations whose cadres were dissatisfied with the inefficient way in which the MTS carried out their work as contractors and increasingly resented the interference of MTS Party officials in the management of the *kolkhoz*. In December 1957 MTS Party instructor groups were withdrawn, and in January 1958 the MTS were abolished and their machinery sold to the *kolkhozy*.

The sale of MTS machinery to the *kolkhozy* would, it was hoped, lead to its more efficient use. But this depended critically on how this transfer was carried out, a point which Khrushchev himself understood. He argued that the MTS should be phased out gradually so that *kolkhozy* which could not afford to buy the machinery or could not use it effectively, would not be adversely effected (Volin, 1970: p. 466). Had this principle been followed an effective system of supplying and using machinery might have been developed, allowing *kolkhozy* to decide for themselves whether to purchase equipment or to continue using the MTS as a contracting agency where this was appropriate. In the event, the process of winding up the MTS was virtually completed by the end of 1958 (Volin, 1970: p. 407). As a result *kolkhozy* not only found themselves having to purchase machinery which did not meet their needs and, in most cases, having to go into debt to do so, but also faced additional costs to cover maintenance, repairs and replacement. At the same time, however, *kolkhoz* revenue was substantially increased because they were able to sell produce which had previously been handed over as payment-in-kind for MTS services. On balance the new system left many *kolkhozy* worse off, especially since *kolkhoz* tax continued to be based on gross revenue (Nove, 1964; p. 53; Karcz, 1979c: p. 243).

The elimination of the MTS Party organisation left a gap in the mechanism of control over the *kolkhozy*, which was filled by strengthening the direct line of authority of the *raion* Party organisation over the *kolkhoz* primary Party organisation. This led to growing conflict between the local Party apparatus and the *raion* inspectorates of the Ministry of Agriculture. It also left unresolved the essential weakness of this system – the inability of local managers and officials to control the agricultural workers.

AGRICULTURAL POLICY IN THE PERIOD 1953–7

The way in which managers and Party officials at farm and *raion* level responded to pressure and directives from above was conditioned by their inability to control agricultural workers on whom 'success' ultimately depended. Faced with pressure from above, on the one hand, and an apathetic labour force on the other; these local officials inevitably sought to protect themselves by simulation and falsification of reports and by forming 'family groups' to cover up failures. Attempts by higher officials, themselves under pressure to achieve results and lacking the necessary information, to control lower officials had perverse and irrational consequences. It was therefore essential to introduce more effective incentives for agricultural workers. Under Khrushchev's leadership there was a very significant revival of interest in agricultural economics which was reflected in widespread debate and research on the optimal size of farm units, on the organisation of work on farms, and on farming techniques and practices.

Procurement prices for non-industrial crops had remained virtually unchanged since the 1930s and, by 1952, these prices had fallen well below costs of production. Moreover, as procurement quotas were raised to meet growing urban demand at the end of the Stalin era, the share of 'above-quota' sales to the state (paid for at much higher prices) had fallen to virtually nil by 1952. It was essential to raise *kolkhoz* revenue to make it possible to pay agricultural workers more for their work on the farm. In the four years following June 1953 prices of both compulsory deliveries and 'above-quota' sales were raised substantially and the share of the latter in total procurements was increased. The combined effect of these measures was that the index of state procurement prices rose to 266 in 1957, taking 1952 as 100 (Karcz, 1979a: p. 131), and *kolkhoz* revenue and payments for labour increased substantially.

While raising payments for labour was necessary it posed a dilemma. Increases in procurement prices which substantially raised the disposable incomes of peasant families would further increase the suppressed inflationary pressure already developing within the economy. The leadership was therefore reluctant to raise agricultural procurement prices and constantly urged the need to raise yields and reduce costs. This required a transformation of peasant attitudes to work on the farms. Lack of motivation was the fundamental reason for low output, making it necessary to impose relatively heavy procurements to meet demand. This left the farms with little to distribute to peasants in payment for their work, forcing them to supplement their incomes by working private plots and to regard work on the farm simply as a requirement imposed upon them, an attitude which resulted in low yields and the consequent heavy burden of procurements. Khrushchev clearly recognised the need to reduce the burden of procurements and break out of this vicious circle, but the state could not do without the procurements. To escape this dilemma, in January 1954 Khrushchev proposed that grain output should be increased by expanding the sown area in the Virgin Lands of the east. The adoption of this policy in March 1954 was a radical turning-point in post-war Soviet agricultural policy and signified the leadership's acceptance that further economic growth could no longer be based on extracting a 'surplus' from agriculture regardless of the effects on its development.

Over the period 1954–60 41.8 m. ha of new land were ploughed, with west Siberia and Kazakhstan accounting for about 75 per cent of this. Taking account of land which went out of use the arable area increased by over 30 m. ha (McCauley, 1976: pp. 82–3). By 1960 the possibilities of further significant increases in sown land had come to an end (the limiting factor being lack of precipitation in the Virgin Lands regions) and further increases could only be achieved by assimilating submarginal virgin land or by draining and clearing idle land in established agricultural regions, both of which required very large capital expanditure. The Virgin Lands project paid off both in terms of the total output and the marketed output of grain. The average annual output of grain increased from 80.9 m. tonnes in 1949–53 to 110.3 m. tonnes in 1954–8 to 124.7 m. tonnes in 1959–63 (McCauley, 1976: p. 96). Of the 43.8 m. tonnes increase between 1949 and 1953 and between 1959 and 1963, the Virgin Lands regions contributed 28.89 m. tonnes (McCauley, 1976: p. 96). State grain procurements increased from an annual average of 32.8 m. tonnes in 1949–53 to 46.5 m. tonnes in 1954–63, despite a reduction in grain procurements in non-Virgin Lands regions in the period 1955–7 (McCauley, 1976: p. 98). This reduction was the result in a shift in policy towards increasing livestock production in established agricultural regions.

As output of food grains increased in the east, land in other regions was reallocated to producing feed grains to reduce the fodder shortages that were holding back livestock production. An important aspect of this change in policy were measures taken to encourage private livestock production. In 1953 taxes and compulsory delivery quotas imposed on the private sector were reduced, and Party and state agencies were instructed to assist actively in supplying peasant households with better pasture facilities and fodder. Moreover, payments-in-kind increased substantially between 1953 and 1955. As a result private livestock herds increased rapidly, holding back the expansion of public sector herds. There was growing concern among the leadership at this trend, but until 1956 they felt unable to take any action which might set back the resulting improvement in food supplies (Wädekin, 1973: pp. 256–7, 259–61). However, the initial successes of the Virgin Lands project led the leadership to believe that the private sector was no longer essential. In 1956 measures were taken to restrict the size of private plots on *kolkhozy* and a ban was imposed on the purchase of grain to feed private livestock in towns. In 1959 a ban was imposed on private livestock in large towns. These measures severely restricted private livestock production in towns where access to grazing was limited and urban livestock holdings fell, but this fall was offset by a continuing increase in private livestock herds in rural areas where the 1956 measures were largely ignored by managers and Party officials (Wädekin, 1973: p. 269).

CHANGES IN POLICY IN THE PERIOD 1958–64

In the period 1953–8 the performance of the agricultural sector improved dramatically. Global output increased by about one-third between 1953 and 1957 and by about one-half between 1953 and the bumper harvest of 1958. Grain output increased from an annual average of 80.9 m. tonnes in 1949–53 to 110.3 m. tonnes in 1954–8 (Narkhoz, 1967: p. 370) and grain yields from an average of 7.7 centners per ha to 9.1 centners per ha (Narkhoz, 1967: p. 370). Cattle numbers increased steadily from 56.6 m. in 1953 to 66.8 m. in 1958, and pig numbers from 28.5 m. to 44.3 m. (Narkhoz, 1967: p. 425). Gross output of meat increased year-by-year from 5.8 m. tonnes in 1953 to 7.7 m. tonnes in 1958, and of milk from 36.5 m. tonnes to 58.7 m. tonnes (Narkhoz, 1961: p. 391). These impressive increases in output were largely due to the initial successes of the Virgin Lands project and to favourable weather, but they strengthened the position of powerful vested interest groups within the Party and state apparatus who opposed the increased priority being given to agriculture at a time when there was growing competition for resources to meet the needs of other sectors of the economy. These groups argued that the problems of agriculture were not primarily due to lack of equipment but to the inefficient way in which equipment was used and that the reforms introduced in the period 1954–8, especially the abolition of the MTS, would result in the more efficient use of machinery so that production of this equipment could be reduced (Karcz, 1979c: p. 241, Hahn, 1972: p. 169). In 1958 there was a sharp reduction in investment by the state, and although this reduction was partly offset by increased investment by *kolkhozy*, the rate of growth of investment in agriculture fell from 12.8 per cent in 1958 to 7 per cent in 1959 to 2.4 per cent in 1960 (Karcz, 1979a: p. 137). In the period 1958–64 annual deliveries of important items of equipment such as trucks, grain combines, cultivators, mowers, seeders and maize silage harvesters fell below the levels of 1956–7 so that on-farm stocks were only maintained by reducing rates of scrapping leading to higher costs for maintenance and repairs and increased breakdowns (Karcz, 1979c: p. 233).

As a result of this change of policy the share of agriculture in total investment fell from 17.6 per cent in 1956 to 14.2 per cent in 1960 rising to 17.4 per cent in 1964 (Narkhoz, 1961: p. 541; Narkhoz, 1967: p. 619). In an attempt to offset the effects of inadequate levels of investment Khrushchev increasingly resorted to campaigns to change cropping patterns in order to achieve the increases in output required (Tatu, 1969: pp. 166–9; Karcz, 1979b: p. 193). This policy had begun in 1965 when Khrushchev initiated a campaign to increase the sown area under maize to improve fodder supplies. Under relentless pressure from above, the area under maize was increased so that in many areas maize displaced crops more suited to local soil and climatic conditions. Between 1953 and 1963 the area under rye was reduced by one-quarter, and under oats by just under two-thirds. Maize displaced winter wheat in the Ukraine and the North Caucasus (Volin, 1970: pp. 496–503; Anderson, 1967: pp. 116–26). Shortages of proper equipment for growing maize resulted in delays in sowing and harvesting which compounded the problems of inappropriate soil and climatic conditions so that average yields were low and the feeding quality was poor (Volin, 1970: pp. 499–501; Anderson, 1967: p. 113).

As output increasingly failed to keep pace with growing demand the policy of changing cropping patterns was further developed from 1961 onwards when Khrushchev toured the country arguing that too much land was given over to unproductive grasses and clean fallow. As a result of a vigorous campaign the area under grass was reduced by about one-half and under clean fallow by almost two-thirds between 1960 and 1963 (Karcz, 1979c: p. 259). Such intensification of land use was feasible provided proper methods were used to maintain fertility and, especially in the east, to conserve moisture. These methods required substantial inputs of appropriate equipment, fertiliser and weedkillers, which, in the event, were not available. The potentially disastrous consequences of this policy were exacerbated by the introduction of early sowing in the Virgin Lands regions, where in 1959 a good crop was partially lost because harvesting was not completed before the onset of frosts and bad weather. A number of agronomists lead by T. D. Lysenko advocated early sowing on the grounds that, whereas late sowing might produce higher yields, this was of no advantage if the crops did not ripen in time to be harvested before the onset of autumn frosts. Opponents warned of the dangers of soil erosion and weed infestation, and insisted on late sowing. Khrushchev strongly supported Lysenko and by 1962 the early sowing technique was imposed on many farms in the Virgin Lands regions (McCauley, 1976: pp. 161–7; Hahn, 1972: pp. 26–8). This, together with the effects of the policy of reducing the area under fallow without adequate supplies of weedkiller resulted in such weed infestation that crops were choked, and more frequent ploughing was urged to counter this. But because of shortages of suitable ploughs the techniques used made the soils particularly vulnerable to wind erosion (Hahn, 1972: pp. 111–12). In 1963 an early spring thaw and drought caused the soil to dry out in the Virgin Lands regions and the result was a disastrous harvest failure and the destruction of millions of hectares of cropland by wind erosion.

The 1963 crop failure exposed clearly that changes in cropping patterns were no substitute for investment. Khrushchev himself was aware of this. Following a disappointing harvest in 1960 he had argued that agricultural output could not be increased by so-called 'voluntary methods' ('by raising even higher the enthusiasm of the masses for work') and that more investment was required (Tatu, 1969: pp. 168–9; Hahn, 1972: p. 86). But he was unable to overcome the powerful groups who were opposed to increasing resources for agriculture. He took up the issue again at the March 1962 C.C. Plenum when, in his opening report, he argued that neither administrative reorganisation nor changes in cropping patterns could be successful without increased inputs of machinery and fertiliser. But he was forced to give way on the issue and, in his closing speech, he warned farmers against false hopes of more equipment and declared that 'the main and most urgent thing now' was to make better use of existing equipment (Hahn, 1972: pp. 87–8). Following the 1963 crop failure, agricultural investment was increased and an ambitious programme to increase output of fertilisers was approved. But even this faced considerable opposition and was only approved after Khrushchev promised that the plans for the defence and heavy industry sectors would not be affected (Hahn, 1982: pp. 114–15).

EFFECTS OF POLICY CHANGES IN THE PERIOD 1958–64

Khrushchev's attempt to substitute changes in cropping patterns for the required inputs of equipment and fertiliser failed because the changes themselves required substantial inputs of machinery and chemicals to be effective and because, in the absence of these inputs and under pressure from above to implement changes, local officials and managers responded in inappropriate ways with perverse consequences. Despite this, output continued to increase. Taking four-year averages to discount the effects of bad weather output of grain and livestock products were significantly higher in 1961–4 than in 1957–60 (Narkhoz, 1961: p. 391; Narkhoz, 1967: pp. 370, 434).

TABLE 6.1 *Average Annual Output (million tonnes)*

	1953–6	1957–60	1961–4
Grain (excl. unripe maize)	98.8	120.3	132.1
Meat	6.3	8.2	9.1
Milk	41.7	59.2	62.7

This cannot be described as a failure. The problem was that output fell far short not only of expectations, but also, more importantly, of demand at existing prices. The Seven-Year Plan was launched in January 1959 and its targets implied that in the period 1959–65 disposable incomes would increase by 53 per cent. Given the rate at which spending on food was increasing in relation to increases in disposable income in 1958, this implied that spending on food would increase by about 50 per cent over the same period (Karcz, 1979c: p. 247).

Global agricultural output was expected to rise by 70 per cent and per capita output by about 56 per cent, leaving a comfortable margin for the unpredictable effects of weather. In the event total population increased by 33 per cent more, and the urban population by 2.5 times more, than was envisaged in the Plan (Karcz, 1979c: p. 224), while global agricultural output in 1964 was only 13 per cent higher, and in 1965 only 14 per cent higher, than in 1958 so that the actual increase in output was only 20 per cent of the planned increase (Karcz, 1979c: p. 224). In per capita terms global output and marketed output barely increased at all throughout the period 1959–65 while disposable money incomes were 46 per cent higher in 1964 than in 1958, and in 1965 61 per cent higher (Karcz, 1979c: pp. 225–9). The consequences of this underestimation of demand and overestimation of output would have been less severe if, as one might have expected, spending on food had increased less rapidly than increases in income. However, except in 1961, spending on food increased significantly more rapidly than disposable income in the period 1959–64 (Karcz, 1979c: pp. 229–30). One reason for this was the shortage and poor quality of non-food consumer goods so that increases in total spending tended to spill over into higher spending on food. This was exacerbated by shifts in the distribution of income favouring low-income families and pensioners with a relatively high propensity to spend on food. But the increased spending on food was also to a significant extent due to the way the leadership reacted to the problem.

To meet the increasing demand purchase quotas for both grain and livestock products were raised so that in the period 1960–3 these quotas were primarily determined by demand rather than output (Karcz, 1979b: pp. 207–8). Because prices paid for livestock products were on average below costs, these increased quotas added to the financial pressures imposed by the abolition of the MTS and by increased investment by *kolkhozy*, so that although *kolkhoz* revenues continued to increase after 1958, money payments to *kolkhoz* workers fell in 1959 and rose only slowly thereafter (Karcz, 1979c: p. 236). More significantly, increased purchase quotas for grain, together with the increased fodder requirements of larger livestock herds, led to a decline in payments-in-kind in the period 1959–63 (Wädekin, 1973: pp. 293–5). Grain accounted for about 80 per cent of the value of produce issued as payments-in-kind or sold by *kolkhozy* to peasant households (Wädekin, 1973: pp. 209–10), and, as noted above, this grain was essential to peasant subsistence both as a basic food and as fodder for private livestock. The reduction in payments-in-kind, together with the restrictions on private livestock herds in towns introduced in the period 1956–9 (see above), had a serious effect on the private sector supply in towns, especially small towns, forcing up free market prices and increasing the demand for livestock products in state and co-operative stores (Wädekin, 1973, pp. 302–3). The leadership attempted to meet this by further raising purchase quotas so that *kolkhozy* were forced to expand their livestock herds and reduce fodder supplies to private livestock. To accelerate the expansion of public sector livestock herds, Khrushchev introduced a policy of 'encouraging' peasant households to sell private livestock to *kolkhozy* and state farms but, given the pressure they were under to meet purchase quotas, local officials began forcing peasant households to sell livestock on a massive scale (Wädekin, 1973: pp. 277–83). The number of privately-owned livestock declined, largely offsetting the increases in public sector livestock and sharply increasing the overall costs of livestock production. In addition, because peasant households received insufficient payments-in-kind to cover their own consumption needs, they were obliged to turn to state trade outlets, so further increasing the pressure of demand of the public sector (Karcz, 1979c: p. 255).

Thus, the policies adopted had the effect of increasing spending on food in state and co-operative stores and led to a deterioration

in the situation of agricultural workers. This not only increased the
rate of rural-urban migration so reducing the labour available for
work on the farms, but also negatively influenced peasant attitudes
to work on the farms. These policies therefore aggravated the fundamental problem of the agricultural sector – peasant apathy and the
lack of effective control over what happened on the farms. Khrushchev attempted to deal with this by introducing further administrative
reforms.

ADMINISTRATIVE REFORMS IN THE PERIOD 1958–64

The abolition of the MTS in 1958 left a gap in the mechanism of
control over *kolkhozy*. As pressure from above further alienated an
already apathetic labour force whose co-operation was essential to
'success' and over whom it was impossible to impose effective
control, local officials responded by concentrating on those targets
and campaigns which appeared to be of greatest importance at any
given moment in ways that undermined the overall objectives of
policy, and by submitting false reports and forming 'webs of mutual
involvement' to cover up failures. A disappointing harvest in 1960,
and the discovery of major fraud in production reports, resulted in
a further reorganisation. In January 1961 the Ministry of Agriculture
was downgraded to a research and advisory service, with Gosplan
taking over control of state farms and the Central Statistical Administration responsibility for gathering production data and statistics. A
new State Committee for Agricultural Procurement, operating
through Regional Procurement Inspectorates, was set up to establish
purchase quotas with wide powers over the planning of production
on *kolkhozy* to ensure that purchase quotas were met. Thus, by
splitting the management of farms among a number of differing
agencies which were less susceptible to local pressures, this reorganis-
aton was a further attempt to impose effective control over local
decision-making. But the reform failed to define clearly the responsibilities of different control agencies, particularly the role of the *raion*
Party organisation.

   In March 1962 the State Committee for Agricultural Procurement
was abolished and a new unified administrative structure was set up,
headed by an All-Union Committee for Agriculture and supervised
by a hierarchy of Party-dominated agricultural committees. The basic
units of this structure were nearly 1000 Territorial Production Associ-

ations (TPAs). To strengthen Party control at local level a Party organiser (Partorg) with 2–4 instructors was assigned by the *obkom* to each TPA to supervise and assist the primary Party organisations on the farms. The TPA partorg staff were responsible for sixty or more farms, and their size was deliberately restricted to prevent them from becoming too closely involved in the routine affairs of each farm and thus being drawn into 'family groups'. The TPA partorgs' function was to act as the agent of the *obkom* to ensure that the TPAs and farms complied with central directives. This reorganisation greatly reduced the role of the *raikom* and, since the territories of the TPAs were not coterminous with those of the *raikoms*, this gave rise to considerable confusion and tension between the two organisations.

This reorganisation was carried further in November 1962 when the *oblast* and *raion* organisations of the Party and local government were reorganised on a production basis. Each *obkom* and *oblispolkom* was divided into separate committees covering agriculture and industry respectively. At the lowest level the *raion* was replaced by 'zones of industrial production' and, in rural areas, by the TPA, with the *raikom* being absorbed into the TPA's Party structure. The objective of this division of the Party was, once again, to reinforce control over local decision-making. This reorganisation seriously affected the position of individual *obkom* and *raikom* secretaries and gave rise to significant opposition. It did not however in any way diminish the power of those at the top of the Party apparatus. Despite subsequent vilification by the Party leaders who replaced Khrushchev in October 1964 there was little opposition among them at the time and Khrushchev was able to secure wide agreement within the Presidium for his proposals (Tatu, 1969: pp. 249–51).

The reforms of the period 1961–3 were further developments of the policy of imposing more effective control over local decision-making, but, as in the case of the reforms of the period 1954–8, they failed. In April 1964 Khrushchev complained that the TPAs were behaving in the same way as previous administrative agencies had done because they were made up of the same people with the same habits and style of work. The continual changes in the structure of control and supervision in this period were not only very disruptive, but did not resolve the problems that were created by the failure to provide farms with equipment of the quality and specification appropriate to local conditions, and the inability of farm managers and Party officials to exert control over an apathetic labour force whose active co-operation was essential if yields and productivity were to be increased. Under these conditions it was inevitable that local officials would continue to respond to pressure from above by bullying and coercing workers and so increasing their alienation. This problem of control was not primarily due to the very large size of farms which resulted from merging *kolkhozy*, but to the way in which work was organised on the farms and to the attitude of officials towards the worker. Individual workers were indifferent to what happened on the farms and reacted to the harassment of managers and officials in stereotyped and inefficient ways that were inappropriate to local conditions. Local officials were forced to strike an uneasy balance between their inability to control the labour force and the pressure from above to fulfil procurement quotas and other success indicators. This led them to concentrate on those targets and campaigns to which their superiors were devoting greatest attention at any given moment and in ways that were inappropriate to local conditions and detrimental to long-term development, and to form 'webs of mutual involvement' to simulate successful performance and cover up failures.

The problems of local officials were compounded by the fact that prices bore little relation to costs and conflicted with the purchase quotas imposed on farms. In particular the prices paid for livestock products did not cover costs of production on the average farm so that higher purchase quotas increased the financial burden imposed by the abolition of the MTS and reduced the farms' ability to pay their workers. In 1962 procurement prices for meat and milk were raised and, in order to reduce the pressure on the state budget, these increases were passed on to the urban consumer in the form of higher retail prices, giving rise to protests and discontent. But the problems of livestock production were not fundamentally due to the lack of profitability. The pressure to increase livestock herds when grain output fell far short of requirements led to shortages of fodder and low yields. It also led to a run-down of grain reserves so that, following the bad grain harvest in 1963, large quantities of grain had to be imported. Despite this, it was necessary to introduce bread-rationing and to slaughter livestock, especially pigs, because of lack of fodder.

Khrushchev attempted to overcome these difficulties by launching a series of campaigns to highlight particular problems and change methods of production, and by embarking on extensive tours of the country during which he harassed local officials and frequently dismissed those who disagreed with him. But, under Soviet conditions where successful farming depends so critically on the timely performance of basic tasks, these proved no substitute for the policies required to transform peasant attitudes and provide the farms with the inputs they required.

KHRUSHCHEV'S LEGACY

Khrushchev's most significant contribution to agricultural policy was that he persuaded the Party leadership that it was no longer possible to go on extracting the maximum possible 'surplus' from agriculture by means of a coercive centralised system of control, and that the further development of the economy as a whole depended on raising agricultural output and productivity. He also understood that this required not only increased investment, but a higher level of technical competence among farm workers and managers and more effective control over local decision-making. But his faith in the Party as an institution capable of achieving this was misplaced. This was partly because the neglect and low-priority of agriculture in the Stalin era inevitably affected Party officials' attitudes to this sector, but mainly because the successful development of agriculture depended on the attitude of agricultural workers, and not on that of Party officials. His policies failed because they failed to mobilise an apathetic and alienated labour force so that Party officials responded to pressure from above in ways that undermined the overall objectives of agricultural policy.

Despite this the system of control and supervision established in the period 1954–8 achieved substantial increases in output because it was capable of (very inefficiently) organising a vast expansion of the sown area in the Virgin Lands regions. But this was not enough to solve the 'grain problem'. The minimum amount of grain required to meet all requirements and maintain adequate reserves was estimated in 1955 to be 160 m. tonnes (McCauley, 1976: p. 74). This was over 20 per cent more than the average annual output in the period 1961–4. Moreover, due to problems of drought, soil erosion and weed infestation, state grain procurements in the Virgin Lands regions were on average only 7 per cent higher in 1959–63 than in 1954–8 and were well below planned levels (McCauley, 1976: p. 99). Khrushchev himself acknowledged that the 'grain problem' could not be solved by assimilating virgin and idle land, and that it was necessary to raise yields by introducing improved cropping patterns and agro-techniques (McCauley, 1976: p. 81). He also recognised that such improvements required not only increased research and debate, but also substantial inputs of agricultural machinery and chemicals (Hahn, 1972: pp. 84–8). But, particularly from 1958 onwards, this latter policy was opposed by powerful vested interests at the top of the Party and state apparatuses.

Those who were opposed to giving investment in agriculture greater priority wrongly argued that the supply of inputs was adequate, but they were fundamentally correct in arguing that the crucial problem was the effectiveness with which this investment was used. The way in which apathetic farm workers misused and abused machinery and equipment resulted in enormous waste and low yields, a problem which could not be solved by simply pouring in even more resources. Moreover, to the extent that ineffective investment in agriculture reduced investment in other sectors of the economy such as light industry, transport and construction, this reduced the non-agricultural sector's capacity to supply agriculture with the inputs it required, not only of machinery and chemicals, but also of the construction materials and consumer goods required to retain and motivate workers, particularly skilled workers. Agricultural policy in the post-Khrushchev period has been undermined by the failure to resolve these problems.

After quickly reversing the administrative reforms introduced in the period 1960–3 and restoring the system of control and supervision essentially to what it had been in the period 1958–60, the post-Khrushchev leadership have maintained the basic strategy advocated by Khrushchev but with greater consistency. The TPAs were eliminated and the division of the Party into agricultural and industrial sectors was abandoned. The Ministry of Agriculture was restored with its former powers, and the *raion* administrative structures reconstituted, with *raikom* officials having a key role in setting delivery obligations and supervising work on the farms. There was strong criticism of Khrushchev's 'hare-brained' schemes and excessive use of campaigns, and a greater appreciation of the interdependence between the public and private sectors and of the fact that excessive controls on the latter impeded the development of the former. Agricultural prices were raised and it was announced that investment was to be substantially increased. But, as happened in the period 1958–63, actual investment and deliveries of equipment fell far short of what was planned as, following a record harvest in 1966, resources were redirected to industry, especially into increasing the output of consumer goods in an attempt to absorb the inflationary pressures of rising household disposable incomes (Hahn, 1972: pp. 189–94). As a result there were growing shortages of foods, especially meat, which were exacerbated by fear of the political consequences of raising retail prices and by the effect of increases in the incomes of agricultural workers which reduced their willingness to cultivate private plots and increased their purchases of food from the public sector (Smith, 1981: pp. 45–6).

Since 1970, with Brezhnev's emergence as *primus inter pares*, the needs of agriculture and of industries producing inputs for agriculture have been given a high priority (Hahn, 1972; pp. 225–31). Procurement prices have been further increased and investment substantially raised both absolutely and relatively. Expensive programmes have been carried out to increase output of livestock products and to develop production in the non-black-earth regions, which had been neglected in the Khrushchev period. As a result the share of agriculture in total investment increased from 23 per cent in 1961–5 to over 27 per cent in 1976–80, and investment in the 'agro-industrial complex' (i.e. agriculture and industries supplying and servicing the agricultural sector) increased from 28 per cent of total investment in 1961–5 to over 35 per cent in 1976–80 (Smith, 1981: p. 46). To ensure that the expansion of livestock herds was not held back by shortages of fodder, feed grains have been imported in substantial quantities (Goldman, 1983: p. 65). Because the increased resources that Khrushchev demanded, but was unable to obtain, have been made available, it has been possible to pursue the policies that he advocated with much greater consistency. Moreover, since shortfalls in the output of grain relative to requirements have been met by imports, it has not been necessary to embark on under-funded 'hare-brained' schemes to deal with this problem. In place of administrative reorganisations and campaigns the post-Khrushchev leadership have sought to raise yields and output by pouring resources into the agricultural sector. Unlike Khrushchev they have not directly intervened in the research and application of improved agro-techniques and crop policies, and disputes among them have concerned the relative priority of agriculture and the reorganisation of production to achieve greater regional specialisation and closer integration of activity between farms and the processing of food products.

As a result impressive increases in output have been achieved. In 1976–80 agricultural output was on average about 50 per cent more per year than in 1961–5 and the quality of the Soviet diet has improved considerably (Narkhoz, 1982: pp. 227, 447). But the costs of this have been enormous for two main reasons. First, because of the inefficiency of industry and the distribution system, much of the increased supply of equipment and agro-chemicals has been of the wrong specification and not available at the time when it has been needed. This, together with frequent breakdown and shortages of the right spare parts, has resulted in long delays in completing basic tasks which, under Soviet conditions, has caused large reductions in yields and increased costs. With increased mechanisation, a perfectly motivated farmer (however defined) can do little unless the non-agricultural sector can provide reliable inputs at the time when they are required (Smith, 1981: pp. 16–25). Moreover, inadequate supplies of construction materials and consumer goods have blunted the incentive effect of the increased incomes of agricultural workers and have contributed to the continued large-scale migration of young trained workers from the farms to the towns. Inefficiencies in the trade and industry sectors have thus increased costs and reduced yields and productivity in the agricultural sector (Smith, 1981: pp. 61–3), and it has been necessary constantly to raise procurement prices. Because the leadership has feared the political consequences of passing on these increases to the urban consumer in the form of higher retail prices for food, the substantial burden of agriculture on the state budget due to higher investment has been further increased by the huge cost of subsidies, and rising urban incomes and the relatively low retail prices have meant that demand has outstripped supply, especially for meat. The second main reason why increases in output have only been achieved at enormous cost is that, because the way in which work has been organised on the farms has not significantly changed, neither has the apathetic attitude of agricultural workers despite considerable increases in labour payments. Consequently, because successful farming depends critically on the way in which workers adapt to specific local conditions, the effectiveness of investment in terms of increased yields and productivity has remained very low. Moreover, because they have been unable to control effectively this apathetic labour force, local managers and officials have continued to respond to pressure from above in much the same way that they did in the Khrushchev period.

The post-Khrushchev leadership's agricultural policy has therefore been a continuation of that of Khrushchev, but they have been prepared to pour resources into this sector on a scale that Khrushchev himself would probably have considered excessive. While this has resulted in impressive increases in output at least until 1980, the costs have been enormous because, as in the Khrushchev period, the policy has failed to resolve the fundamental problem: the inability of managers and local officials to control an apathetic labour force. Because they have been prepared to make up for shortfalls in grain output by importing, it has not been necessary for the post-Khrushchev leadership to resort to campaigns, constant administrative reorganisations and 'hare-brained' schemes. They have implemented Khrushchev's policies in a more lavish and consistent way than in the Khrushchev era and, in doing so, have shown that these policies cannot resolve the problems of Soviet agriculture and ensure that the Soviet population's demand for livestock products, fruit and vegetables is met at a cost which the economy as a whole can sustain.

7 Labour

D. FILTZER

On Stalin's death the Soviet regime faced a host of truly daunting economic difficulties, not the least of which were the behaviour and performance of the industrial workforce. As with industry in general, the problems were structural and systematic. Stalinist industrialisation during the 1930s had created a highly specific system of production relations within the Soviet industrial enterprise (Filtzer, 1986). The combination of dire material scarcity and a chronic labour shortage made discipline difficult to enforce: job changing and absenteeism were high throughout the decade, as workers moved from factory to factory in search of better conditions and felt confident that breaches of discipline regulations would provoke few sanctions from managers desperate not to lose workers. More important was the pattern of worker–manager relations that the labour shortage imposed. Workers, deprived of any possibilities of collective resistance or collective defence of their position, responded by appropriating control over the one area left open to them – the indivdiual labour process. Workers retained considerable control over the use of work time. They squandered substantial portions of each shift on personal diversions and took advantage of internal disorganisation (non-arrival of supplies or instructions, inability to find needed tools or parts) to ease the strains of the work regime. Even periodic campaigns, such as Stakhanovism, designed to break their control over the work routine were undermined by management's need to reach accommodation with a basically uncooperative workforce under conditions where labour was scarce. This meant not only tolerance of slow work and what in the West are known as 'restrictive practices', but also active attempts to protect workers' earnings through the artificial suppression of output quotas (called 'norms' in Russian) and the illegal or semi-legal manipulation of wages. Only in 1940–1 did the regime finally manage to exercise greater authority over worker behaviour through a succession of drastic measures: the criminalisation of job changing and truancy; the introduction of compulsory labour service for youth; and the assumption of the right to direct skilled workers and specialists to jobs anywhere in the country (ibid. ch. 5). The war, of course, strengthened the regime's capacity to restrict workers' freedom of action (Schwarz, 1952: pp. 119–29).

By the early 1950s the worst aspects of the system created in the 1930s had assumed almost grotesque proportions. Shortages of parts and materials were aggravated by an unwieldy and hopelessly inefficient distribution network (Davies, 1956: pp. 314–15; see also *Izvesitya*, 7 Jan, 13 May 1954, *Komsomolskaya Pravda*, 28 Feb 1954). The stress on gross output militated against the introduction of new technology, since production might fall during 'teething' stages and, in the longer term, a cheapening of output due to technical improvements could lead to plan 'underfulfilment' (Davies, 1956: pp. 322–3; *Pravda*, 24 May 1955). So baroque had the system become that some Ministries adopted the bizarre practice of allocating to factories supplies from non-existent enterprises still under construction (*Izvestiya*, 30 June 1956).

It was therefore clear to all parties involved in the post-Stalin leadership struggle that on economic grounds alone the system was in need of alteration. Hence Khrushchev's ill-conceived and ill-fated experiment with limited administrative decentralisation through the *sovnarkhozy* (Councils of the National Economy), whose failure lay not so much in their bureaucratic cumbersomeness as in the fact that none of the proposed solutions actually challenged the root of the problem – the system itself.

In terms of labour policy the need for reform was equally transparent. Workforce morale was low. Waste of resources, large volumes of defective production and general inefficiencies stemmed not merely from the bureaucratic rigidities of the planning mechanism, but equally from the negligence and indifference of the workers. The draconian labour legislation of 1940–1 was becoming increasingly difficult to enforce and was a hindrance to industrial efficiency. The wages and norm-setting system had gone completely out of control. Thus, abstracting from the possible political motivations behind Khrushchev's liberalisation of Soviet society, the fact was that fundamental reforms of labour policy, including attempts to relegitimate the regime in the eyes of its working population, were essential to raise productivity and improve worker motivation. Put simply, economic reform was impossible without some form of political liberalisation. This is not to deny the existence of other pressures pushing towards 'de-Stalinisation', including the desire by the bureaucracy to regularise its position within society, but the problem of productivity was paramount. This is demonstrated by the fact that all the main contenders for power – Khrushchev, Malenkov and Beria – recognised the gravity of the situation and had drawn up reform programmes (Brus, 1975: pp. 117–19; Service, 1981: pp. 235–6).

Any reform of labour policy presented the Soviet élite with a fundamental dilemma. If terror was no longer an acceptable or efficacious mode of social control, how could the workforce be compelled to work? Before Khrushchev's secret speech in 1956 the regime had no coherent answer. Labour policy had been allowed to drift. Only after the XX Party Congress were major changes introduced in the vital fields of labour law, incentive systems and 'reform' of the trade unions. Although sweeping in character, and able to eliminate some of the more glaring excesses of the inherited system, they failed to alter the fundamental features of Soviet production relations created under Stalin. In this sense the Khrushchev era can be seen as a transitional period between the Stalin years and the present day. If Stalinist industrialisation had set in place the basic inherent features of the modern Soviet system it was also able to keep them from fully manifesting themselves thanks to the combination of terror and a dynamic for extensive growth. With the end of terror the constraints on these essential tendencies were removed, while the regime found no new means to counteract them. The system was thus free to evolve into its contemporary form.

CHANGES IN LABOUR LAW

On 25 April 1956 the regime repealed the Edict of 26 June 1940, which had criminalised job changing and absenteeism. The Edict had stipulated that workers who left their jobs without permission were to be tried in the People's Courts and sentenced to between two and four months' imprisonment. To prevent workers from using absenteeism or gross violations of labour discipline to force their dismissal (the penalty for these offences since November 1932) truants and 'malicious disorganisers of production' were to do up to six months' corrective labour at their place of work with up to a 25 per cent loss of pay. Criminal penalties for job changing and truancy had been partially relaxed in 1951 and 1952, but the decrees announcing these changes were never published. Although after 1951 handbooks on Soviet labour law began publishing the 1940 Edict without listing its criminal sanctions, prosecutions did take place after that date (Gliksman, 1956: p. 22). But there is evidence to suggest that prosecutions were rare. In 1954 nearly 25 per cent of Soviet industrial workers and some 50 per cent of workers in construction left their jobs (Davies, 1956: p. 324; Fakiolas, 1962: p. 18). Although some of them did so due to retirement, redundancy or conscription into the Soviet Army, criminal sanctions had clearly ceased to deter large numbers of workers from quitting of their own free will. Moreover, between 1952 and 1956 both managers and People's Court judges began to enforce the 1940 law with increasing laxness. Managers often failed to refer violators for prosecution and judges frequently handed down illegally lenient sentences (Gliksman, 1956: p. 22). It is worth noting that managers and lower court judges had responded in identical fashion following the law's introduction in 1940, and for exactly the same reason: the new restrictions had been economically unworkable (Filtzer, 1986: ch. 9).

The April 1956 decree was not, however, a total liberalisation. It left in force the highly repressive provisions of the law of 28 December 1938, which had tied receipt of disability and pension benefits to an exceptionally long length of service at one and the same enterprise. Although these provisions were partially relaxed in February 1957, to exempt those injured on the job or contracting an industrial disease (*Trud*, 6 Feb 1957), they were not repealed *in toto* until 1960, when all workers, regardless of length of service, were given the right to receive full social insurance payments. It is perhaps significant that the 1960 liberalisation was opposed by some labour economists on the grounds that it deprived the regime of a necessary weapon against labour turn-over (*Sotsialisticheskii trud*, 8/1964: p. 128; *Trud*, 7 Dec 1962).

In July 1958, as part of the general trade-union reform, the procedures under which managers could dismiss workers were also considerably changed. The trade unions now had restored to them the right to review management decisions to fire workers for violations of labour discipline (*Vedemosti Verkhovnogo Soveta SSSR*,

1958, no. 15, art. 282), a prerogative the unions had exercised with considerable diligence in the 1920s and early 1930s (and even later in isolated cases) through the Rates-Conflict Commissions (RKK). In 1957 the RKK themselves were replaced by Commissions on Labour Disputes, made up of equal numbers from the trade unions and management, and it was made easier for workers to appeal dismissals directly to the factory trade union or to the People's Courts (*Trud*. 14 Feb 1957). Here, too, policy under Khrushchev was returning to a situation that had existed two decades earlier, at the height of Stalinist industrialisation.

LABOUR TURN-OVER

It should not be surprising that following the decree of April 1956 turn-over, taken in the narrow sense of those quitting voluntarily or fired for violations of labour discipline (i.e. excluding retirements, those entering military service, or redundancies), rose sharply, from 15 per cent of the workforce in 1950 to 38 per cent in 1956 (Feshbach, 1966: p. 732). Clearly workers took advantage of their new freedom to change employment despite the loss of social insurance benefits this still entailed. As most job changers were young this was not likely to be an effective sanction in any case (ibid., p. 734; *Sotsialisticheskii trud*, 8/1964: p. 129). Three features of the turn-over statistics are of note. First, turn-over declined markedly after 1956, to 19 per cent of the work force in 1960 and 20 per cent in 1961 and 1962 (Feshbach, 1966: p. 732). Second, although Feshbach considered these levels extremely high, the rate of *total* separations (i.e. turn-over plus those leaving for administrative or other involuntary reasons) was not very different from separation rates recorded in the West (Fakiolas, 1962: pp. 20–1). Third and most significant is the fact that even the relatively high figure for 1956 was well below the astronomical levels of job changing recorded in the 1930s, when even the best years showed the average Soviet worker switching jobs nearly once a year (Filtzer, 1986: ch. 2).

When assessing the economic impact of turn-over it is important to keep in mind that the regime's policy of opening up new industrial areas, primarily in Siberia and the eastern republics, required a certain degree of labour mobility. Nevertheless turn-over caused considerable economic difficulties. From the point of view of the economy as a whole job changing usually brought with its lower productivity and increased labour costs, as enterprises had to train new workers to replace those who had left, and the latter were themselves less efficient while acclimatising to their new jobs. In addition those leaving rarely took up new employment straight away; on the contrary, in 1960 the time between quitting one job and starting a new one ranged from two to six weeks, depending on the region, during which period the worker was engaging in no useful economic activity (Fakiolas, 1962: pp. 28–9). Moreover, even if the global figures for turn-over were not alarming, the haemorrhage of workers from certain industries or construction sites was sufficient to cause bottlenecks and delays with inevitable repercussions in other areas of the regional or national economy. Construction projects in the Kuzbass in 1962 were finding it difficult to hold on to recruits and were losing nearly as many workers as they were taking on (*Trud*, 7 Oct 1962). The same problem plagued construction sites, factories, and collieries in the southern Urals, Kuibyshev *Sovnarkhoz* and Armenia (*Trud*, 17 Nov, 7 Dec, and 26 Sept 1962). To some extent these workers left because of poor amenities, especially housing, a pattern typical of Soviet job leavers, who more frequently cited working and living conditions rather than wages as reasons for quitting (Feshbach, 1966: pp. 728–9; Nemchenko, 1974: p. 36). Yet in the cases given here housing was not the main problem. A more prevalent cause was the inability of young workers to fulfil their norms, leading to a fall in earnings and a desire to look elsewhere for work. Others left because the bonuses available under the wage reform were too low (*Trud*, 8 June 1962). The connection between poor norm fulfilment and turn-over also affected more established industries and enterprises. In coal mining, pit managers in the Kuzbass in 1959 claimed that they had to improve the earning potential of locomotive drivers in order to deter them from quitting (Dovba, *Sotsialisticheskii trud*, 1/1960: p. 50). In engineering, machine operators, whose norms were made more difficult to over-fulfil following the wage reform of 1956–61, responded by giving up these jobs and seeking work involving more manual operations where overfulfilment payments would be easier to earn (Batkaev and Markov, 1964: p. 209). The pressures that the threat of losing workers exerted on managers to violate prescribed norm-setting poli-cies will be discussed below.

LABOUR DISCIPLINE

Like labour turn-over, no comprehensive statistics on absenteeism have been published since 1936. Press reports complaining of increased days lost at some factories because of truancy are difficult to put in perspective because they do not indicate what percentage of the workforce was involved (*Trud*, 15 May 1962, 3 Apr 1964; *Sotsialisticheskii trud*, 5/1957: p. 33). Even less precise is the information available on other forms of discipline violations, e.g. so-called 'hooliganism' and alcoholism. Although press and journal commentaries reveal that these have always posed chronic problems for industrial efficiency this is clearly an area where further detailed research is needed.

Despite the difficulties posed by overt violations of discipline the issue of control over the labour process and use of work time has always had a more fundamental effect on the functioning of the Soviet economy. Studies carried out in the 1930s demonstrated that although the enormous losses of work time recorded in that period were to a large extent attributable to the chaos and confusion besetting Soviet industry, they were equally caused by overt squandering of time by workers and their persistent defence of the right to take advantage of industrial disorganisation to slow down the pace of work (Filtzer, 1986: ch. 6). Numerous surveys conducted during the Khrushchev years indicate that losses of work time continued to be substantial, roughly on the order of fifty minutes a shift per worker, depending on the enterprise, industry and region (*Sotsialisticheskii trud*, 5/1957: p. 34; 7/1957: pp. 89–90; Zanin, *Voprosy ekonomiki*, 9/1961: p. 74); Prudenskii, *Voprosy ekonomiki*, 1/1960: p. 54). Actual losses were probably far higher, since factories often failed to record brief interruptions (*Trud*, 8 May 1956) or grossly under-reported stoppages (Prudenskii, *Voprosy ekonomiki*, 1/1960: p. 54). So substantial were total losses that Zanin, (*Voprosy ekonomiki*, 9/1961: p. 74) could claim, perhaps with a touch of hyperbole, that reserves for raising labour productivity through better use of work time were greater than those created by improved technology. What is more, enterprises apparently had little difficulty in meeting their plan targets despite the lost time (*Trud*, 10 May 1957, 25 Mar 1964) – a fact which indicates that both plans and norms were being kept within manageable limits. Unlike the 1930s, however, these studies almost universally ascribe the overwhelming share of losses to 'organisational' or 'production' failures, and only an insignificant proportion to violations of labour discipline.

Losses of work time due to serious disruptions to production or supplies are, of course, a familiar feature of Soviet industry. Workers would fail to receive job assignments on time or would be unable to locate materials, tools or parts. Supplies would arrive late or in incomplete batches unsuitable for assembly. Workers might find that the materials delivered were defective. Equipment was badly looked after or poorly repaired, and so was repeatedly going out of service. Considerable time was lost rectifying products or semi-finished goods that were either defectively manufactured or damaged through improper storage (*Trud*, 5 Mar and 10 May 1957; 12 May, 11 Sep, 14 Sep 1962; 24 Mar 1964). The limited surveys available suggest, however, that workers were well able to take advantage of this inherently unstable situation to appropriate additional time for themselves: they would arrive late or go home early, take their time preparing and starting up machinery, take long dinner breaks, use forays after job assignments or tools to stop and chat with workmates, etc. (*Trud*, 12 July 1959, 24 Mar 1964). While most studies maintained that the average worker wasted no more than six to ten minutes out of each shift on such actions (*Trud*, 8 May 1956; *Sotsialisticheskii trud*, 5/1957: p. 34; Bykov and Epshtein, *Sotsialisticheskii trud*, 7/1964: p. 63), this has been disputed by some labour economists, who have asserted that workers were, and remain, more directly responsible for poor efficiency (Sonin, *Sotsialisticheskii trud*, 3/1977: p. 96). It is important to keep in mind that throughout the Khrushchev period the press was extremely reluctant to criticise industrial workers, almost certainly in order to contrast the Khrushchev regime's alleged championing of workers' interests with the attitude during the Stalin period, when the regime repeatedly blamed its own failures on 'self-seekers' and 'malicious disorganisers of production'. More important is the point that formally recorded losses of work time are only an imperfect measure of the pace of work and the ability of workers to use the disorder of the industrial routine to protect their position. This has become generally accepted by both Western and Soviet commentators on the contemporary USSR, but has been less well documented for the Khrushchev years. Here, too, additional research is required.

TRADE-UNION REFORM

Because the trade-union reform has been described so extensively in the standard Western literature (Brown, 1966; McAuley, 1969), it will only be discussed here in passing. The reform was clearly part of the larger campaign following the XX Party Congress about the restoration of 'socialist democracy', one of whose aims, we have argued, was to restore the regime's legitimacy in the eyes of the workforce in the hope that this would improve morale and with it labour productivity. This was indicated quite strongly in a leading article in *Trud*, which argued that everyone would now have to make sacrifices if the country were to advance, and that this in turn made totally avoidable cases of negligence or managerial abuse 'intolerable' (*Trud*, 15 June 1956).

Consistent with this line two of the main features of the trade-union reform were campaigns against unfair dismissals of workers by enterprise directors and attempts to revive socialist competition. The law of 15 July 1958 had stipulated that workers could only be fired with the approval of the factory trade-union committee. Throughout the period the press and journals complained that managers were continuing to dismiss workers either without trade union consent or with the unions merely rubber stamping management decisions without proper hearings or consideration of workers' rights. An indication of the validity of these charges is the fact that approximately half of the cases brought by workers to People's Courts seeking to have their dismissals overturned were successful – often despite trade union approval of the original discharge (McAuley, 1969: pp. 213 ff.; see also *Sotsialisticheskaya zakonnost*, 12/1959: pp. 20–2, *Sovetskaya yustitsiya*, 7/1960: pp. 12–14, and *Trud*, 13 Sep 1962, 12 Jan 1964). Nevertheless it should not be assumed that managers had suddenly begun indulging in an orgy of dismissals or that the unions routinely turned a blind eye to abuses. In the wake of the trade-union reforms of 1957 and 1958 the number of reinstatement cases coming before the courts dropped sharply, so that in Moscow and Leningrad (the country's two largest industrial centres) in 1962 there were roughly 2000 and 1000 such cases respectively (McAuley, 1969: pp. 205–6). Despite the press campaigns the legal changes introduced by Khrushchev had provided *de facto* guarantees of a worker's security of employment: workers were now free to change jobs at will, while management found it extremely difficult to fire them or to make dismissals stick if appealed. This was clearly one of the concessions that the regime felt it had to make in order to regain the overall co-operation of the workforce.

The impact of appeals for socialist competition is more difficult to assess. Socialist competition has always been largely devoid of any content and genuine commitment from most workers. However, the possibility must at least be examined that in the wake of de-Stalinisation the regime might have enjoyed some temporary success in enlisting more than token enthusiasm. The daily accounts in the press of the various achievements of competing brigades or factories are no indication either of the veracity of the claims made or of the spirit with which workers took part. It is perhaps significant that, by late 1962, Grishin, then head of the All-Union Central Council of Trade Unions (VTsSPS), complained of widespread 'formalism' in competition, with trade unions and *sovnarkhozy* awarding honours and bonuses to enterprises and workers who had not in fact met targets for growth in productivity, cutting costs or improving quality (*Trud*, 25 Dec 1962).

THE WAGE REFORM OF 1956–61

The most important element of labour policy under Khrushchev was the wage reform of 1956–61. The system of determining norms and wages had remained basically unchanged from the First Five-Year Plan until the reform's introduction. The basic wage, paid to those fulfilling their norms by 100 per cent, was kept low so as to compel piece workers (the overwhelming majority) to overfulfil their quotas. At the same time there was a wide disparity between piece and time rates, to the detriment of time workers. The result of this system was that managers resorted to a number of devices in order to allow workers to achieve reasonable earnings. For piece workers they deliberately kept norms low so that workers could overfulfil their targets relatively easily (Batkaev and Markov, 1964: p. 201). In addition the use of so-called 'progressive' piece rates was widely practised, whereby piece rates were increased for each percentage of norm overfulfilment. In some industries, e.g. coal mining, progressive payments were paid for less than 100 per cent norm fulfilment as to workers in industries where working conditions made norms more difficult to meet (Davies, 1956: p. 326). The result was that average norm fulfilment prior to the reform was quite high, in some industries nearly 200 per cent (Table 7.1). In the 1930s this

TABLE 7.1   *Average Norm Fulfilment in Selected Industries*

Industry	Prior to wage reform	October 1963
All industry	169	120
Iron and steel	137	115
Non-ferrous metallurgy	142	115
Coal mining	123	106
Oil extraction	134	127
Engineering and metalworking	209	133
Chemicals	158	120
Woodworking	170	120
Building materials	144	113
Textiles	146	111
Sewn goods	155	113
Meat and dairy	157	107*
Baking	134	111*
Printing and publishing	184	112*

*Figures obtained by special survey conducted after introduction of the wage reform; the date is unspecified, but probably 1957 or 1958.

Source: Batkaev and Markov, 1964: p. 198.

process of retarding norm rises had led to norms being set well below plan targets, so that if all workers in an enterprise fulfilled their norms by 100 per cent the plan would be underfulfilled, sometimes substantially. This practice apparently carried on until the reform (Meerzon, *Voprosy ekonomiki*, 7/1960: p. 39).

For workers on time wages, whose earnings could not be adjusted by manipulating norms, managers resorted to a baroque system of bonuses, many of which were illegal or for fictitious work, to allow these workers to close the differential between themselves and piece workers. Other devices were to put workers into higher skill and wage grades than they had been trained for, or to pay them at so-called 'fictitious' piece rates for work that should have been done on a time basis and where the 'norms' then set were extremely easy to overfulfil (Batkaev and Markov, 1964: p. 203). The manipulation of both norms and bonuses formed part of a general pattern, according to which managers were more or less compelled to protect workers' earnings in order to stem discontent during times of low living standards and when labour was in short supply. Understandably wage costs prior to the reform consistently exceeded planned levels.

The reform of 1956–61 sought to remedy this situation through a number of measures.

1 Basic wage rates were raised, together with output quotas, in order to cut levels of norm overfulfilment and reduce the share of overfulfilment payments in total earnings;
2 Piece workers were switched from progressive piece rates (which had played a large role in spiralling wage costs) and even straight piece rates to various bonus systems, bonuses now being paid out for such items as plan overfulfilment, quality and cost reductions. This was designed to reverse the long-standing emphasis on gross physical indices of individual performance;
3 Differentials between skills were narrowed by simplifying the network of so-called 'skill and wage grades' [*razryady*], reducing the number of grades in most industries to six;
4 Certain groups of piece workers were put on to time wages, the emphasis being on those carrying out maintenance operations or jobs requiring precision, where piece work was deemed detrimental to results;
5 Norm-setting procedures, under which norm rises for each industry and occupation were announced annually from the centre, were decentralised, giving enterprise managers authority to determine the timing and size of increases theoretically in line with improvements in technology and productivity.

Both Soviet and Western assessments make it clear that at least certain objectives of the reform were achieved. Average levels of norm fulfilment declined, in most industries dramatically (Table 7.1). The share of basic wages in earnings rose and that of norm-overfulfilment payments correspondingly fell. In the six industries that had completed the wage reform by 1960 (coal, chemicals, cement, reinforced concrete products, non-ferrous metals, and iron and steel) the basic wage as a proportion of piece workers' earnings had risen from 61 to 77 per cent (Meshchaninov, *Sotsialisticheskii trud*, 2/1961. p. 30). By 1961 the basic wage represented just over 70 per cent of earnings for all piece workers and 73 per cent of earnings for piece and time workers combined (Batkaev and Markov 1964: p. 221). The percentage of workers on time wages also incresed, although piece work remained the dominant form of payment: By August 1962 time workers were nearly 39.5 per cent of the workforce (ibid. p. 208). By 1961 the number of industrial workers on straight or progressive piece rates (as opposed to piece rate plus bonuses) had fallen from two-thirds to one-third (Kirsch, 1972: p. 23) and of these only a tiny fraction were on progressive scales (Meshchaninov, *Sotsialisticheskii trud*, 2/1961: p. 32). Finally, the reform brought the growth of *money* wages into line with planned levels for the first time (excluding the Second World War) since the First Five-Year Plan (Nove, 1964: pp. 213, 219). Yet for all its achievements it is doubtful that the reform succeeded in its main objective, namely to develop an incentive system that would lead to the production of regular, high levels of output of reliable quality.

It is possible to identify a number of factors leading to the reform's failure. One was the regime's inability to develop a system of 'technically based' norms, according to which norms would be set not on the basis of average local conditions, including allowances for stoppages, time lost due to non-delivery of supplies, etc., but in line with the full technological potential of the equipment at hand (Kirsch, 1972: pp. 50–1). In fact the failure to apply technically based norms dates back to the 1920s (Siegelbaum, 1984; Filtzer, 1986: ch. 8), and is itself an important aspect of Soviet economic life that needs to be explained.

Second, the reform prejudiced the earning potential of several groups of workers, forcing managers to find various means of compensation. In the engineering industry, for example, those workers carrying out highly repetitive mechanised operations saw their earnings suffer because their norms could be more precisely set, leaving them less scope for substantial overfulfilment (Kirsch, 1972: p. 68). As already noted, Batkaev and Markov (1964: p. 209) cited this as a major cause of high turn-over among machine operators in the engineering industry where, according to the authors, workers had a positive preference for jobs involving more manual operations, where norms were of necessity looser and the worker had greater leeway for overfulfilment. It is possible that managers attempted to compensate by keeping the norms for these workers low, since overfulfilment throughout the engineering industry was very high 'as a result of which workers of average and even lower skills were receiving very high wages, the size of which did not reflect actual expenditures of labour' (ibid. p. 210). The same disparity applied to production versus auxiliary workers, who, because their jobs were poorly mechanised, had ever since the 1930s been able to record far higher degrees of norm overfulfilment than workers in basic production. The wage reform had intended to rectify this by raising the basic wages of auxiliary workers relatively more than of production workers, but *at the same time* making their norms more difficult to overfulfil through the application of technically based norms. As this would have endangered auxiliary workers' earnings managers in a number of industries either shifted them into higher skill and wage grades or kept their norms low (Meshchaninov, *Sotsialisticheskii trud* 2/1961: pp. 30–1). By 1961 it was clear that auxiliary workers were enjoying levels of norm overfulfilment far higher than industrial averages (Amelchenko, *Sotsialisticheskii trud*, 7/1961: p. 65). Despite the various controls the reform placed on piece earnings (or perhaps because of managerial circumvention of them) piece workers as a whole remained in a favoured position relative to time workers, even those in key areas of production (Batkaev and Markov, 1964: p. 204). This clearly threatened the earnings of piece workers shifted on to time rates and there is evidence that management, at least in some industries, made good the losses by abusing the award of bonus payments (Nevolin, *Sotsialisticheskii trud*, 6/1960: pp. 55–6; Grishin, *Trud*, 28 July 1962).

Finally, the switch to bonus systems failed to offer adequate incentives to increase productivity. Instead workers came to look upon bonuses as a stable and regular part of earnings (Manevich, *Trud*, 4 Oct 1962; Kirsch, 1972: p. 69). In theory the new bonus systems were to compensate workers for the loss of wages paid for norm overfulfilment. In reality they failed to do so. While piece-work overfulfilment payments fell as a percentage of earnings, other bonuses did not make up this loss. Total earnings remained roughly the same thanks to the rise in basic pay (Kirsch, 1972: pp. 46–7), but this meant that the largest determinant of earnings was virtually guaranteed. Bonuses could not function as a variable element designed to encourage improved performance because they were too small and in any case had themselves become a more or less fixed part of take home pay rather than being made conditional upon results. For example, in the engineering industry of Kuibyshev *sovnarkhoz prescribed* bonuses ranged from 10 to 30 per cent of the basic wage rate of production workers (versus 40 to 60 per cent of the salaries of technical specialists and engineers). In actual practice bonuses for production workers were much less – a mere 6 per cent of earnings. Elsewhere in the region, where bonus systems were allegedly applied more extensively than in engineering, workers fulfilling their norms by 105–15 per cent were earning a derisory bonus of three rubles a month. In addition the fact that bonuses for piece workers were tied to the plan fulfilment of an entire section, and hence made dependent on the performance of other workers, was also alleged to be a disincentive (Kromskii, *Trud*, 8 June 1962). The Kuibyshev region was not unique in this regard. Figures provided by Batkaev and Markov (1964: p. 221) produce a rough estimate that in 1962 bonus payments for piece workers were approximately 6 per cent of earnings throughout industry.

No doubt as a response to this situation managers found ways of increasing bonus payments. In Leningrad managers would keep shadow workforces not listed on their establishments whom they would move into hard-pressed sections during storming. Their output would be credited to the regular workforce, thus earning the entire section a bonus for 'improved' productivity (*Trud*, 26 Feb 1959). We have already noted that managers in some industries simply put all workers on to bonus systems irrespective of regulations. Where this did not work they could always promote workers into higher skill and wage grades. Therefore the bonus, which was designed to offer incentives to improve output, productivity and quality, merely took over the role that low norms had fulfilled in the 1930s and early 1950s, *a guarantor of earnings*. The assumption of this function virtually precluded it from carrying out the task for which it had been intended.

To a large extent the application of a bonus system which tied workers' earnings to collective results was clearly incompatible with the retention of most workers on piece rates. Manevich (*Trud*, 4 Oct 1962), whose laments on the failures of Soviet norm-setting changed little over the next decade and a half (*Voprosy ekonomiki*, 8/1976; p. 122), complained that bonuses for such indices as improvements in quality or reductions in costs either did not exist at most enterprises or were extremely small, making up less than 1 per cent of the total enterprise wage fund. But this is not surprising in a system where the overriding emphasis was, and remains, on gross physical output. Despite the arguments of some labour economists that the development of technology had made piece rates counterproductive, they remained the dominant form of payment. In the end this was almost certainly a political decision, consistent with the conditions under which the Soviet élite consolidated its position under Stalin and has retained it since. In the 1930s the mass application of piece rates was an essential part of the policy of individualising work organisation and remuneration and was instrumental in allowing the regime to break down collective resistance and atomise the workforce

(Filtzer, 1986: ch. 3). For all the economic drawbacks of retaining poorly integrated production processes – and with them a poorly integrated workforce – the regime has drawn the political advantage that they help keep the workforce atomised and hence politically controllable. Any attempt to abandon piecework would have to confront the potential political implications of such a move.

It is interesting in this light to examine the fate of so-called 'collective' piece rates under Khrushchev. Like the production communes of the 1930s (Filtzer, 1986: ch. 3) workers on collective piece rates frequently took the independent initiative of pooling their earnings and sharing them out on various egalitarian lines. It is inconceivable that this system could have posed any kind of political threat to managerial authority or to the basic fabric of wages policy (as the communes *did* do in the 1930s), yet it came under bitter attack for breeding 'egalitarianism' (Shkurko, *Voprosy ekonomiki*, 5/1962: p. 43; Grishin, *Trud*, 28 July 1962).

Both the inability to extend the application of technically based norms and the expectation by workers that bonuses would become a guaranteed part of earnings must be seen as *effects* of the wage reform's failure and not as causes. Complaints that technical norm-setting was poor because inadequate resources and effort were invested in collecting the data necessary to set unified, centrally determined norms (Grishin, *Trud*, 28 July 1962; *Trud*, 19 Oct 1962) cannot be taken seriously. In like manner the fact that, as Manevich (*Trud*, 4 Oct 1962) claimed, 'the bonus (especially in engineering) has become an organic part of earnings and is often paid independently of results' derived from managers' need to protect the earnings of workers whose incomes had suffered under the new system and would otherwise give up their jobs. The same pressures drove managers in a number of industries openly to subvert the prescribed norms. The devices were the familiar ones used from the 1930s to the present. Managers would hoard technological improvements: small improvements in equipment or work organisation would be made which on their own might not warrant norm rises. Such improvements would, of course, accumulate, enabling substantial gains in productivity, but the norms would not be changed (Shkurko, *Voprosy ekonomiki*, 5/1962: p. 41). In the coal mines of the Kuzbass managers simply set norms below those stipulated in official handbooks. In addition the amount of work actually performed was not properly recorded, overestimating workers' real output. Where this did not suffice, workers were placed in higher skill and wage grades

– a practice allegedly prevalent throughout the coal industry and not just the Kuzbass (Dovba, *Sotsialisticheskii trud*, 1/1960: pp. 50–1). In late 1962 the press complained that norms in some industries and regions, e.g. Ukrainian gas and oil construction and Leningrad city, were so low that workers on some jobs could easily fulfil them by 250–300 per cent – something that would only have been possible if management had been deliberately keeping norms depressed (*Trud*, 26 Sep, 10 Oct 1962).

An interesting device was the introduction of temporary norms for new lines of production, ostensibly to allow for the difficulties and reduced output associated with the manufacture of new products. Managers in fact had the option of transferring workers on to time wages to protect their pay during the initial settling-in period. Instead they opted by and large to apply lower temporary norms, which became increasingly easy to overfulfil as production difficulties were ironed out over time. Naturally workers resisted attempts to replace the temporary norms by permanent, technically based ones, since this would have reduced earnings. Where permanent norms were installed they were very often raised only by a token amount. Perhaps more significant is the fact that where rate-setters insisted on substantial rises shop-level trade unions and foremen opposed them, trying to keep the norms low (Mikhailov, *Sotsialisticheskii trud*, 5/1964: pp. 122–5; *Sotsialisticheskii trud*, 10/1964: pp. 118 ff.; 11/1964: pp. 113 ff.; see also *Trud*, 22 Sep 1962).

The inability to impose technically based norms reflected itself in highly uneven patterns of norm fulfilment between industries, as shown in Table 7.2.

Whereas in October 1962 some 31 per cent of piece workers in coal mining were unable to meet their norms, the average was only 11 per cent for industry as a whole, and was as low as 7 per cent in engineering and 5 per cent in chemicals. And while iron and steel and light industry showed nearly half the piece workers fulfilling at just about 100–110 per cent, in engineering over 50 per cent of piece workers were meeting their quotas by 120 per cent or more. These figures, while showing the great unevenness between industries, reveal little about the patchy pattern of norm fulfilment between trades within industries, which, as has already been noted, tended to show better results for auxiliary and manual workers and relatively poor performances by those whose jobs were highly mechanised.

The fact is that uneven norm fulfilment, like the inability to inculcate technically based norms, is endemic to the Soviet system. Kirsch

TABLE 7.2 *Share of Piece Workers at Different Levels of Norm Fulfilment for Selected Industries October 1962*

Industry	Level of fulfilment (%)					
	90 or less	90– 100	100– 110	110– 120	120– 150	150 or greater
All industry	5.2	6.2	30.0	20.4	27.0	11.2
Iron and steel	1.5	3.6	46.6	23.1	21.9	3.3
Coal mining	14.7	16.7	28.8	20.3	16.7	2.8
Engineering and metalworking	4.3	2.6	16.1	16.6	27.2	23.2
Chemicals	1.7	3.2	33.5	24.9	29.7	7.0
Woodworking	4.4	6.6	26.6	23.0	30.6	8.8
Light industry	4.3	7.9	43.7	21.9	18.9	3.3
Food	8.5	9.5	36.0	22.2	19.1	4.7

Source: Batkaev and Markov, 1964: p. 208.

has tried to explain this in terms of managers' need to retain a certain slackness in the norms in order to compensate workers doing difficult jobs or working under unfavourable conditions for possible losses of earnings (Kirsch, 1972: pp. 66–7, 129–30). The nature of Soviet production indicates that the problem is far more systematic than this explanation suggests. The difficulties in job reclassification, the impossibility of dismissals, the permanency of the enterprise (factories cannot go 'bankrupt' if they overrun their costs) and the shortage of skilled workers combine with the well known host of intra-enterprise production difficulties to make norms unenforceable. From the worker's point of view his or her performance depends on too many extraneous factors, e.g. breakdowns, non-arrival of supplies, shortages of (or the inability to locate) tools and parts, non-standardisation of parts and equipment and continual changes in production plans and product mix. The result is that virtually *all* workers can at any given time find their earnings threatened; what is more it is often quite unpredictable which groups of workers will be affected at a particular moment. All of these various factors have led to a long-standing resistance by both workers and management to technically based norms, precisely because the conditions of Soviet production require that managers retain the ability to insulate workers' earnings from the perpetual irregularities of Soviet economic life. A good illustration is what happened in the non-ferrous metal industry in Siberia and Central Asia when the work day was shortened in the late 1950s. Norms for many production and auxiliary workers were not raised after the wage reform, and so norm fulfilment and earnings shot up. At the same time, because the shift to the seven-hour day was poorly prepared nearly a third of workers were unable to meet their norms due to the ensuing disruptions. Managers compensated by putting workers into higher wage grades, paying workers on routine jobs for allegedly doing heavy or dangerous work or paying bonuses above established maxima (Smirnov, Rudnitskii, *Sotsialisticheskii trud*, 2/1960: pp. 66–7).

The apparent failure of the Khrushchev wage reform has added significance given the fact that the Brezhnev era saw few fundamental changes in the wages and norm-setting system. It therefore raises the question of whether any system of incentives based on norms can be developed under Soviet conditions.

CONCLUSION

The major aspects of labour policy under Khrushchev were addressed to quite specific and urgent conomic necessities. The legalisation of job changing and the removal of criminal sanctions for truancy were probably inevitable even in the absence of de-Stalinisation: the increasingly widespread failure of managers and the lower courts to enforce the legislation are evidence that at shop-floor level the laws had become impediments to the smooth functioning of the enterprise. Similarly the trade-union reform cannot be seen as any genuine attempt to allow the working masses directly to control their own destinies. There was never any question of permitting them to establish truly independent trade unions, much less political organisations. In many respects the reform merely gave back to the unions rights which they had exercised up to the middle of the 1930s. Rather the reform was part of an attempt to relegitimate the regime in the eyes of the population and to offer political incentives to raise productivity.

The fate of the wage reform is perhaps a more complex issue. It has been argued above that no reform of the wage- and norm-setting system can genuinely succeed under Soviet conditions. It remains then to examine the structural factors that make changes in the norm-setting mechanism so difficult. Here concessions over norms and wages should be seen as part of a much larger pattern of worker–manager relations which requires management to make various accommodations to the workforce due to the latter's considerable control over its own work process. Future research must, therefore, examine how this relationship manifested itself on the shop floor.

The substantial losses of work time in Soviet factories in this period has already been noted, as well as the conflicting views of labour economists over the role of the worker in slowing down the pace of work. Here it must always be kept in mind that in the Soviet system what presents itself to one group of workers as an 'objective' difficulty (lack of parts or supplies, equipment breakdowns, etc.) is usually the result of the 'subjective' behaviour of workers and managerial staff at an early stage of production or distribution. Non-arrival of supplies, defective production, poor maintenance and so on, arise not simply from the bureaucratic nature of the planning system, but equally from the regime's inability to develop a credible system of incentives or sanctions. Workers have little fear of unemployment while the wage system, combined with the severe shortage of consumer goods, offer insufficient inducement to raise the intensity of labour. Ultimately it is the labour shortage which creates the conditions that make it possible for workers to work as poorly as they do while at the same time compelling managers to keep norms within achievable limits. But the labour shortage has a definite morphology and cycle of reproduction. By providing workers with the 'freedom' to violate discipline, to work slowly or to produce goods of inferior quality, the workers are re-creating those tendencies within the system which require managers to hoard labour, thus keeping labour scarce throughout the economy as a whole. The individual worker is thereby constantly reproducing the conditions which grant him or her this relative control over the labour process. Having abandoned coercion, being afraid to face the political consequences of reintroducing unemployment, and at the same time proving incapable of providing the population with any genuine political or economic incentives, the Khrushchev regime showed itself unable to break this cycle.

8 Social Policy

ALASTAIR McAULEY

8.1 INTRODUCTION

The Khrushchev period witnessed a crucial shift in social priorities and Khrushchev himself has been given too little credit for this. It is true that no one person can bring about a social revolution, but the nature of the Soviet political system is such that the direction of policy is very much influenced by the attitudes and preferences of the man at the top. So, in what follows, innovations in policy or philosophy will often be attributed to Khrushchev personally although these properly belong to the inner leadership more generally.

It was during the Khrushchev era that the living standards of ordinary Soviet families began to rise significantly, that the population began to reap the benefits of a quarter of a century of rapid industrialisation. It was in these years that the first concerted effort was made to solve some of the pressing social problems that had accumulated over twenty-five years of central planning. This break with the Stalinist past owed much to the new First Secretary's vision of communism. Yet, he has received no credit for his contribution to the building of socialism from the Party; rather, Brezhnev and his propagandists tried to claim the credit for making growth in the people's standard of living a primary objective of the Party's economic policy (Borodina and Fursov, 1983: pp. 3–4). This chapter should be seen as a small attempt to redress the balance.

In a contribution to a recent assessment of Soviet policy in the 1980s this author suggested that social policy in the USSR could best be understood as the set of decisions relating to the formation and disbursement of social consumption funds, *obshchestvennie fondy potrebleniya* (McAuley in Brown and Kaser, 1982: pp. 146–70). In the context of this paper, however, such a definition is too narrow. The formulation of social policy in the 1950s and early 1960s involved more than the making of decisions about the level of funding to be received by particular programmes. It involved a re-examination of the goals of social policy and, perhaps, an attempt to return to basic Marxist–Leninist formulations. It involved a reconsideration of the processes by which policy was made and the instruments through which it was implemented. It resulted in the emergence of a new conception of the appropriate relationship between state and society, citizen and government. These wider issues should be included in the discussion.

Although Karl Marx made a point of not providing a detailed blueprint of the policies to be followed by a future socialist government, his writings contain a general framework for social policy. This framework was endorsed by Lenin in his various writings and was accepted (at least in principle) by later Stalinist Politburos. In practice, however, the policies pursued by the Soviet government in the 1940s and early 1950s differed radically from these models. Under Khrushchev this divergence was recognised, a concerted attempt was made to identify shortcomings and to formulate policies that were in closer accord with ideological precepts. These developments are discussed in Sections 8.3 and 8.4 of this chapter. Section 8.2 contains a brief description of the heritage of socialist ideas about social policy and contrast it with the reality of Soviet society in about 1950. (Some of the issues raised here are discussed at greater length in McAuley in Collard *et al.*, 1980: pp. 238–57.) This chapter ends with an assessment of the significance of Khrushchev's contribution to the evolution of social policy in the USSR.

8.2 SOCIAL POLICY IN THE LATE STALIN PERIOD

In his *Critique of the Gotha Programme* Marx argued that the ultimate goal of a communist society must be distribution according to need; but he recognised that this could not be adopted until society had achieved material abundance and until work itself had become a source of satisfaction for all. In the first post-revolutionary phase (what is now called 'socialism') the principle of distribution would be: from each according to his ability to each according to his labour. What is being asserted here is that, under socialism, labour earnings should form the main source of support for the vast majority of families. Only in this way will available supplies of goods and services be distributed fairly while at the same time ensuring that *all* who are capable of it contribute to social labour. This same idea was expressed by Lenin by means of the biblical quotation 'he who does not work, neither shall he eat'. In fact Marx goes further: he argues that earnings must be differentiated to reflect differences in skill and conditions of work if individuals are to be encouraged to acquire the skills needed for economic development, if they are to be induced to undertake essential but unpleasant jobs.

In the *Critique*, however, Marx recognised that earnings would not constitute the only source of consumption expenditure in a socialist society. In addition he wrote of income maintenance payments for those not able to support themselves and of the public provision of such services as medical care and education. In this he was only echoing a wider European radical tradition.

Finally, there is the question of the growth in living standards. This is not something that is discussed explicitly in the *Critique*; but, it was not something that was dealt with at length in the economics literature of the period when Marx was writing. (Indeed, emphasis on year-by-year increases in real income as a source of political legitimation is a largely post-Second World War phenomenon.) But a steady improvement in the well-being of the working class is implicit in the logic of Marx's argument: approaching abundance must entail a continuing decline in scarcity.

The social and economic conditions enjoyed by the Soviet population at the time of Stalin's death differed in a number of ways from what is implied by this socialist heritage. Far from there having been a continuous growth in popular living standards under Stalin, real wages in 1952 were very little different to what they had been in 1928 (Gordon *et al.*, *Rabochii klass i sovremennyi mir*, 2–3/1974: p. 59). And there was little for the population to spend its money on. Urban per capita food supplies were lower than before the war and supplies of industrial consumer goods were inadequate.

The distribution of earnings was also characterised by substantial inequality. It is reported that the ratio of the ninth and first deciles of the distribution of state employees by monthly earnings in 1946 was as high as 7.24 (Rabkina and Rimashevskaya, *EKO*, 5/1978: p. 20. The ninth decile of the earnings distribution is a monthly wage such that nine-tenths of all recipients earn less than it. The ratio of deciles (known as the 'decile coefficient') is a favourite Soviet measure of dispersion. Western economists prefer to use the Gini coefficient. A figure of 7.24 is quite extreme; in Britain in the late 1960s, for example, the decile coefficient on earnings was only 3.6). Although earnings inequality was reduced after 1949 when the wages of the lowest paid were raised in conjunction with the derationing of bread, it was still substantial in 1952. This was not the only source of inequality, however. In 1954 the average earnings from the *kolkhoz* of the collective farm peasantry were 16 roubles a month; the earnings of industrial workers in the same year were 76 roubles a month. On almost half of these farms, *kolkhozniki* were paid less than 46 kopeks a day – under 16 per cent of the average industrial wage (McAuley, 1979: pp. 33–4). Of course, these peasants also derived income from their private plots, but even so the gap between them and state employees was enormous.

Extensive inequality, of course, almost always implies substantial poverty. And this is true of Stalin's Russia. It was not only *kolkhozniki* who were poor, however; the wages of many state employees were low and those who were no longer able to support themselves were also very badly off. In 1950 the average value of a state pension was only 10 roubles a month (McAuley, 1982: p. 160). This was less than 50 per cent of the lowest state wage and only about one-fifth of average earnings. Worse, few of those entitled by age to a pension were in fact in receipt of one. Even in 1959 there were only 4.4 million old-age pensioners out of a total of 25.3 million persons of pensionable age. In 1950 there were less than a million (ibid. p. 157).

At the time of Stalin's death, then, the USSR was characterised by a stagnant standard of living, by substantial inequality and extensive poverty. It could not even be claimed that Soviet provision of key public services was adequate. There was a serious housing shortage; this had been aggravated by the destruction of the Second World War, but housing problems were already acute in the 1930s. On the other hand, medical care was readily available and the state had invested heavily in education but even these services were organised in a rather élitist way. There were separate hospital facilities for higher Party officials for example; and parents were required to pay for secondary education.

In one respect at least the situation in the Soviet Union in 1952 was even more depressing than the description given in the previous paragraphs suggests. None of the statistical information used to characterise the deplorable living standards endured by the population was in the public domain – and some of it was not even known to the authorities. This widespread public and official ignorance can be attributed to two factors: fear of criticism and bureaucratic overload.

Under Stalin the central organs of the Party and government claimed the exclusive right to initiate and formulate policy. And during the stresses of the early Five-Year plans they had taken increasing exception to the assessment of their performance by academic economists and other specialists. To prevent criticism and to conceal failure the net of official secrecy had been spread wider and wider: the last pre-war statistical handbook was published in 1936; almost no details of later plans of their fulfilment were published at the time. More, economists were discouraged if not prevented from undertaking independent research into the determinants of living standards. And it was maintained that Marxism constituted the only valid sociology for a socialist society: no purpose would be served by empirical social research.

This ban on academic inquiry was complemented by widespread official neglect of issues relating to popular welfare. For example, so far as one can tell, the first post-war census of earnings was held in 1956; the first inquiry into the distribution of income in 1957 (McAuley, 1979: pp. 54, 218). In part this neglect can be attributed to the fact that Stalin's government considered such questions to be of secondary importance. (This is shown by the abolition of the People's Commissariat of Labour in 1933 and the failure to replace it by any central body capable of exercising responsibility over questions of general welfare.) But it is also the case that in the pre-computer age there is a limit on the amount of information that can be collected and processed – even by a bureaucracy as large as Stalin's. And in the 1950s Soviet officialdom was fully occupied with the information collected for the planning of output. As a result, despite claims of omnipotence, Stalin's totalitarian state lacked the effective power needed to solve the widespread social problems that the government faced in 1952. It lacked knowledge of the scale of particular problems; it lacked theoretical or empirical insight into their determinants; it lacked the cadres who might carry out the necessary inquiries; finally, in many areas it lacked the administrative structures needed to implement policies designed to alleviate problems when they had been identified.

8.3 THE KHRUSHCHEV REVOLUTION IN SOCIAL POLICY

This was the rigid and joyless society that Khrushchev inherited in 1953. And this was the system that he changed radically. The impetus for this change sprang in part from the leadership's concern with the need to maintain high rates of growth of output; for example, it can be argued that new policies towards agriculture, adopted as soon as the new government took office, were prompted by a belief that stagnation on the farm was acting as a brake on productivity growth in manufacturing.

But change was also the result of Khrushchev's rather naïve views about the attainability of communism. These were set out in the 1961 Party Programme; they suggest that conditions of material abundance would be approached by the 1980s. This literal belief in the imminence of Marx's Utopia resulted in the change of emphasis in the Party's social policy. A much higher priority was attached to increases in personal consumption. (Although it is virtually imposs-ible to document this, Khrushchev's travels, and those of his immediate associates, also contributed to this shift. They were able to see at first hand what conditions were like in advanced capitalist countries, in the People's Democracies, even in the Third World. And this will have made them look more critically at living conditions at home.)

The two factors mentioned so far may explain the shift in Party priorities, they do not necessarily account for the fact that in the 1950s, the way in which Soviet social policy was made also underwent fundamental changes. By 1965 the government was routinely collecting (and publishing) much of the information needed to monitor changes in popular living standards. In the preceding decade or so a range of research institutes had been established with a duty to investigate pressing social problems and even to propose possible solutions. The teaching of sociology had been introduced into the university curriculum; the teaching of economics was in the process of being reformed. Much greater emphasis was being placed on empirical work. A cadre of specialists in social science was in the process of being built up. In short an apparatus for the provision of specialist advice on social policy had been established. In fact, more had been achieved. As argued below, the first-fruits of this new more rational policy-making process had already been reaped: the first post-war reorganisation of wages had been completed; the country's pension system had been fundamentally recast and state old-age pensions had finally been made available to the mass of indigent collective-farm peasants. And a more radical all-embracing investigation of the extent (and determinants) of poverty had been set in train.

There is one feature of Soviet development under Stalin that might explain this growth of pragmatism in the formulation of social policy – although there appears no way of proving its importance. In the 1920s and even more in the 1930s the Soviet government invested in the education of its new élite. Many of those who rose to occupy positions of political power were given a higher education and more often than not this education was in engineering. Is it too fanciful to suppose that these new graduates transferred what they had learned to the field of *social* engineering?

At all events this fundamental shift in the Soviet social policy and the way in which it is made took place while Khrushchev was First Secretary of the Party. He certainly consented to the changes and actively encouraged many of them. It would be too simple to claim that he brought about the 'revolution' single-handedly. But it reflects his personal vision as well as the deeper changes that had been taking place in the training and attitudes of the Soviet governing élite. And it is not wholly inappropriate to call it the 'Khrushchev revolution'.

8.4   THE EVOLUTION OF LIVING STANDARDS UNDER KHRUSHCHEV

The 'Khrushchev revolution' of Section 8.3 was identified with the increased priority that the Soviet government gave to questions of consumer welfare and the new pragmatism with which social policies were formulated. The first of these developments is described here; the second will be discussed in Section 8.5.

In 1950 the average money earnings of state employees in the USSR were 64 (new) roubles per month; in 1955, on the eve of the first major post-war reorganisation of the wage and salary system, they were 72 roubles. In 1965, the year after Khrushchev's ouster, they had risen to 96 roubles. Thus, over the twelve years or so of the Khrushchev period, earnings increased at an average rate of 2.8–2.9 per cent per year.

Of course, these figures relate to nominal earnings; no allowance has been made for changes in the price-level. But such an adjustment makes little difference to the figures (for the period 1950–64, the real-wage index increased at an average rate of 2.94 per cent per year (McAuley, 1979: p. 244)). Moreover, the interpretation of real wages as an index of consumers' welfare poses certain problems for a Soviet-type economy. Real wages are defined as money wages deflated by a cost-of-living index. In a market economy changes in the availability of goods are reflected in their prices – and hence in the cost of living. If prices are set by the state and are not adjusted to ensure that consumers' goods markets are in equilibrium, as has frequently been the case in the USSR, movements in real wages need not correspond to changes in the amounts of goods and services that can be acquired with the relevant money wage.

(In actual fact the Khrushchev period was one in which official retail prices were constant for the most part (and Western-calculated price indices show only modest growth (ibid: p. 326); the range and quantity of goods available also increased substantially. There is therefore no reason to assume that the real-wage index is misleading in this instance.)

The increase in average living standards was accompanied by a reduction in inequality. For state employees this was the result of a major reform of wage and salary scales. *Kolkhozniki* benefited from higher and more regular labour-payments; some of those belonging to the poorest and most backward farms also benefited from the farm-conversion programme.

The measure of inequality in wages most favoured by Soviet economists and statisticians, the decile coefficient, is not at all sensitive to changes in the tails of a distribution, but it does give an idea of the gross dispersion involved. In 1956 the decile coefficient of the distribution of state employees by monthly earnings was reported as 4.9. In 1964 this had fallen to 3.3 – a reduction of a third (ibid. p. 222).

But the wage reform did much more than reduce overall dispersion in wages. In addition it changed the composition of earnings, increasing the relative importance of basic rates at the expense of supplementary payments. This made it possible to link bonuses much more closely with above plan performance. This in turn made it easier for the authorities to encourage genuine increases in productivity. The reform also went a long way towards eliminating inconsistencies and irrationalities in the wages paid by different enterprises and Ministries. The 1900 or so wage scales that had been in use in Soviet industry under Stalin were reduced to 10; the several thousand base rates were reduced to 50. This introduced coherence in the place of chaos and produced a structure that was seen to be fair by a majority of Soviet workers.

Wage reform and the growth in earnings led to a decline in poverty among state employees; and this was reinforced by the changes in income enjoyed by other social groups. There is some doubt about what should be taken to constitute poverty in the Soviet Union. One can argue plausibly for a poverty-line income of 30 roubles a month per capita in 1955. For the end of the Khrushchev period, say 1965, one can take either 30 roubles a month or the higher figure of 50 roubles proposed by Sarkisyan and Kuznetsova. On balance the former figure is preferable (ibid. ch. 4 for the derivation of these poverty lines and the statement of the reasons why 30 roubles a month is preferable. See also Sarkisyan and Kuznetsova, 1967).

Soviet figures on the extent of poverty (in either 1953, 1965 or any intervening year) are not readily available. But the following estimates have been made in the West. In 1958 there were some 68 million state employees and their dependents living in families with a per capita income less than 30 roubles (ibid. p. 75). In 1960 the average per capita personal income of *kolkhozniki* and their dependants was 328 roubles a year – 27.3 roubles per month (ibid. p. 29). At that date there were 67.3 million *kolkhozniki*; it seems plausible to infer that at least 33 million collective farmers received a per capita income below 30 roubles a month in 1958. Thus at least 100 million people were below the notional poverty line in 1958 – and the figure would have been greater in 1953.

In 1967 there were approximately 30 million persons with a per capita income below 30 roubles a month – 19 million *kolkhozniki* and 11 million state employees. There were only some 80–5 million persons living in families with a per capita income below 50 roubles per month! (ibid. p. 75). These figures demonstrate the scale of Khrushchev's success in his struggle to raise Soviet living standards.

This achievement can be attributed to the decision to raise the minimum wage substantially, the continuing increases in agricultural procurement prices – and hence *kolkhoznik* earnings – and, third, the reorganisation of income-maintenance programmes. In 1953 there was no legal minimum wage, although the lowest rate paid to state employees has been reported as 20–22 roubles a month. A minimum wage clause was adopted in 1956 and the minimum was set at 27–35 roubles (depending upon branch and place of employment). In 1959 the minimum was raised to 40–45 roubles for those branches whose wage-scales had been reorganised. This had become universal in the state sector by 1965. Thus the Khrushchev period had witnessed a doubling of the minimum wage in twelve years (ibid. pp. 203–6).

The increases in wage-rates and earnings enjoyed by collective farmers over the same period are even more striking. As mentioned above, the average earnings of *kolkhozniki* in 1954 were only 16 roubles a month; in 1965 they were 54 roubles (ibid. p. 33; Narkhoz, 1975: p. 414). There were equally dramatic changes in the value and availability of pensions during this period. In 1950 there were only 846 thousand old-age pensioners in the USSR. The vast bulk of the 18.3 million pensioners at that date were in receipt of disability pensions; they were those who had been crippled by war or by industrial accidents. Fifteen years later there were 32 million pensioners in the country – of whom 16 million were receiving old-age pensions. At the same time the average value of a state (and, in 1966, a collective-farm) pension increased from 10 roubles a month to 27.6 roubles (McAuley, 1982. pp. 157, 160). These two types of change combined to raise millions of old people out of poverty.

The 'Khrushchev revolution' involved more than these increases in money income, of course. The Soviet government in these years continued to invest in such public services as health care, education and housing. And considerable progress was made towards satisfying demand. In addition, in education at least, reforms were introduced to make access more open, to make the system less élitist. (For an account of this reform of education in 1958 see Matthews, 1982.)

8.5 KHRUSHCHEV AND THE DEVELOPMENT OF SOCIAL POLICY

The evolution of living standards under Khrushchev provides evidence that the Soviet government had made a decisive break with the Stalinist past. The changes in ideas about the role of the Party and the state, called the new pragmatism above, constitutes an equally if not more fundamental departure from Stalinism. The nature of this departure and its consequences for the Soviet political system are the subject of this section.

It was argued above that Khrushchev's naïve belief in the attainability of communism contributed to a change in government priorities: it focused attention on the need to raise living standards and to eliminate unjustified inequality. This in turn led policy-makers (and their specialist advisers) to re-examine the structure of society and the economy, to explore the way in which they worked and the obstacles that they posed to the attainment of government objectives. The problems that were revealed in this process led the government to support the establishment of empirical sociology and the revival of applied economics. The growth of a social research establishment has in its turn modified leadership perceptions; it has undermined their literal faith in the Marxian Utopia and eroded belief in other ideological tenets. The nature of these interactions will be illustrated by a discussion of Khrushchev's reorganisation of wage- and salary-scales.

In 1956 the Soviet authorities embarked on a far-reaching reform of the country's wage and salary structure, the first coherent change to the system in twenty years. It has already been pointed out how important the role played by wages was in the determination of living standards in the Soviet conception of socialism. The content of the reformed wage- and salary-scales should therefore be seen as evidence of contemporary views on what was feasible or desirable by way of raising the standard of living for particular groups, reducing differentiation and so forth. The reform is also important for the light that it throws on the way that the Soviet government's ideas about the formulation and implementation of policy was changing at this time. These two issues form the major theme of this discussion. Before addressing them, however, it is desirable to say a few words about the wider context in which the wage reform of the 1950s took place. (Ideas on the political significance of these changes have been influenced by the analysis in Hauslohner, 1984, esp. ch. 2.)

The middle 1950s witnessed major changes in the social and political environment in which Soviet workers operated; the reform of wage and salary structures was only a part of this renegotiated social contract. The new deal also included a repeal of Stalin's 1938–40 laws restricting a worker's right to quit his job voluntarily and an attempt to revive the trade unions, thereby creating organisations that would protect the individual from the arbitrary and illegal acts of management.

The laws of 1938–40 contained criminal sanctions for use against workers who were late for work, who were absent without the consent of management; they made it an offence to leave one's job without the permission of the enterprise's management. Employers were given the right to transfer skilled workers and professionals between enterprises and regions if such transfers were justified by the interests of production; managers did not have to seek the consent of those involved before ordering the transfers. These acts constituted an extraordinary infringement on the freedom of workers. And they cannot be justified as emergency powers similar to those taken by all governments in time of war. Rather they should be seen as the culmination of a process of legislative encroachment on freedom of labour that took place during the 1930s.

The 1940 law prohibiting unauthorised quits was not always enforced and criminal sanctions against certain infringements of labour discipline were dropped in 1951 (but this fact was not made public at the time.) However, the 1938–40 legislative framework was a powerful weapon for use by management against their workers. And it was a weapon that continued to be used; even in 1955, the Leningrad courts were still hearing cases under the 1940 laws. More often than not those charged were convicted and were often sentenced to periods of corrective labour (at the same enterprise but at a reduced wage) (McAuley, 1969: p. 47).

The decision to abandon this weapon, to repeal the laws which had been the cause of substantial resentment, was a dramatic and public gesture, a signal that the government wished to redefine its relationship with society, or rather, with the working class. By allowing those who were dissatisfied with their conditions of work (or with the treatment that they had received at the hands of management), the right to quit at no greater cost than the loss of an uninterrupted work-record, the government significantly altered the context of industrial relations on the factory floor. And the Soviet government under Khrushchev went further; in a series of decrees in 1957–8 it modified the procedures for the settlement of workplace grievances and, in the process, greatly strengthened the role of the factory trade-union committee. The developments of this period were intended to encourage the imposition of legal norms on to management–worker relations and inhibit the arbitrary exercise of power that had been a feature of Soviet managerial practice up to that time. Although progress was halting at first, the courts (and the unions) did show themselves willing to defend the workers' newly established rights. And this too has contributed to the changed context of social policy formation in the post-Stalin USSR (ibid.; *passim*; Hauslohner, 1984; pp. 102–5).

By its decision to deprive managers of a potent weapon for use in the struggle to impose labour discipline, and by its decision to somewhat redress the balance of power on the shop floor, the Soviet government initiated a process of disengagement from direct involvement in the struggle for industrialisation and growth. Under Khrushchev the role of the central organs as arbiters between different social interests (if not interest-groups) was strengthened. But this disengagement necessitated the creation of alternative mechanisms to fulfil those functions previously discharged by an *engagé* state. This implied a need to introduce a framework of incentives to ensure that individual workers would voluntarily seek jobs in the sectors and regions necessary for the attainment of the government's social and economic goals. And, second, it implied the need for incentives that would elicit sufficient on-the-job effort. These were the productionist objectives of the wage reform.

The nature of the solution that was found to these demands was conditioned by the general Soviet (and Marxist) lack of faith in the ability of autonomous social institutions to attain optimal outcomes. It was also influenced by more general socialist commitments towards equity and equality. The major thrust of both Marxist theory and Russian administrative tradition is that the market will provide a worse solution to the problem of designing an efficient structure of wage differentials than an administrative institution. Consequently the decision to embark upon a wage reform was accompanied (or preceded) by a decision to set up a new body to oversee that reform. This was the State Committee on Labour and Wages, which was established in 1955 but apparently only became active in the following year (Kirsch, 1972: ch. 1; Hauslohner, 1984; ch. 2; McAuley, 1969: pp. 198 ff.). This body was given the task of formulating a socialist wages policy and introducing new wage- and salary-scales which conformed to that policy. It was thus intimately involved in the post-war revival of labour economics in the Soviet Union.

From both the administrative and the socialist ethical point of view it was accepted that wage- and salary-scales should embody the principle of equal pay for equal work. If this were not the case, it was suggested, there would be an incentive for workers to move from job to job in search of higher pay. The elevated levels of turnover that this would entail would reduce the economy's production potential. Hence the issue that had to be resolved by the State committee and the new discipline of labour economics was: what was meant by equal work? The answer that was given to this question settled the course of wage-determination for the next quarter-century or so.

Soviet labour economists based their analysis of the determinants of wages on the Marxist labour theory of value. If the value of different commodities was determined by the differing amounts of labour they contained, it must be possible to convert the amounts of work done by people with different skills into some abstract or undifferentiated labour. And indeed, Marx claimed that 'skilled labour was simply unskilled labour multiplied up or raised to some power'. Knowledge of the coefficients involved in this reduction process would allow the wage-setting authorities to determine the amount of 'labour' involved in different occupations and make wages proportional to that amount.

In principle two approaches to the identification of these reduction coefficients are consistent with Marxist theory. The first emphasises outputs, or the effects of applying labour; the second emphasises inputs, or the characteristic of the labour that is applied. In 1956 the State Committee and its theorists chose the second approach. They argued that differences in the wages paid in different circumstances should primarily reflect differences in the quality of labour supplied. (In this they were developing ideas that had been advanced in the 1920s and early 1930s.) Some attention was paid to working conditions in the determination of labour quality, but primary emphasis was placed on skill. For Soviet labour economists skill was more than just the adeptness with which particular occupations were undertaken; it was a continuous and inter-occupationally comparable dimension of work. After the establishment of a conversion-scale (which translated units of skill into roubles, making due allowance for other factors) the wage reform became an all-embracing job-evaluation programme. Industry by industry, trade by trade, job-specifications were prepared and job content compared; equivalent jobs were assigned equal wages. It was this process that resulted in the 1900 or so different wage-scales that had been used by state enterprises under Stalin being reduced to ten; the 700 or so salary-scales were cut to 150.

This simplification, regularisation and codification reduced the scale of formal inequality. But it was accompanied by official claims that the government had only limited power to change the extent of differentiation and a continued insistence that egalitarianism, *uravnilovka*, was anti-socialist. Theorists argued that the extent of inequality in earnings was determined by the pattern of skills to be found in the labour force; only as this changed, only as the unskilled or uneducated workers disappeared, would differentials narrow. Official attempts to move too fast, to reduce the spread of pay scales artificially, would eliminate the incentive to acquire desirable skills and thus slow down the rate of growth, put off the arrival of full communism.

The wage reform of 1956 demonstrates three characteristics of the new Soviet approach to the formulation of social policy under Khrushchev. First, it reveals that the voluntarism implicit in a belief in the all-powerful state had been abandoned. The government and Party no longer proclaimed the slogan; there are no fortresses that the Bolsheviks cannot storm. Rather it is now recognised that social evolution proceeds according to social laws. This recognition gave rise to the second feature of the new approach: the desirability of basing social policy upon the results of social inquiry. It is for this reason that the leadership revived empirical economics and established the new sociology. Recognition that the political power of government was limited also contributed to the third feature of social policy-making after Stalin, the emergence of a more neutral state. If the state was no longer *éngagé*, if its reputation, its very existence was no longer bound up with its attainment of particular (economic) goals, the nature of politics and political commitment was changed. In the Soviet (or, possibly, the Russian) context, this did not mean that autonomous social organisation and action was to be permitted. But it did mean an increase in administrative regularity and a reassertion of the primacy of legal norms.

By 1964, then, when Khrushchev was removed from office, the Soviet government had been provided with administrative machinery capable of formulating and implementing a coherent wages policy. The State Committee on Labour and Wages not only had the formal power to decide questions of wage-levels and relativities, it had the personnel needed for such work and a theory to provide it with a guide to action. And it had used its authority to effect a substantial change in social policy. This is but one example of the administrative and political evolution that had occurred under Khrushchev. In other areas of social policy too, Stalinist *diktat* had been replaced by legal norms and by an administrative machinery armed with its own operational theory. In total this new and self-conscious specialist intelligentsia has been able to challenge the pre-eminence of the Party apparat and erode its ideology. (For a recent, thought-provoking analysis of the interrelationship of ideology and social research in an area related to social policy see Yanowitch, 1985.)

8.6 CONTINUITY AND CHANGE IN SOCIAL POLICY UNDER KHRUSHCHEV

In Section 8.5 the innovative character of both policy content and policy formulation under Khrushchev has been stressed. Here a note of caution should be introduced. Despite the changes that occur, there are strong elements of continuity that link the Khrushchev period with its Russian and its Soviet past. It is not being argued that Khrushchev was either a European liberal or a radical egalitarian!

The social values implicit in the reformed structure of wages or in the newly codified system of social security mentioned in Section 8.3, remain within the Marxist-Leninist tradition. Both the necessity of inequality and the desirability of ensuring maximum participation are reasserted.

In the wage-system this is brought out most clearly in the decision to set the minimum wage at (or only marginally higher than) the notional poverty line. This implies acceptance of the proposition that the minimum wage is not intended to provide for the subsistence of dependants. It is also implied by the refusal of the authorities, for many years, to introduce non-work-related income supplement programmes for the alleviation of poverty. (The first such programme was introduced only in 1974. See McAuley, 1979: ch. 4.) There is still no adequate Soviet public assistance programme. This stress on the need to work was increased under Khrushchev by official campaigns against idlers and the adoption of so-called 'anti-parasite laws'.

The codification of pension and social security legislation also provided the occasion for a reaffirmation of Soviet values. First, the new law provided for the payment of old-age pensions that were related to prior earnings; earnings-relatedness was also a characteristic of disability pensions, of sickness benefits and maternity allowances. And Soviet commentators explicitly condemn flat-rate pension schemes. They start from the principle that benefits paid must not exceed earnings while in work; the contrary is held to undermine the incentive to participate in social labour. With even a moderate degree of differentiation in earnings – this principle implies that the flat-rate pension or benefit must be set so low as to entail some hardship for a majority of recipients (Lantsev, 1976; p. 100). Second, old-age pensions and most other social security benefits were made to depend upon prior participation. And the value of the benefit was often increased for those with appropriate work-records. The most commonly identified features here were continuous employment, *neprerivnyi stazh*, and membership of a trade union. Third, the law did not regard all forms of participation in social labour as equivalent. Employees in some sectors or industries received more favourable treatment than those in others. The most glaring discrimination in this respect concerned the failure to extend the state's schemes to cover members of collective farms. Not only were *kolkhozniki* not entitled to state pensions in old age, they did not qualify for disability pensions in the case of industrial accidents, they were not eligible for sickness benefits or maternity allowances. But differences in treatment were more pervasive than this. In addition to receiving higher benefits because their previous earnings were higher those employed in heavy industry (and particularly in underground mining) enjoyed more favourable eligibility conditions and so on.

These three characteristics of benefits payable under the 1956 Pension Law reveal a continued commitment to the idea that 'the principle of each according to his labour should operate in the field of social security as well'. This so-called 'socialist doctrine', as we have seen, is supposed to determine the overall distribution of income in the USSR; but its explicit extension to income mainten-ance was a feature of the Stalin period (see Archarkan, *Sotsialisti-cheskii trud*, 11/1974: pp. 119–29). In this respect then there was continuity between the Khrushchev period and its predecessors. However, the attempt to use income-maintenance programmes to encourage desirable behaviour or the acquisition of appropriate atti-tudes was unfortunate. It got in the way of their primary aim. For example, if maternity benefits are supposed to provide support for mother and new-born child they should be paid to *all* women who give birth; payment should not depend upon such irrelevancies as whether or not the mother is a member of a trade union.

The new welfare programmes made few allowances for variations in family or other circumstances. They were thus liable to generate horizontal inequalities. The arrangements contained in the 1956 laws seemed to have been chosen as much for the sake of administrative convenience as to ensure that due allowance was made for variations in personal circumstances. In part these choices seem to have reflected the somewhat oversimplified conception of Soviet social structure that was (and still is) characteristic of official rhetoric; perhaps the political leadership was a prisoner of its own conceptual straightjacket. (But at the time when the legislation was first drafted it was not only the leadership that suffered from the ideological and empirical blinkers of the Stalin period. Officials and specialists had no satisfactory evidence of social complexity that might lead them to advocate a more flexible framework for response.) In part, however, administrative simplicity was a rational response to the constraints under which these social programmes would operate. In 1956 the Soviet government did not have at its disposal a network of offices, staffed by trained social workers, capable of administering a sophisticated programme of welfare supports. In such circumstances it is not clear that a more complicated system of benefits will necessarily result in a more equitable pattern of support.

Under Stalin the Soviet government had shown little concern for the conditions of the peasantry, of the elderly, of the disabled. It could not have been interested in the distribution of earnings since it made no attempt to find out what that was. Under Khrushchev, however, all of these questions become topics for specialist inquiry and official action. Not surprisingly, these government responses to social problems that had accumulated over a quarter of a century or more were limited and partially misdirected. In this they reflect the inadequacy of Marxism—Leninism's conceptual framework for the analysis of social action in a socialist society; they also suffer from the fact that empirical inquiry into Soviet reality had been suppressed for more than two decades.

The new socialist welfare state was committed to the value of labour. For those who had found work in the new industries, who had been able to acquire skills, whose behaviour conformed to one of the simple stereotypes of the Soviet family, the system provided support in adversity and comfort in old age. It had much less to offer the unskilled and incompetent, those not able to cope with the pressures of modern society, social misfits, the mentally unstable. Soviet policy-makers steadfastly set their faces against accepting the principle that the state has a duty to provide a safety net, a minimum standard of consumption below which no one's income should be allowed to fall. This Beveridge principle was seen to be in conflict with socialist distribution, and its acceptance was supposed to encourage idleness. This lack of compassion in Khrushchev's social security policy should be seen as a reflection of a deeper property of post-war Soviet thought – the commitment to meritocratic values. (For further development of this idea see McAuley in Collard *et al.*, 1980, and Dunham, 1979.) And this has continued into the 1980s.

9 Eastern Europe

MICHAEL SHAFIR

The blissful state of being presented with the memoirs of one's protagonists is seldom afforded the Sovietologist. Viewed from this angle Soviet–East European relations in the period after Stalin's death constitute an outlandish topic. The researcher benefits from the reminiscences of Imre Nagy (1957), from the (grantedly distorted, but none the less genuine) perspectives of Nikita Sergeevich Khrushchev (1971 and 1974) and is even graced by Enver Hoxha's remembrances (1980). In addition the published memoirs of Mićunović (1980), one of those East European officials who could observe Soviet policy-making at arm's length, are an invaluable primary source. And as if this were not sufficient, there is a plethora of biographies (Pálóczi-Horváth, 1960; Crankshaw, 1966; Frankland, 1966; Medvedev and Medvedev, 1976; Medvedev, 1982), supplemented by numerous studies, some of which are expressly devoted to Eastern Europe (Brown, 1966; Brzezinski, 1967). Indeed the period's facets are in fact so well known that this chapter takes for granted the reader's familiarity with historical detail. Nevertheless, two decades and more after Khrushchev was sent into oblivion by his colleagues, the task of producing definite judgements concerning the impact of his role on Eastern Europe is still complex. This is primarily due to the fact that the analysis easily renders itself to opposite, or rather non-coterminous, perspectives; it is also due, however to several queries concerning Khrushchev's *personal* contribution to the scenario of East European events and their eventual outcome. This contribution attempts to provide a bridge between these conflicting interpretations, one of which could be labelled as 'intra-systemic', the other as 'inter-systemic'. Apart from attempting to cope with the relevance of those question marks that still hang over the Soviet leader's responsibility for the 1956 events, this chapter will address the issue of Khrushchev's legacy as it affected both his political successors and East European society at large.

One possible angle of approaching the inquiry is the intra-systemic perspective. This involves examining the declared and undeclared objectives pursued by the Kremlin in the region between 1953 and 1964, as well as the new institutional and ideological devices geared to preventing or solving conflicts among the system's components. Should one opt for this horizon the conclusion that Khrushchev was the personification of failure is simply unavoidable. Having inherited from Stalin a socially shattered and economically unviable, yet monolithic 'empire,' he bequested to his successors a shrunken 'periphery', which was still socially tense and in relatively poor economic shape, but one which, in addition, was divided by personal, national and ideological rivalries. Attempting to cope with Stalin's dysfunctional legacy, Khrushchev strove to replace the necessity for direct supervision of, and interference in, the components members' affairs, by a 'socialist commonwealth' united by ideological incentives, the institutionalised forms of which were the Warsaw Pact (WTO) and a revived CMEA which would function on the principles of mutual benefit; he sought to woo Yugoslavia back into the camp; and, finally, to secure the voluntary acknowledgement of the Soviet Union as leader of the 'socialist world'. Instead, by the time he departed from the political stage, East European leaders were still subject to Moscow's directives and/or attempts to depose those reluctant to conform; Soviet tanks had been deployed against the Hungarian insurgents; Tito had defied all of Khrushchev's designs; Albania had joined China in denouncing Moscow's apostasy from the 'true' doctrine; and Romania, having rejected the 'division of labour' endorsed by Soviet-supported integrationist schemes for Comecon, issued a statement denying the existence of 'parent' and 'son' parties (*Scînteia*, 24 Apr 1964).

Yet the legacy of the Khrushchevist period appears in an altogether different light when the intra-systemic perspective is replaced by the inter-systemic one, i.e. by the analysis of the impact produced by Khrushchev's role on the evolution of Eastern Europe's social and political life. Indeed, remembering Hegel's remarks concerning mankind's great leaders who, while 'absorbed in their mundane interests' are but 'history's unconscious tools and organs' (1967: p. 217), one can hardly underestimate Khrushchev's contribution to the immediate or belated tremors which significantly changed the face of Stalinist Eastern Europe.

The Hegelian approach is the more fruitful one. One should, in other words, strive to distinguish the man from the events which he fostered and from their systemic and ideological import. Khrushchev and Khrushche*vism*, are not necessarily similar. At this point an elucidation of terms seems necessary. 'Khrushchevism,' as employed in this chapter does not refer to a coherent body of ideology. One can hardly dispute Fehér's view concerning the First Secretary's 'incapability of thinking a theoretical problem through to the end' (1984b: p. 25). Even such a highly sympathetic biographer of the Soviet leader as Roy Medvedev is forced to admit that he 'was no theoretician' and 'contributed nothing to the theoretical discourse initiated by Lenin or to its successor, that political-theoretical hybrid that came to be known as Stalinism'. Yet not only Medvedev, according to whom Khrushchev's 'instinct for the appropriate course' led him to advance 'ideas that were bold and fresh', thereby stimulating '*indirectly* the development of Marxist theory' (1982: p. ix. Emphasis mine), but also the highly critical Fehér writes that 'the simpleton in cultural and ideological questions' none the less combined such simplicity with [ideational] 'elements of the great statesman' (1984b: p. 26). It is to these ideas or elements, *regardless of the immediate historical circumstances of their propagation* (e.g. Khrushchev's *personal* struggle against such 'hard liners' in the Kremlin as Molotov), that Khrushchevism refers to in this contribution. In other words, the definition is based on 'Khrushchev the 'original leader', even if in many of the internal (Soviet) aspects, the former First Secretary was but a 'transitional leader'. In no circumstances, however, may Khrushchevism be approached from a position which views Khrushchev as a 'Transitory leader'.[1]

In so far as Eastern Europe is concerned the central elements of Khrushchevism appear to be the legitimation of the existence of different paths to socialist construction, the pledge not to interfere in internal Party affairs, the de-legitimation of state terror, the concept of peaceful coexistence and the enunciation of the stage of the 'state of all people'. Yet one should not fall prey to the undialectical temptation of separating the man *in toto* from his words. Khrushchev was not only the person in charge of, above all, *Soviet* interests, and proud to fulfil this function, but also a man conscious of having climbed from the darkness of the pit to world renown under the communist system of rule. As such, to his dying day he remained convinced that the Soviet system was by far the most superior form of political organisation ever produced by history. And the core of this system was the Leninist tenet of unchallenged Party domination of society, one which he never doubted and which was considered by him worthy of universal emulation (Fainsod, 1965: pp. 108–9, 128–9). This component of the man's belief system was part and parcel of Khrushchevism too. In other words, Khrushchevism was to a great extent fenced in by Khrushchev the man. To Eastern Europe this has meant that political change in the sense of going beyond Khrushchevism, implies a strenuous path, the more so as from Brezhnev to Chernenko, Khrushchev's successors inherited all his inhibitions and none of his (albeit sometimes improvised) innovatory outbursts.

To state that Khrushchev was not a name on everyone's lips in Eastern Europe before March 1953 is an understatement. To be sure, with Molotov's partial exception, none of Stalin's heirs had previously entertained wide contacts with leaders of the 'sister parties', for the dictator regarded this realm as one of his many strictly personal prerogatives. Khrushchev's experience before 1953, as one learns from his *Memoirs* (1971: pp. 217–20; 1974: pp. 152–83), was restricted to a war-time encounter with Walter Ulbricht and to the leadership of the Polish party, in whose take-over preparations he became involved in his capacity as head of the Ukrainian Party and government. As war-time 'boss' of the Ukraine Khrushchev had been in charge of the sovietisation of Western (Polish) Ukraine, as well as of those Bessarabian and Bukovinian territories transferred to 'his' republic after the formation of the Moldavian SSR, in the wake of the June 1940 Soviet ultimatum to Bucharest. Reminiscing on the war years, he revealed himself as the typical Great Russian chauvinist. He deplored Stalin's sacrifice of the gains secured in the Ribbentrop–Molotov pact, claiming that the 'concession' had 'failed to take into account the national interests of both the Ukrainians and the Bielorussians'. As such, he is bewildered by the attitude of 'some Polish comrades who were still dissatisfied with the borders Stalin had given them', thinking that 'the border with the Soviet Union should be even farther to the east'. Similarly, for Khrushchev, it is clear that 'Moldavia had never been part of the Romanian state' (1974: p. 232).

His lack of experience in the area's affairs notwithstanding, no politician aspiring to the Soviet leadership mantle can afford to ignore Eastern European developments. Evidence of continued Soviet interference in the internal affairs of the East European countries is abundant (see below), though hardly surprising. Yet it is not less true that after Stalin's death Eastern Europe becomes *an internal factor in Soviet politics*, even if such 'diffusion' (Gitelman 1975) is only rarely generated by voluntary design. Khrushchev is no exception to this pattern. To the extent that the beginnings of his ascendancy coincide with Beria's elimination, Eastern Europe played at least a tangential function. Although the victorious faction in Moscow encouraged similar, if slightly more cautious 'New Course' internal *and* foreign policies, Beria (accused, among others of intending to 'liquidate' the GDR) and the Zaisser–Herrnstadt group in East Germany (which allegedly wanted to abandon the 'construction of socialism') were eventually blamed for the events leading to the uprising of 17 June (*Pravda*, 8 Mar 1963; *Die Neue Zeitung*, 23 Aug 1953; Baras, 1975; McCauley, 1979: pp. 78–9; Féhér and Heller, 1983: pp. 32, 71; Larrabee 1984: pp. 112–14). This was but the first in a long chain of events connecting the career of the Soviet leader with East European developments. Among these the most critical were the years 1956–7, when Khrushchev's opponents attempted to bring about his dismissal on grounds of, *inter alia*, having fostered turbulence in Poland and Hungary by going too far in his denunciation of Stalinism at the XX Party Congress[2] (Medvedev, 1982: p. 116). According to at least one version, internal opposition to Khrushchev's initiative to pursue a more flexible policy towards both German states (with its implied dangers for the GDR), provided the occasion, if not the cause, of his dismissal (Wolfe, 1970: pp. 117–27; Stent, 1984: p. 37). And, whereas the evidence for this interpretation is open to challenge, there is no doubt that among the many accusations thrown in the face of the Soviet leader by M. A. Suslov in October 1964, the mishandling of East European affairs was repeatedly specified (Medvedev, 1982: pp. 237, 241–2).

It is difficult to establish whether the imposition of the 'New Course' on Eastern Europe should be attributed to the Soviet leadership's lack of experience and/or information concerning the 'state of the empire', to the fact that it was too preoccupied by internal Party strife to realise the potential consequences which these limited reforms entailed for Moscow's most loyal viceroys, or to the basically Stalinist persuasion that what was good for the Soviet Union was good for the entire bloc. It was probably a combination of all these factors. There is no evidence that, at this stage in his ascendancy, Khrushchev opposed the Malenkov line. On the contrary it is well known that he associated himself with his colleagues in castigating Rákosi's handling of affairs in Hungary and was instrumental in Nagy's elevation to the premiership (Nagy, 1957: pp. 66, 252). The East German uprising of June 1953, and the intervention of Soviet forces, on the other hand, should be considered an indication of the limits of 'change' the Kremlin was willing to accept in Eastern Europe, as well as an omen for future developments.

At the formal, structural level, the emulation of 'collective leadership' had little impact on Eastern Europe with the exception of Hungary and, though not instantly, that of Bulgaria, where Chervenkov bet on the wrong, Malenkovist horse, by choosing the Premiership and, unlike Gheorghiu-Dej in Romania, failing to correct his mistake (Brown, 1966: pp. 7–8; Shafir, 1985: p. 68). The more important aspects of this change rests in the connection that can be established between leadership upheavals in Eastern Europe and internal Soviet party skirmishes, once the 'collectivity' in the Kremlin began to show signs of falling apart.

In East Germany Ulbricht could act against his adversaries by exploiting the accusations raised against Beria. When the Soviet First Secretary challenged Malenkov's investment policies, Rákosi could act in order to oust Nagy by adopting a 'return to heavy industry', Khrushchevist posture (Kovrig, 1979: pp. 281–2). Similarly, the liquidation of the 'Anti-Party group' in 1957, influenced the evolution of the struggle for power in Romania and Bulgaria (Fischer-Galati, 1967: p. 67, Jowitt, 1971: pp. 172–3; Tismaneanu, 1985: pp. 58–9; Brown, 1970: pp. 78–82). This does not mean, however, that the Kremlin served as a merely passive and somewhat oracular referent in the 'periphery's' leadership cleavages. Khrushchev was personally involved in most of these struggles. Not only was he instrumental in Todor Zhivkov's victory over his adversaries in Bulgaria (Brown, 1970; pp. 113, 126–9, 133–4) and temporarily saved Novotný in Czechoslovakia in the 1960s (Brown, 1966: pp. 30–1; Golan, 1971: p. 48), but, as is well known, he vetoed Zambrowski's election as head of the Polish Party[3] and was personally involved in the attempt to stop Gomułka's comeback in 1956[4] (Brzezinski, 1967: pp. 256–61; Mićunović, 1980: pp. 86, 123; Medvedev, 1982: pp. 106–7), though later, and for good reasons, he became a staunch supporter of the Polish leader's *mała stabilizacja* (Korbonski, 1984b: pp. 63–4). In Hungary he badly mishandled Rákosi's replacement, opting for his *alter ego*, Ernö Gerö, and, after the outbreak of the revolution, at Tito's recommendation, decided to place Kádár at the head of the leadership, after having initially inclined toward Munnich (Mićunović, 1980: pp. 135–6). Having once overcome his avowed misgivings concerning Kádár (Khrushchev, 1971: p. 467), he would then back him in all internal Party struggles (Brown, 1966: p. 49; Kovrig, 1979: pp. 339, 356; Valenta, 1984a: pp. 111–12). Attempts to engineer the ouster of Hoxha in Albania and Gheorghiu-Dej in Romania (Brown, 1966: p. 200; Clissold 1975: p. 74 and Lendvai, 1969: pp. 305–6), two countries where Party monolithism was successfully blended with the exploitation of nationalism, ended, however, in failure.

Not the details of these developments, but their intra-systemic significance, should provide the focus of one's juxtaposition of Khrushchev and Khrushchevism. Statements of intent aside (the 'Belgrade Declaration', which Tito and Khrushchev signed in early June 1955 [text in Clissold, 1975: pp. 154–7], pledged 'Mutual respect and non-interference in internal affairs for any reasons – whether of an economic, political or ideological nature'), Khrushchev's perception of Eastern Europe remained that of an area where the Kremlin's legitimate interests of securing the implementation of its line, if need be through nominations, dismissals and even coups, could not be doubted. This is probably why the ever-submissive Bulgarians appear to have been his preferred East European ally (Khrushchev, 1971: p. 399). The Yugoslavs, at best, were the (temporary, it was hoped) exception to the rule. As Mićunović put it in March 1956: 'We regard the Belgrade Declaration as a sort of socialist Magna Carta, which is to apply to Yugoslavia's relations with the Soviet Union as well as with other socialist states. But the Russians . . . think differently, and believe they can conduct one policy toward socialist Yugoslavia and a different, even opposite one towards the other socialist states' (1980: p. 7.) Viewed from this angle Khrushchev the man acted in defiance of Khrushchevism. In historical perspective (Schöpflin, 1981: pp. 77–8) his successors may be said to have been just as little inhibited by the doctrine as Nikita Sergeevich himself ever was.

There can be little doubt that the de-Stalinisation process launched in earnest at the XX Party Congress and renewed at the XXII Party Congress had an immediate or (in Czechoslovakia's case) somewhat belated impact on the departure of the 'little Stalins' from the political scene. But Tito's role was just as significant, for the Yugoslav leader insisted on his 'pound of Stalinist flesh'.[5] It is also to the *rapprochement* with Belgrade that one should attribute Moscow's endorsement of the principles of 'sovereignty, independence, territorial integrity, equality, mutual respect and non-interference in internal affairs' ('Belgrade Declaration', June 1955), eventually to be adopted by the Romanians as doctrinal trenches in defending their autonomy *vis-à-vis* the USSR.

Given Khrushchev's initial reluctance to attribute the guilt for the Soviet–Yugoslav break to Stalin himself and to Stalin*ism* in general (text of his speech in Belgrade in Clissold 1975: p. 253), in May–June 1955 he was unable to secure more than the re-establishment of normalcy in state relations. It was only after the XX Party Congress had officially sanctified the principle of 'many roads' (text of Khrushchev's formal address in *Current Digest of the Soviet Press*, VIII, no. 4, 1956; 'Secret speech' in Khrushchev, 1971: pp. 656–7) and undeified Stalin that relations between the two Parties were restored (text of 'Moscow Declaration', 20 June 1956 in Clissold, 1975: pp. 261–2). But even this declaration failed to satisfy Moscow. Aware that his visit to Belgrade had merely produced a document written 'by a Yugoslav hand', the Soviets strove to replace it by one bearing a 'Party' rather than a 'state' imprint, which would reflect 'the spirit of "Marxism–Leninism" and "proletarian internationalism" ' (Mićunović 1980; pp. 6–7). But the Yugoslav side refused to assume any obligation with regard to the 'camp' or to sign any document which would refer to 'ideological unity' (Mićunović, 1980: pp. 72–4).

As it soon became clear, what Khrushchev was offering Tito amounted to what Tito had demanded from the Soviets in the late 1940s. It was too little, too late. For if the Kremlin had evolved from Stalinism to Khrushchevism Tito might be said to have moved from initially Khrushchevist to Titoist positions. The Khrushchevist understanding of the 'commonwealth' into which the Soviet leader attempted to lure Belgrade was best summed up in July 1957, in a speech he delivered in Prague (quoted in Brzezinski, 1967: p. 269). As it turned out, while the Soviet Union acknowledged 'different paths', it also demanded 'unity, closed ranks and rallied forces'. The paths were said to mean no more than recognition of the *temporary* existence of 'tributaries' to the 'big river'. Khrushchev's heirs may deplore his foreign policies as 'voluntaristic and adventuristic' (*Dvizhushchie sily vneshnei politiki SShA*, 1965: p. 7 as quoted in Holloway, 1975: p. 49), but inasmuch as 'many roads to socialism' are concerned his legacy stands unchallenged. A decade after Khrushchev's dismissal 'Marxist-Leninists' were urged to 'proceed from the fact that there is only one scientific model of socialism, common to all countries' (Butenko 1974: p. 277). According to Yuri V. Andropov, 'the basic principles of the socialist system' were 'the same for all countries and for all peoples' (*Pravda*, 23 Apr. 1982), whereas K. V. Chernenko was persuaded that 'there is not, nor can there be, any path of socialism in circumvention of the general laws discovered by Marxism-Leninism and *confirmed by the experience of the USSR and of other countries of existing socialism*' (TASS, 4 Jan 1983. Emphasis mine).

Tito, however, certainly no longer saw himself as a mere 'tributary', the more so since the tribute he was asked to pay consisted in renouncing his special status in the non-aligned movement and his special relationship to the West. Yugoslavia, Khrushchev is reported to have told Kardelj and Ranković in 1957, could not go on 'sitting on two chairs' (quoted in Clissold, 1975: p. 71). In his eyes choosing sides amounted to the formal joining of the institutional structures of the 'commonwealth' CMEA and the Warsaw Pact (Miller, 1984: pp. 197, 201). But Tito was unwilling to oblige, the more so as events in Poland and Hungary in 1956, where Yugoslav-like innovations were on the reformists' lips, made him feel confident that the *river Sava* might soon replace the Moskva river. This was anathema to the Soviet leadership. At a 'secret lunch' for CC members and ambassadors from the 'camp', on May Day of that year, Khrushchev warned that the Soviets 'would not permit any "innovations" ' in Poland where, as he complained in a conversation with the Yugoslav Ambassador in mid-July, ' "anti-Soviet" elements . . . were trying to follow Yugoslavia's example although they had no right to do so. They were all, in Poland, in Hungary and elsewhere . . . now quoting Yugoslavia' (Mićunović, 1980: pp. 44, 86). Neither Khrushchev the man nor Khrushchevism could envisage such deflections in the 'big river's' course.

A first attempt to set up a barrage came in the form of a confidential letter dispatched to the bloc's Parties, warning against the emulation of the Yugoslav model (Mićunović, 1980: pp. 94, 107, 109. Text in Clissold, 1975: p. 263). Tito's ambivalent attitude displayed *vis-à-vis* the intervention in Hungary (speech in Pula in Zinner, 1957: pp. 516–41) and towards the subsequent arrest of Nagy as he left the Yugoslav embassy in Budapest (Mićunović, 1980: pp. 145–53, 169–70, 394–404) could only add to the Kremlin's suspicions.[6] In 1957, in best Stalinist tradition, the Soviet leader apparently demanded the right to review the unfinished draft of the new Programme of the LCY (Miller, 1984: p. 199), and, approximately at the same time, he dispatched B. N. Ponomarev and Andropov to Belgrade, with the draft of a common declaration, to be signed at the international gathering planned in Moscow for November (Mićunović, 1980: p. 315). The latter document (ironically enough, adopted in part due to Chinese pressure on the USSR to 'resume' its role as leader of the 'camp') amounted to the promulgation of an obligatory joint policy. Reiterating 'proletarian internationalism' as the 'bedrock of the relations of the world socialist system and all the Communist and Workers' Parties', this 'Declaration' went on to designate the Soviet Union as 'the first and mightiest socialist power'. Relations among socialist countries were said to be based on principles identical with those of the 'Belgrade Declaration', but these, it was hastily added, did not 'exhaust' their 'essence'. 'Fraternal mutual aid' was deemed to be of no lesser importance, and to constitute 'a *striking* expression of socialist internationalism' (*Soviet News*, 22 Nov 1957. Emphasis mine). As Robert Hutchings observes (1983: p. 19), in view of the 'mutual aid' extended to Hungary one year earlier, 'striking' was a rather infelicitous term.

Finally, the 'Declaration' underlined 'the necessity of overcoming revisionism and dogmatism', but placed the former on clear order of preference. This was obviously aimed at the Yugoslavs, and consequently, the official news agency Tanjug announced on 29 October that Tito would be unable to go to Moscow because he was suffering from an 'acute attack of lumbago'. The Yugoslav delegation to the Moscow meeting, headed by Kardelj, had to withstand uninterrupted pressure, with Khrushchev's remarks being 'plainly insulting' (Mićunović, 1980: p. 317). But they refused to sign.

The publication of the Draft Programme in April 1958, with its implied criticism of the still-existing 'distortions' of socialism in the USSR and its affirmation that defence of Soviet Union no longer constituted the 'principal criterion of proletarian internationalism', as it had 'when the Soviet Union was the only socialist country' (Clissold, 1975: pp. 275–7) brought about the so-called 'second Soviet–Yugoslav split'. Although more restrained than the Tito–Stalin dispute (the Yugoslavs were well aware of the Chinese factor and of Khrushchev's need to defend *himself* against the 'revisionist sin'), the 'split' was never really overcome in ideological terms. The Yugoslavs were not invited to the 81 party conference in Moscow in December 1960. Despite a later return to contacts and to 'normalcy' in state relations Khrushchev never succeeded in his efforts to move Yugoslavia back to Soviet ideological and organisational tutelage. Tito's refusal to attend the pending world conference of Communist Parties, shortly before the Soviet leader's dismissal, was the last epitaph on Khrushchev's failure. Twenty years later the bungle appears to have been the more unproductive, since it was his courtship of Yugoslavia, more than any other factor, that brought about Albania's defection.

In his *Memoirs* Khrushchev can claim with a straight face that 'we deliberately avoided applying pressures on other Socialist countries', believing that 'every Communist Party should, and would, handle its own internal problems by itself'. He can state that one cannot 'herd people into paradise with threats and then post soldiers at their gates', and yet be proud of having given Ulbricht the green light for building the Berlin Wall because, as he put it, 'naturally, under the dictatorship of the working class, there can be no such thing as absolute freedom' (Khrushchev, 1971: pp. 397, 566, 506, respectively). Presumably this applies to the bloc at large and to its component members. Just as the 'all-people's state' ceases to be the dictatorship of one class, yet it is still guided by a single vanguard Leninist party, so the 'socialist commonwealth' is no longer the realm of the dictatorship of one state, indeed it even acknowledges the legitimacy of 'different roads', yet these must all lead to Moscow, the capital best suited to interpret 'proletarian internationalism'.

This is why, after some hesitation, Khrushchev could accept Gomułka, but never Imre Nagy. For Nagy's 'sin' consisted of a double negation: by legalising a multi-party system, the Hungarian Premier forsook Leninism; by withdrawing from the WTO, he forsook intra-systemic Khrushchevism. The repression of Hungary not only established the precedent of bestowing a police function on an organisation supposed to defend the 'commonwealth' against an *external* threat, but it also invented the doctrinal justification for intervention, embodied in the claim that it was the 'international *duty*' of the socialist community to come to the rescue of 'socialist conquests' (*Pravda*, 23 Nov 1956). Or, as Khrushchev himself put it on his first visit to Hungary in 1958. 'If provocateurs or enemies of the workers attempt a putsch or counterrevolution in any Socialist country, then I tell them here and now that all the Socialist countries and the armed forces of the Soviet Union will be ready at all times to give the provocateurs the answer they deserve' (*Keesing's Contem-*

porary Archives, vol. IX, 1958: p. 16237). The 'Brezhnev doctrine' was *not* born in 1968.

However, as Valenta (1979: pp. 30, 55, 81, 144) demonstrated, the 'Brezhnev doctrine' should not necessarily be associated with his name, for the Soviet Party leader wavered long between the interventionist and non-interventionist coalitions in the Kremlin. Brezhnev is even reported to have told a Czechoslovak Party leader, three days after the invasion, that he originally opposed the decision, but that 'If I hadn't voted in the Politbureau for military intervention . . . *I probably wouldn't be sitting here*' (Mlynar, 1980, p. 163. Emphasis mine). Khrushchev's case may be one of considerable similarity. To be sure, despite their hesitations, at the end of the day both leaders probably would have inclined for invasion, for their monopolist Leninist value-system, combined with 'Great Russian chauvinist' postures, undoubtedly leaned in that direction. Yet Khrushchev's personal contribution to (or 'responsibility' for) the evolution of the 1956 events warrants reconsideration.

From his *Memoirs* one learns that there were considerable hesitations in the Soviet leadership concerning the 'second intervention' (4 November) in Hungary, or, as he put it, 'I don't know how many times we changed our minds back and forth' (1971: p. 460). The 'first intervention' (24 October) had been relatively low key, involving only a limited contingent of troops which generally avoided engaging the Hungarians in combat (Larrabee, 1984: p. 116). Furthermore, although in doubt about its feasibility, at this stage the Russians still hoped for a *political* solution, as Khrushchev is reported to have told Mićunović on 25 October (Mićunović 1980: p. 127). The conciliatory tone adopted by Moscow *vis-à-vis* the new Nagy government, including the Soviet government's declaration of 30 October (*Pravda*, 31 Oct 1956) are proof that the Soviets still hoped to bring the situation under control without wide-scale armed intervention. On 28 October 1956 an editorial in *Pravda* was still referring to '*Comrade* Imre Nagy' (Emphasis mine).

Khrushchev's personal attitude towards Nagy was by no means one of total hostility. It is true that he tacitly backed Rákosi in 1955, but this posture was dictated more by the necessities of inner *Soviet* strife than by pro-Rákosi sympathies. According to Schöpflin (1984: p. 544) Khrushchev's backing of Gerö, instead of Nagy, to replace Rákosi in June 1956 was mainly due to the fact that 'he was not likely to have been well disposed towards his rival's protégé'. As is well known, Nagy's patron in the Kremlin had been Malenkov. In view of later developments, however, it is not without importance to point out that the person dispatched to Budapest to supervise the process of Nagy's resignation was Suslov (Kovrig, 1979: p. 281). Shortly before Rákosi's resignation Suslov once more went to Budapest. Following *his* report to the Presidium, the Soviet leadership 'decided to give Rákosi their energetic support' because, as Khrushchev put it to Mićunović 'they had no other choice' (Mićunović, 1980: pp. 64, 87). Yet when Rákosi decided to put Nagy in the dock, the Kremlin had to drop him. Already in 1954 Khrushchev had warned that 'We will protect Rákosi's authority only in so far as it is not prejudicial to Party authority' (Nagy, 1957: p. 296). Rákosi was obviously throwing petrol on fire and the Kremlin could not afford that at a time of rising tensions in the region. And, again, it is not irrelevant to indicate that this time not Suslov, but Anastas I. Mikoyan was chosen for the mission (Kovrig, 1979: p. 294). What is less known is that neither Khrushchev nor Mikoyan, whose positions were close to, if not identical with, those of the First Secretary, were satisfied with the 'Gerö solution'. In September 1956 Zoltán Szántó, a veteran member of the Party and the then-ambassador to Poland, was asked by Mikoyan to suggest possible candidates for Gerö's replacement (Fehér, 1984a: p. 211). And when Kádár and Nagy finally took over (if one can believe Enver Hoxha), Andropov, the Soviet Ambassador to Budapest, rejected his Albanian homologue's objections to Imre Nagy, and indicated that 'the Party's political bureau is satisfactory and enjoys our trust' (Gosztony, 1984: p. 374). This evidence indicates that it was indeed only after Nagy proclaimed the establishment of a multi-party coalition on 30 October that Khrushchev's position acquired an interventionist posture. During the post-invasion negotiations in Moscow Brezhnev is reported to have told Dubček: 'I believed you and defended you against the others. . . . But you have disappointed us all terribly' (Valenta, 1979: p. 144). These words could have been uttered by Khrushchev as well, had he encountered Nagy after the crushing of the revolution.

As in 1968, in 1956 there was no homogeneity in the Soviet leadership. Khrushchev's rivals' misgivings concerning the over-zealous de-Stalinisation launched at the XX Party Congress appeared to find corroboration in the Poznań uprising (28 June) and subsequent developments in Poland and Hungary. When in October 1956 a Soviet delegation flew to Warsaw attempting to prevent the leadership upheaval, Mićunović noted in his diary: 'Khrushchev no longer goes on his own, as he did a month ago to Yugoslavia. Something is obviously changing in the Kremlin when Khrushchev and Molotov go together to Poland.' Clearly on the defensive, in subsequent public postures the First Secretary attempted to prove 'that the socialist camp, meaning Soviet domination of Eastern Europe, is as dear to him as it was to any of the well-known Stalinists in the Kremlin' (Mićunović, 1980: p. 124). But at the time of the Hungarian events '*Khrushchev was at his weakest*' (ibid. p. 277). As he later told Egyptian President Anwar Sadat, Molotov 'thought that it was my policies that had led to the trouble in Hungary . . . [and] that my tolerance of Tito had encouraged the Hungarians' (Heikal, 1978: p. 92). The hard core of the future 'anti-Party' group most likely pressed for intervention in order to demonstrate their rival's personal responsibility for the deterioration of the situation in Eastern Europe. Kaganovich's inclusion in the delegation that flew to Warsaw in October (alongside Molotov, most likely as a counterbalance to Khrushchev and Mikoyan) is in this sense an indication of disagreement in the Kremlin concerning the handling of policy *vis-à-vis* the East European October. Malenkov, who lost the premiership in February 1955, was not beyond opportunistic postures, as demonstrated one month earlier, when he had taken the lead in castigating Nagy for pursuing the policies whose main champion he had been (Kovrig, 1979: p. 281). They were in all likelihood supported by Suslov, whose previous staunch support of Rákosi as the one and only viable option makes him an unlikely supporter of anything Nagy stood for.

Viewed from this perspective the two Mikoyan–Suslov missions to Budapest in late October, appear once more to have represented the opposing trends in the Presidium (Fry and Rice, 1983: p. 95). Mikoyan may well have been the most outspoken member of the leadership against military intervention and for reaching a *modus vivendi* with Nagy. It was Mikoyan who, in September, had expressed dissatisfaction with the 'Gerö solution' and who reportedly chided Gerö for his rash decision to ask Moscow to send troops in the 'first intervention' (Zinner, 1962: p. 258). Unlike Suslov, according to the Smallholder Party representative in the Nagy government, Zoltán Tildy (quoted in Kovrig, 1979: p. 305) he displayed a conciliatory position during the talks in Budapest. And as Valenta points out (1984b: p. 100), it was probably Mikoyan whom Khrushchev had in mind when, after the crisis, he mentioned in a speech in Budapest 'one or two of our comrades' who had doubted whether the Hungarians would 'take it in the right spirit if we hastened to come to their aid'.

While there is no indication that Khrushchev's position was identical to Mikoyan's, it is more than likely that, as in most other matters, the two were not far apart. The vacillations mentioned by Khrushchev reflect divisions in which Mikoyan's vote was simply not powerful enough to have obstructed intervention. Three main factors may have finally persuaded Khrushchev to change his position: first, the *institutionalisation* of a multi-Party system on 30 October (v. its *de facto* existence since 27 October), with its infringement of the Leninist norm of the 'leading role of the Party';[7] second, pressure from the military establishment, which he probably resisted up to 30 October; and, finally, the panic-striken voices of other East European allies, combined with the danger of 'contamination' which could possibly affect even the Soviet Union (Medvedev, 1982: pp. 137–8; Féhér and Heller, 1983: pp. 49–66; Korbonski, 1984a; Valenta, 1984b: pp. 99–100; Nekrich, 1984: pp. 93–7).

During the encounter on the island of Brioni on the eve of the invasion Khrushchev told his Yugoslav hosts that 'There were people in the Soviet Union who would say that as long as Stalin was in command everybody obeyed and there were no big shocks, but that now, ever since they had come to power . . . Russia had suffered the defeat and the loss of Hungary.' 'They' apparently referred to the 'de-Stalinisers', for the First Secretary went on to specify that 'this was happening at a time when the present Soviet leaders were condemning Stalin'. Such unanimity in the deceased dictator's condemnation, was, of course, illusory. But the 'hard-liners' faction now apparently succeeded in mobilising the military establishment to its side, for 'Khrushchev said that this might be said primarily by the Soviet Army, *which was one of the reasons why they were intervening in Hungary*' (Mićunović, 1980: p. 134. Emphasis mine). From the Yugoslav Ambassador's *Memoirs* one learns that, even before the outbreak of the revolution in Hungary, Marshal Zhukov expressed public dissatisfaction with the compromise reached with Gomułka, indicating that 'we could have crushed them' (1980: p. 141).[8] Another powerful military figure who seems to have pressed for drastic measure in Poland, as well as in Hungary, was the commander of the Warsaw Pact, Marshal Konev (Fry and Rice, 1983: pp. 93–4). It is very likely that Khrushchev's remark concerning the vital military indispensability of continued stationing of Soviet force in Poland (Khrushchev, 1974: p. 199) reflected Konev's views. With Rokossovsky, who had also urged military action in Poland (ibid. p. 203), now back in the USSR, the military appear to have played a central role in the decision-making process. Once more this may be considered a prelude to the events in 1968, when the interventionist faction in the Politburo found support among powerful élites in the Soviet armed forces (Valenta, 1979: pp. 108–14). Last but not least, albeit with significant alterations,[9] Moscow's allies exercised pressures in favour of intervention in Hungary in 1956, in Czechoslovakia in 1968 and in Poland in 1980.[10]

None of the above should, however, be taken as an attempt to demonstrate that military intervention in Hungary would have been eventually avoided, were the composition of the Presidium to have been more Khrushchevite in 1956 than was actually the case. Not only is Khrushchev's version of events in Hungary utterly distorted (Khrushchev, 1971: pp. 456–73), but, unlike other events, *vis-à-vis* which his *Memoirs* display some measure of *post-factum* remorse,[11] no regrets whatever are expressed for the way Nagy and/or the insurgents were handled. Viewed from this angle Khrushchev's hesitations before joining the interventionists is but a footnote which illuminates yet another obscure corner in the Soviet decision-making process.

Whatever doubts the First Secretary might have entertained concerning Hungary's invasion he 'was not interested in presiding over the dissolution of the Soviet camp' (Brzezinski, 1967: p. 206). And in Khrushchev's perception the 'camp' allowed neither an infringement of the Party's 'leading role' nor Yugoslav-like diversionist postures. By 1957 Molotov and his friends had been ousted. As long as they were still in the leadership Khrushchev had missed few occasions to hint to the Yugoslav Ambassador that Tito's stubbornness weakened his own position (Mićunović, 1980: p. 83), 'threatening that the Stalinists might come to power if something that Moscow wanted was not done' (ibid: p. 381). And, indeed, Molotov's negative attitude towards the *rapprochement* with Yugoslavia was officially recorded in the resolution denouncing the 'anti-Party group' (text in Clissold, 1975: pp. 273–4). But in May 1958 Belgrade's envoy was noting in his diary that since 'The influence of the so-called Stalinists . . . ceased to be a factor in Khrushchev's policy after June 1957', he no longer had any doubts in his mind 'that the principal initiator of the current anti-Yugoslav moves . . . was Khrushchev himself' (Mićunović, 1980: p. 381).

What was altered in the wake of the Polish and Hungarian events of October 1956 were not the *goals* but the *means* of Soviet policies in Eastern Europe. Emphasis was now more and more placed on the institutional instruments of conflict prevention and/or resolution, the Warsaw Pact and CMEA. Soviet efforts to foster military, political and economic integration of the 'commonwealth', were, however, only marginally successful during Khrushchev's tenure. Joint military manoeuvres were first conducted only in 1961, the Political Consultative Committee of the WTO met only four times between 1955 and 1961, and other policy-coordinating bodies of the alliance were practically inactive (Johnson, 1984: pp. 261, 262; Hutchings, 1983: p. 22). Following Marshal Grechko's appointment as WTO's Commander-in-Chief in 1961 the USSR began to put more emphasis on the military capabilities of the East European armies, but even then, the pact's High Command was more 'an administrative and co-ordinating agency for the East European armies . . . without command-and-control responsibilities' (Mackintosh, 1984; p. 46). Khrushchev's legacy to his successors was in this sense more than dubious. Faced with the wastefulness of parallel Stalinist industrial development policies in Eastern Europe, as well as with ever-growing indications that the Soviet Union was gradually beginning to subsidise East European industries and/or exports to *Western* markets (Khrushchev, 1974: pp. 211–19), Khrushchev envisaged intergrationist policies for CMEA and proposed to transform the organisation into a supranational organ, thereby arousing Romanian nationalism (Montias, 1967: pp. 187–230; Marer, 1984: p. 261; Shafir, 1985: pp. 47–8). In the 1960s Khrushchev's successors had to cope with the 'spill-over' effects of these postures, with Romanian and Czechoslovak officials questioning Soviet domination of the WTO structure and policy-making processes (Remington, 1971: pp. 84–8, 101; Johnson, 1984: pp. 263–4). And despite subsequent reforms in CMEA and the WTO, integration, in all its aspects, remains unsatisfactory from the Soviet vantage-point.

Inasmuch as Khrushchev's quest to ensure Soviet interests in the region by replacing direct control with a mutually beneficial relationship is concerned, one cannot but conclude that it has ended in failure. Even the 'coalition warfare' doctrine instituted by Grechko is open to the strong suspicion of being but one more facet of the control and policing function fulfilled by the WTO in Eastern Europe (Jones, 1981: pp. 111–16, 1984: p. 109). Some observers (e.g. Larrabee, 1984: p. 122) argue that in the 1968 invasion of Czechoslovakia the Soviets acted 'in concert with their allies' and that consequently, in this case, 'the Warsaw Pact served as an instrument of policy coordination and implementation'. However, 1968 was *not* a WTO operation (Johnson, 1984: p. 264), and, as Larrabee himself concedes, the East European military contribution was mainly symbolic, serving chiefly to shift some of the opprobrium from the Soviet Union (1984: p. 127). Ironically enough it seems that in 1968 Brezhnev was following the advice Tito volunteered to Khrushchev in 1956, i.e. that intervention 'should not be based exclusively on the weapons of the Soviet Army' (Mićunović, 1980: p. 135).

Turning from the intra- to the inter-systemic impacts of Khrushchevism, one must ask what would Eastern Europe look like today without the Khrushchevian episode. The answer is frightfully simple: at worst (give or take a few Shehus) it would look like Alia's Albania; at best (give or take a few Baráks), it would look like Novotný's Czechoslovakia at the end of the 1950s. One tends to forget, however, that before Khrushchev, the Baráks were just a handful, but the barracks of concentration camps were innumerable. De-Stalinisation has not only meant the dismissal of those responsible for the crimes of the past, but also, due to Khrushchev's attacks on the Stalinist theory of the 'intensification of the class struggle on the eve of socialist edification' ('Secret speech' in Khrushchev, 1971: pp. 628–9), the discrediting of terror as a legitimate systemic feature of communist rule. Nothing illustrates this better than Husák's 'normalised' Czechoslovakia. Post-April 1969 CSSR is certainly no paradise-come-true. But not even under Husák is terror employed unselectively.

The de-legitimation of terror can be traced back to Molotov's enforced recantation of his statement that the USSR had not yet built socialism (*Kommunist*, 14/1955). Since socialism was now proclaimed to exist and the USSR to be constructing *communism*, one could no longer justify terror on class criteria. To be sure Stalin had proclaimed the advent of socialist society as early as 1936, but within the caveat of the 'encirclement' of the Soviet Union by world imperialism which allegedly activated internal remnants of the bourgeoisie and its implanted agents. The adoption of a 'peaceful coexistence' line destroyed the base of that argument. The announcement of the 'final and complete' victory of socialism at the XXI Party Congress (1959) was thus combined with the proclamation of the end of capitalist encirclement and that of class-based oppositional political crime, thus rendering impossible the use of Stalinist justifications for a state of siege against the population at large (Breslauer, 1982: p. 76). The blend practically amounted to a repudiation of 'revolution from above' (Lowenthal, 1970: pp. 85–98; Féhér, 1984: pp. 29–31). In the East European context this meant, in addition to other aspects affecting the Soviet Union, that some ruling élites (e.g. Romania) were being provided by Khrushchev himself with the ideological instrument necessary for the vindication of their search of support in the West, geared at resisting *Soviet* pressure.

An additional major contribution to change in Eastern Europe generated by Khrushchev consists in his having triggered a chain reaction in which reformists learn from each other's mistakes. Zdeněk Mlynář, one of the main architects of the Prague Spring, attests that the Czechoslovak reform movement could not have come into being without the proclamation of the 1961 CPSU Programme, with its theses that communism necessitates a sold basis of productive forces (and hence the need of economic reform) and the development of social self-government hailed in the theory of the 'state of all people' (Mlynář, 1984: pp. 234–6). In a seminal article on theories of socialist development in Soviet–East European relations Sarah M. Terry (1984: pp. 221–53) provides an in-depth analysis of this process. Unfortunately Terry's article insists unwarrantedly on the concept of 'developed socialism' and pays only implicit attention to that of the 'all-people's state'. Even though first employed in Czechoslovakia, 'developed socialism', as acknowledged by Terry, has little if anything in common with its 'real socialism' variant of later vintage. Consequently the focus of attention should not be transposed by what is a mere semantic accident. Rather than stressing the legitimacy of the existing power structure, as 'developed socialism' in its Brezhnev version does, the Richta group and other Czechoslovak reformers *challenged it*. And this challenge was directly linked with Khrushchev's concept of the 'state of all people'[12] (Golan, 1971: pp. 174–6; Skilling, 1976: pp. 125–9, 270–1). As launched in the CPSU Programme adopted at the XXII Party Congress in October 1961, the 'state of all the people' formula was based on the assumption that the 'dictatorship of the proletariat' had ceased to be exercised in the Soviet society, where social classes were now deemed to have become homogenous. 'The dictatorship of the proletariat' it was stated, 'has fulfilled its historic mission' and the state which arose out of it 'has become . . . a state expressing the interests and the will of the people as a whole' (1961 Programme of the CPSU in

Triska, 1962: pp. 97–8). To be sure the affirmation could be traced once more back to Stalin (Kanet, 1968), but again, within the caveats mentioned earlier. The major innovation brought about by the Khrushchevian formula, consisted, however, in its explicit stress on the participation of ever-increasing numbers of representatives of these 'homogenous' classes in the daily management of the community's affairs. As Breslauer (1976) points out, Khrushchev's encouragement of mass participation went well beyond the Leninist notion of *privlechenie* ('drawing in'). Kenneth Jowitt (1975) refers to the main features of this formula as 'inclusion'.

Yet 'inclusion' does not provide for 'participation' in the Western sense of the term. As Breslauer put it elsewhere, 'participation' on Khrushchevian terms was not synonymous with increased individual autonomy (1982: p. 56). 'Whereas Khrushchev was arguing for new areas of politics and less explicitly administrative control, his emphasis on social control did not sanction liberalization or diversification' (Breslauer, 1982: p. 76). The stage of the 'state of all people' was one where the Party would maintain its unchallenged leading role, though, grantedly, under the label of a Party 'of the entire people'. The Party was to be 'the brain' of the epoch, showing the people 'scientifically motivated roads along which to advance'. In fact, not only would its role not diminish, but it was to be enhanced (1961 Programme of the CPSU in Triska, 1962: p. 125). Since setting the goals of the future remained the strict prerogative of the sole organisation that 'understands the laws of social development', participation was in fact restricted to the 'output' dimension of the system. It could have read '*Party*-cipation' just as well.

Whereas the 'Khrushchevian earthquake' undoubtedly signified departure from such system-embracing 'rules of the game' as mass terror on the leader's ability to make unconstrained decisions, its limitation rested in the stubborn negation of any sign of institutionalisation of a 'public political arena'. That arena, as Rigby points out (1980: p. 26), remained as empty as ever, with debate limited to the *means* of achieving *regime-designated* goals. In other words, Khrushchevism evolved from the provision for a change in the number of 'rule-makers' (collective leadership) to the negation of the rule-makers' right to terrorise society, but it never envisaged a change in the 'name of the game' (Shafir, 1985: p. 56).

That task was historically left to the Czechoslovak reformers. As Mlynář was to put it later, while in the USSR the thesis of the 'all-people's state and the development of an all people's democracy and social self-government . . . had always remained mostly abstract slogans' in Czechoslovakia this 'was formulated more concretely: in order for "the interests of the whole society" to be able to be expressed correctly it is necessary that the [*non*-homogeneous] interests of all social groups and individuals be freely expressed, and thus by democratic means a genuine total social interest must be constituted out of the conflict of interests of the parts' (Mlynář, 1984: pp. 233–4). While it is true that Dubček himself remained ambiguous as to the future modality of the implementation of the Party's leading role, the April 1968 Action Programme of the Czechoslovak Party signified a substantial shift from Khrushchevist postures (Rupnik, 1981). Khrushchev was thus the 'unconscious tool' of historical developments, having, in Mlynář's words, created *'indispensable conditions'* for the reform movement which he had unwittingly *'inspired'*. At the same time, *'It is clear that the contents of the resulting reformist concepts as elaborated by the Czeshoslovak communists, far overstepped the framework of the ideological concepts of Khrushchev's CPSU Programme'* (Mlynář, 1984: p. 236. Emphasis mine).

This is why qualifying Dubček's Czechoslovakia as 'Khrushchevist', as Féhér and his associates do (Féhér, Heller and Márkus, 1983: p. VIII) is a gross misinterpretation. Furthermore, their contention that 'Kádár's Hungary is the only Khrushchevite country in a post-Khrushchevite environment' (Féhér and Heller, 1983: p. x) is quite incorrect. Kádárism, to be sure, stops substantially (and safely!) short of Czechoslovak acknowledgement of *institutionalised* autonomy. It is based on 'negative legitimation', on 'marginalisation' of dissident intellectuals combined with co-optation of other segments of this stratum, and on consumerist (which *is* Khrushchevist[13]) privatisation (which is *not*!) of large parts of the economic sector (Schöpflin, 1979 and 1982; Volgyés, 1984). However, pockets of autonomy, as Féhér himself acknowledges, are tacitly condoned; there is unofficial tolerance of existing pressure groups and a private sphere of economic and cultural pursuits is encouraged. The latter, albeit aimed at the depoliticisation of society (Féhér, 1984: pp. 221–5), creates the *potential*[14] for a future rebirth of civil society. These elements are untypical of any envisaged Khrushchevist designs. To qualify Kádárism as 'politics of limited reform' is accurate enough. To call such politics 'Khrushchevism' (Féhér and Heller, 1983: p. 30) is to pay compliment where compliment is undue. For, as the Hungarian dissident social scientist Mihály Vajda put it, 'If

Sweden or [the colonels'] Greece represent alternatives within the capitalist system, then Hungary under Kádár's rule is indeed an alternative within "existing socialism" ' (Vajda, 1981: p. 132).

Dubček's failure taught following generations of reformers that self-government cannot be achieved 'from above', necessitating instead the creation of structures of 'parallel politics' (Skilling and Prečan, 1981), entrenched in civil society (Rupnik, 1979). Czechoslovak reformism ultimately had to pay the price of its 'original sin', namely that of seeking legitimacy where it could not be found – in its Khrushchevist inspiration. The Polish Solidarność (but also such KOR-KSS-inspired initiatives as the VOSN in Czechoslovakia and the SZETA in Hungary) were the outcome of this process of historical learning. The process, as Touraine[15] and his associates remark, can be traced back to the 1956 events. It entails the erosion of 'the gap between revisionist criticism coming from the top . . . and mass resistance to an artificially imposed regime'. This gulf is gradually replaced 'by a united movement centered on economic demands but broadening out into a struggle against the Party's pervasive domination of society'. Having learned from past failures, opposition members 'will not be satisfied with partial adjustments to the ideological line or economic policy; their concern is to defend society against the regime, and they rest upon the awareness of a fundamental conflict between the people and its rulers' (Touraine *et al.*, 1983: pp. 19–20).

Khrushchev, or rather Khrushchevism, thus became the involuntary midwife of an appeal to democratisation. Were it not for Khrushchev's recognition of different paths to socialist construction and for the de-legitimation of state terror, Eastern Europe might never have known the days of October 1956. Were it not for 'peaceful coexistence' and for the 'state of all people', the Czechoslovak reformers might have never found the ideological justification for the process which they fostered. And were it not for the lessons of these aborted attempts, Solidarity might never have come into being. As we know from Hegel (1967: p. 218), however, the 'deed of the world mind' is not 'the aim and object' of history's makers. *That* deed remained for ever 'concealed' from the First Secretary and from his successors.

NOTES

1. For the distinction between 'transitory', 'transitional' and 'original' leader and its impact on possible approaches to Khrushchevism see Martin McCauley's chapter in this volume.

2. When in November 1956, in the wake of the Soviet intervention in Hungary, the Yugoslav Ambassador to Moscow, Veljko Mićunović, mentioned the Congress' achievements to Khrushchev, the Soviet leader 'commented reluctantly that "there are people amongst us who think that the new decisions are responsible for everything bad that has happened" ' (Mićunović, 1980: p. 159).

3. According to Brzezinski (1967: p. 245), on grounds of his Jewish origin, which would alienate the Poles. Khrushchev indeed seems to have resented the attitude of the Berman–Minc–Zambrowski group *vis-à-vis* the (non) promotion of native cadres and the patronage displayed towards Jewish members of the party (Khrushchev, 1974: pp. 178–81). But the veto was also consonant with the policies adopted in the Kremlin immediately upon Stalin's death, which were aimed at the 'nationalisation' of local leaderships, geared at generating support for the ruling Parties. Beria, for instance, is reported to have mocked Rákosi for trying to become Hungary's 'Jewish king' (Váli, 1961: p. 5).

4. Khrushchev claims that 'we knew full well that Gomułka's release from prison meant his subsequent appointment to the top post. We anticipated that and we accepted it'. But then he goes into a candid description of the preparations for military intervention in Poland (Khrushchev, 1974: pp. 201, 203–5).

5. Tito's resentment was particularly strong in Rákosi's case, but he also demanded the replacement of Chervenkov and (unsuccessfully) that of Novotný and Hoxha, as well as the rehabilitation of such 'Titoites' as Rajk, Kostov and Slanský (Royal Institute 1958: p. 271; speech in Pula, 11 November 1956 in Zinner, 1957: pp. 523–4; Mićunović, 1980: p. 63; Brown, 1966: p. 9).

6. Khrushchev's sense of injury might have been enhanced by what he probably interpreted as Tito's violation of his pledge to support the invasion. Reminiscing on their meeting on the island of Brioni on the eve of the invasion, the Soviet leader writes: 'I expected even more strenuous objections from Tito than the ones we had encountered during our discussions with the Poles. But we were pleasantly surprised. Tito said we were absolutely right and that we should send our soldiers into action as soon as possible. He said we had an obligation to help Hungary crush the counterrevolution . . . we had been ready for resistance, but instead we received his wholehearted support.' (Khrushchev, 1971: pp. 463–4.)

7. Those analysts (e.g. Larrabee, 1984: pp. 117–18) who consider that the declaration of neutrality and the withdrawal from the WTO (1 Nov) was *not* what determined the Soviet intervention are absolutely correct. Czechoslovakia's saga in 1968 in the best proof of this thesis. For a different view see Valenta, 1984a: p. 273. However, Valenta 1984b: pp. 120–4 appears to reach somewhat different conclusions.

8. This evidence is overlooked by Fry and Rice (1983: pp. 93–4), whose interesting analysis in many ways reaches conclusions similar to those here. The two authors are persuaded that Zhukov's position was similar to that of Khrushchev.

9. E.g. Gomułka's anti-interventionist posture in 1956 v. his prointerventionist stance in 1968, and Romania's volunteering of troops in 1956 as against her denunciation of the intervention in Czechoslovakia (Valenta, 1979: pp. 52–3, 114–18; Khrushchev, 1971: p. 463; Radványi, 1984: p. 260).

10. With Bulgaria and the GDR once more insisting on the 'duty' of members of the 'socialist community' to come to each other's rescue (Ascherson, 1981: p. 198).

11. E.g. the Polish October: 'Looking back on it now, I think we were too hotheaded' (Khrushchev, 1974: p. 200.)

12. As Ronald J. Hill's contribution to this volume demonstrates (chap. 3), the concept of the 'all-people's state' was never really jettisoned by Khrushchev's successors. But it is important to emphasise that it was very much emptied of those diffuse variables which were liable to 'adaptations' of the kind produced by the Czechoslovak reformists. Cf. Terry, 1984: pp. 239–46; Hill, 1984: pp. 111–16.

13. It was Khrushchev who, during his last trip to Budapest in the spring of 1964, referred approvingly to Kádár's economic policy as 'goulash politics' (*The New York Times*, 2 Apr. 1964). On Khrushchevist consumerism see Breslauer, 1982: pp. 84, 98, 100 and *passim*. On 'consumerism' and its impact on Eastern Europe see Liehm, 1975; Rupnik, 1979; Gitelman, 1981: pp. 199–202; and Mlynář, 1983: pp. 4–8.

14. For example, the so-called 'secondary economy' encouraged by the regime, creates substantial inequalities, generating social tensions in an environment where the private sphere destined to pre-emptive purposes thus may turn against the system itself (Vajda, 1981: p. 138).

15. Both Touraine and V. V. Kusin rely on the evolution of Polish dissident thought in their description of this phenomenon. See in particular Michnik, 1976. According to Kusin, in its simplified form, the theory of 'parallel institutions' suggests that 'both popular uprising [1956] and reformism having failed, the dissaffected public could no longer relate to the government . . . Hence the emphasis was put on building alternative organisations, communication and even education' (Kusin, 1983: pp. 52–3).

10 Foreign Policy

HARRY HANAK

'He was a man of great warmth and totally belligerent.' (NIXON speaking of Khrushchev, *Time*, 13 Aug 1984)

Was Khrushchev's approach to foreign policy a continuation of Stalinism or did it initiate different methods and different aims? As long ago as 1947 George Kennan had argued in the 'Z article' that whenever the Soviets wanted something badly enough they would thrust into the background some negative aspects of their policy. These were tactical manoeuvres. Real changes would only take place when the 'internal nature of Soviet power changes' (*Foreign Affairs*, 4/1947: pp. 566–82).

It was the opinion of such an acute observer as the Yugoslav Ambassador to Moscow, who wrote in his diary on 28 May 1956 that while Khrushchev had condemned Stalin in one speech, in the main political report which he also delivered at the XX Party Congress he said that the system was not to be changed since it was the best that history had ever known. 'The political line of the Soviet Communist Party had, apparently, always been correct, even though it was laid down until his death by none other than Stalin' (Mićunović, 1980: p. 56).

Khrushchev perceived that information was necessary; that the foreign-policy decision-making process would work better if it were better informed. He records in his memoirs the ignorance of everyone in Moscow concerning what Camp David was or where it was, to which Eisenhower had invited him: 'I couldn't for the life of me find out what this Camp David was' (Khrushchev, 1974: pp. 371–2).

To overcome such a deplorable situation a specialist élite had to be trained. The Institute of World Economy and World Politics, headed by Eugene Varga, had been disbanded after the Second World War, a fact which Mikoyan was to regret in his address to the XX Party Congress. Indeed the Institute was reconstituted under a different name in April 1956. Its main task was to study the economies of capitalist states and the relations between them. It began publication of a journal in July 1957. In 1962 Boris Ponomarev complained of the shortcomings of the study of history. Latin American and African studies were being particularly neglected. Even the study of the history of socialist countries was notable not for growth but for contraction (*Voprosy Istorii*, 1/1963: pp. 3–15). The process of remedying all this began after the XX Party Congress.

While it was obvious that the Soviet position internally and externally was more favourable than in 1939, Khrushchev understood that little use was being made of this change of circumstance. There was no reason why the Soviet Union should not be accepted as a partner in a world dominated by two superpowers. It was necessary to revise the Leninist concept of war and Khrushchev did this at the XX Party Congress. War was not fatalistically inevitable, he said, because mighty social and political forces possessed the means to prevent the imperialists from unleashing war. Attacking the Chinese at the Romanian Workers' Party Congress on 21 June 1960 he poured ridicule on those who believed that war with imperialism was inevitable even though the imperialist countries 'may be as small as, say, a coat button.' And he went on to ask: 'What then? Should we then also look up in the book what Vladimir Ilych Lenin said quite correctly for his time, and simply repeat that wars are inevitable inasmuch as capitalist countries exist? It is quite true that the nature of capitalism, of imperialism, does not change, even if represented by small countries. We all know that the wolf is just as blood-thirsty as the lion or tiger, though he is incomparably weaker. That is why a man is much less afraid of meeting a wolf than a tiger or a lion. True, the lesser beasts of prey can also bite, their nature is the same, but their capacity is not. They are not as strong, and are rendered harmless more easily' (Khrushchev, 1961a: pp. 62–3).

As a corollary to this Khrushchev stressed peaceful coexistence with the capitalist world. It would be difficult to find a speech by him dealing with foreign policy where the achievements of peace and peaceful coexistence were not highly praised and prized. Whether the capitalists liked it or not, he said in Bombay, 'the socialists and the capitalists have to live side by side on one planet' (*Pravda*, 26 Nov 1955). Khrushchev's diplomacy was personal in a way that Stalin's had never been. Khrushchev was a great traveller. No doubt he had an insatiable curiosity about other countries, a curiosity stifled in Stalinist Russia. But his travels and his meetings with foreign statesmen had other reasons than pure self-education or tourism. He believed that he could overcome opponents in direct confrontation. He also believed that he could judge a situation best by himself rather than by reading the reports of others. Why else would he have made the journey to Warsaw in 1956 to meet Gomułka? In any case the nature of the collective leadership, even after he had overcome his most open opponents, imposed on him the necessity of dealing at first hand and personally with foreign statesmen and not allowing others to do it. His personality and his activity caught the imagination of the West. The fact that he took his wife on some of his trips abroad, and that he was prepared to argue with journalists, gave the Western public the impression of a man whose image approximated to that of the democratic politicians of the West. Such a vision was, of course, false. Whether the Soviet citizen shared this Western view of a 'folksy' leader is doubtful. We know that Khrushchev's colleagues did not.

It would be a work of supererogation to mention all the countries that Khrushchev visited and all the foreign statesmen that he met. The importance, however, of one country and of its leaders superseded all the others: America. Khrushchev had this to say of his journey to the USA: 'I'll admit I was curious to have a look at America, although it wouldn't be my first trip abroad. After all, I'd been to England, Switzerland, France, India, Indonesia, Burma and so on. These were all foreign countries, but they weren't America: America occupied a special position in our thinking and our view of the world. And why shouldn't it? It was our strongest opponent among capitalist countries, the leader that called the tune of anti-Sovietism for the rest.' And thinking about his journey just before his plane landed in Washington on 15 September 1959 Khrushchev felt proud 'that we had finally forced the United States to recognise the necessity of establishing closer contacts with us. If the President of the United States himself invited the Chairman of the Council of Ministers of the USSR, then you know conditions have changed' (Khrushchev, 1974: pp. 369, 374).

One of the purposes of the visits was to establish this personal contact with the President that Khrushchev regarded as vital. Speaking in Moscow in August 1959 announcing his forthcoming visit, Khrushchev outlined what he understood to be the nature of personal relations with the President and thus of the relations of the USA and the Soviet Union: 'In the course of these visits we shall have unofficial conversations, just conversations and not negotiations. But I do not attach any special importance to the form of our exchange of opinions – whether it will be negotiations or unofficial discussions. The important thing in this exchange of opinions is to find a common language and a common understanding of the problems that we have to solve' (Khrushchev, 1960: p. 64).

And again in New York on 17 September Khrushchev said: 'I have never gone in for diplomacy but I have a good understanding of diplomatic language in relations between states. If I tell you frankly what I think, let the diplomats with their diplomas not judge me too severely for possible deviations from protocol' (ibid., p. 122).

The purpose of all these contacts with Eisenhower was to be the fading of the cold war, 'with a warmer climate setting in . . . a climate similar to that of California or . . . to that of the southern coast of the Crimea . . .' (ibid. p. 198) as he told his audience in Los Angeles on 19 September.

At that time in 1959 it had been intended that Eisenhower should visit the Soviet Union. Such a visit never took place and the May 1960 Paris meeting was aborted after the U–2 incident. But Khrushchev did meet Kennedy in Vienna in 1961 and the nature of the contact between them at the time of the Cuban missile crisis can be judged by the ten private letters which the two leaders exchanged between 22 and 28 October 1962. So essential was contact between them that the establishment of the hot line followed shortly after the conclusion of the Caribbean crisis.

It was clear to Khrushchev that the very survival of the Soviet Union and of the camp of socialism did not depend on petty satraps in Eastern Europe or even on Mao Zedong, but on the USA. The Americans alone were in a position to inflict unacceptable damage to the USSR. A number of consequences followed from this premise. First, it was essential for the Soviets to build up a military posture which would act as a deterrent to America. Khrushchev and his successors pursued military strength with great determination. Rather typically Khrushchev sought to solve the financial and economic dilemma of greater arms spending by concentrating on the glamorous weapons of the new technological age. His successors gave equal military and political value to nuclear bombs, missiles and conventional forces. Second, it was to avoid conflict, to defuse military escapades which could get out of hand, to preach peaceful coexistence. There was therefore a special relationship between the Soviets and the Americans: a relationship of rivalry and partnership at the same time. It was essential to undermine the positions of the capitalists everywhere in the world but it could not be done in such a way that they might resort to war. Third, Chinese codetermination of the camp could not be tolerated. What was good for China was not necessarily good for the Soviet Union. No Soviet leader could allow his policy to be dictated by foreigners.

There were other reasons for Khrushchev's peace policy. The Eisenhower administration in which Dulles served as Secretary of State had come to power on a wave of anti-communist rhetoric. Communism was to be 'rolled back', and the 'captive nations' were to be 'liberated'. The USA moreover was not to shrink from 'going to the brink' even if it was a nuclear brink. It is not clear to what extent the new Soviet leadership was impressed or even frightened by this vocabulary. Certainly by the time of the 1956 Hungarian revolution it was seen how empty these phrases were. But what was more significant was the acquisition by the USA of a strategic capability for inflicting massive damage on the Soviet Union. By 1955 the total number of American bombers capable of attacking the Soviet Union with nuclear weapons had risen to 1350. The Soviets had perhaps 350 such bombers. The concessions that the Soviets were prepared to make in these years were directly attributable to this American capability.

Therefore the Soviet leadership must have watched with disbelief and astonishment the failure of the West to exploit Soviet difficulties in Poland and Hungary in 1956. They must have been even more amazed at American actions in forcing the British and French out of Suez. It may be assumed that this striking illustration of the contradictions of capitalism would never have been foretold in the Kremlin. The Soviets now realised that the West would use its military superiority only if certain of its vital interests were affected. The West was not aggressive. A more active Soviet policy can be dated from early 1957. It was with some justification that Khrushchev noted in 1961 that the possibilities of restoring capitalism to the socialist camp no longer existed.

The more aggressive posture was seen in Khrushchev's espousal of the Third World and the national liberation struggle which he made in this speech in 1961. It was delivered on the eve of Kennedy's inauguration as President. Arthur Schlesinger wrote that Kennedy was alarmed by the speech and took it as an authoritative statement of Soviet intentions. Khrushchev regarded nuclear world war as a disaster to the world and thus for communism – 'We know that the first to suffer in the event of war would be the working people and their vanguard – the working class' (Khrushchev 1961–6: p. 21). Equally unacceptable were limited wars, and these had to be stopped the way the Soviet Union had stopped the Suez war. Wars of national liberation on the other hand would continue for as long as colonialism existed. But Khrushchev was at pains to point out that the national liberation struggle did not develop independently of the struggle for socialism. 'The imperialist powers,' he said, 'above all the United States, are doing their utmost to chain to their system the countries that have cast off the colonial yoke and thereby strengthen the position of world capitalism, to infuse fresh blood into it. . ..' (ibid. p. 38). In this the imperialists would not succeed because communists were revolutionaries 'and it would be a bad thing if they failed to see new opportunities' (ibid. pp. 49–50). It was the international duty of the working class of the socialist countries to help the peoples of developing countries to smash the chains of colonial slavery.

The concept of the national democratic state was the new opportunity of which Khrushchev spoke. Such a state fought against imperialism and colonialism, promoted agrarian reform, nationalised foreign capital and socialised what industry there was. It was expected that the revolutionary democrats leading these states would pursue a foreign policy in close accord with the Soviet Union and would give it voting support in the General Assembly of the United Nations. All this could be done in the absence of a significant and class conscious working class. In an extremity, it would even be done without the services of a Communist Party. The existence of the USSR would provide the impetus which a local working class could not.

Khrushchev's foreign policy therefore rested on the two pillars of peaceful coexistence and a far from peaceful national liberation struggle. He sought among the charismatic leaders of the anti-imperialist struggle for those to whom Soviet favour could be extended in the hope that they would take their countries on to the non-capitalist path of development and thus eventually espouse the cause of

Marxism–Leninism. This marked a radical change in Soviet policy. While Stalin measured the extent of communism as the area covered by the Soviet soldier, Khrushchev saw communism as arising in every nook of the world where a Soviet presence could be represented by arms, experts, loans and verbal aid. The socialist camp could therefore no longer be monolithic. Differences and divergences had to be accepted. In the last resort Soviet interests would prevail through Soviet pressure. For those who could not be fitted into this scheme, perhaps because of their size – after all another China would have been unbearable – the policy of non-alignment or positive neutralism was prescribed and approved, as in the case of India. There were, in any case, a number of candidates: Nkrumah, Sukarno, Lumumba, Gizenga, Mobido Keita, Sekou Touré were all at one time or another favoured. Some of them were addressed as 'comrades'; others became recipients of the Lenin peace prize. All of them became recipients of development aid and in some cases also of military aid. But for one reason or another none of them were appropriate. More promising were Nasser in Egypt, Ben Bella in Algeria and Kassem in Iraq. No Lenin prizes for them. Nasser and Ben Bella together with Field Marshal Hakim Amer became Heroes of the Soviet Union! Much effort and much money was invested in Nasser and in spite of ups and downs Khrushchev visited Egypt in May 1964 to be present at the ceremonies at the Aswan Dam. What was perhaps more important for the Egyptians was a 250 million rouble loan.

Castro and Cuba was the first and the only example in Khrushchev's time of the success of this policy. The existence of a communist regime at the very gates of capitalism was intoxicating. Castro's credentials for inclusion in a communist world were not of the best. But what did that matter?

The Cuban missile crisis, or the Caribbean crisis as the Soviets call it, permits of no dogmatic explanation. Why did Khrushchev act thus? Why did he act so much out of character? Or did he? How was it possible that a man who sought to avoid war would allow the world to go to the nuclear brink? Indeed, at the height of the crisis, Kennedy wrote to Khrushchev to voice his surprise that any 'sane man would, in this nuclear age, deliberately plunge the world into war which it is crystal clear no country could win and which could only result in catastrophic consequences to the whole world, including the aggressor' (22 Oct 1962). Khrushchev answered in a characteristic but very un-Leninist way in his letter of 26 October:

'We communists are against any wars between states at all. . . ' (US Dept of State *Bulletin*, 19 Nov 1973, LXIX, no. 1795, pp. 635–55).

Castro's regime in Cuba was recognised by the Soviets in January 1959. Initially Soviet comment was brief and restrained. They did not know which way the Castroist experiment would develop. Not until February 1960, when Mikoyan visited Havana and an agreement was signed by which the Soviets purchased sugar and provided Cuba with credits did Khrushchev mention Cuba. The tone was still non-committal. He said that the Soviet Union supported countries like Cuba and would give them aid (*Pravda*, 13 Feb 1960). It seems that by the summer of 1960 Khrushchev was quite intoxicated by the success of the Cuban revolution and by the developments on 'the island of liberty' (Clissold, 1970: p. 263–5). It is worth while remembering that at this time détente with the USA had gone sour after the U–2 incident, that the Berlin problem was no nearer solution, that the quarrel with the Chinese had become public and that relations with Nasser had reached a low point and resulted in Nasser's emissary Sadat being subject to a tirade of invective by Khrushchev in Moscow. Castro and Cuba were more than a substitute for Nasser and Egypt. For the first time the revolution had leaped across the Atlantic. Under these circumstances Khrushchev was ready to accept Castro's self-proclaimed Marxism. On 18 April 1961 Castro boasted that the Cubans had carried out a socialist revolution under the very noses of the USA and on 1 December 1961 he announced that he had always been a Marxist–Leninist and would be to the last day of his life. He also gave hope that his revolution would be an example to Latin America which would 'turn the Andes into the Sierra Maestra of the American continent' (Levesque, 1978: p. 21). In Khrushchev's vision of world affairs Castro had become an asset of such value that he could not be dropped. It is evident that support for Cuba had become intermingled in Khrushchev's mind with a missile threat to the USA. The Soviet inferiority in the sophisticated hardware of nuclear bombs and rockets could be compensated by this fortuitous transformation of a populist leader into a communist. Thus while in a *Pravda* interview of 16 February 1960 Mikoyan explicitly denied any intention of sending arms to Cuba, a little later in June 1960 the Director of the Cuban Institute of Agrarian Reform quoted Khrushchev in a different vein. Khrushchev had assured the Cubans that the Americans would not launch an attack on Cuba because they were afraid of a Soviet reaction similar to that at the time of the Suez crisis, i.e. the threat of nuclear attacks on Britain.

When Khrushchev was asked whether it was Soviet policy to put military bases on Cuba he answered that it was not necessary as 'the Soviet Union has only to press a button in any part of the Soviet Union for rockets from that country to fall on any other part of the planet' (Clissold, 1970: pp. 255–66). On 9 July Khrushchev, addressing a teachers' conference, warned the Americans that the Soviets had rockets 'capable of landing precisely on a given square at a distance of 13 000 kilometres' (Khrushchev, 1963: pp. 369–423). Khrushchev elucidated his meaning in an interview which he gave to Cuban journalists in October 1960. Asked by one of them what his attitude was to the Western belief that the use of ICBMs in the event of armed aggression was merely symbolic, he agreed that it was so if no aggression took place, but implied that there were plenty of rockets in readiness if the attack did take place. In January 1961 Khrushchev denied that rockets were being placed on Cuba. And this denial Khrushchev repeated to Kennedy after the Bay of Pigs invasion. In February 1962 this promise was repeated. In his report to the USSR Supreme Soviet in December 1962 concerning the missile crisis Khrushchev justified placing missiles on Cuba on the grounds that they were intended to defend the island. This justification had also been given by Khrushchev to Kennedy in their correspondence between 22 and 28 October 1962. It was repeated in the articles in *Voprosy Istorii* written by Anatoly Gromyko, son of Foreign Minister Gromyko (7/1971: pp. 135–44; 8/1971: pp. 121–9). In his memoirs Khrushchev wrote that he worried much about the Cuban situation and the blow that the revolutionary process would receive if communism were wiped out in Cuba. While attending the Bulgarian Party Congress in May 1962 he suddenly had the idea of defending Cuba by installing missiles. There is no reason to doubt the statements given by Khrushchev, although it does not answer the reason why Soviet troops armed with conventional weapons could not have carried out the task just as well. But Khrushchev answers that too in his memoirs. He wrote: 'In addition to protecting Cuba, our missiles would have equalised what the West likes to call "the balance of power" ' (Khrushchev, 1974: pp. 454–5.) The former Hungarian diplomat Janoš Radványi records a briefing of Soviet-bloc diplomats in Washington given by Mikoyan on 30 November. Mikoyan confirmed that the purpose of the operation had been both to defend Cuba and to achieve a definite shift in the power relationships between the socialist and capitalist camps (Radványi, 1972: p. 137).

But while Khrushchev could, within limits, deal with the USA and her allies, he could not deal with the Chinese. The Ulbrichts, the Novotnýs, the Gomułkas, the Kádárs, the Zhivkovs could be manipulated. Even Castro could be forced to come into line and be made to realise that without Soviet support his days were numbered. Tito, of course, could not, but the working relationship established with him was not unsatisfactory. When it came to the Chinese no amount of manipulation or cajolery would help. The Soviet conception of the communist world was one where the Soviets ruled and the others obeyed. In return the others were given protection from both internal and external enemies. Given the weakness of virtually all communist regimes such a scenario was by no means unfavourable to the smaller socialist states, and in particular to the Communist Parties ruling them.

The Chinese viewed the world communist movement as one where decisions were to be reached on a basis of consultation and the evolution of joint policies. The Chinese said that the world communist movement had to have a leader and that could only be the Soviet Union. Militarily and technologically the Soviets were superior. To some extent the Soviets were prepared to go along with Chinese wishes. The phrase 'the socialist states led by the USSR and PRC' became the commonplace of public announcements. The trouble was that the Chinese expected the Soviet Union to lead in a particular direction. The Soviets were already disturbed by Chinese intervention in Eastern Europe in 1956. They hardly needed Chinese advice or support over Hungary and Poland and Zhou Enlai's tour of Hungary and Poland in January 1957 must have irritated them. Shortly afterwards the Bulgarians attempted their own version of the great leap forward until they were called into line. Even the GDR gave exaggerated praise to the Chinese experiments.

But worse was to come. Before the great leap forward turned out to be an economic disaster it posed a serious political threat. It had far-reaching ideological implications. The Soviets held to the ideological precept that communism could only be achieved after the successful construction of socialism. True enough Khrushchev had promised that communism would arrive in the foreseeable future, during the lives of 'our children'. To the Chinese this was not fast enough. In 1958 they expected that the great leap forward would land Chinese society on the stage of communism by 1961. During the period following the Caribbean crisis when criticism was no longer muted and the polemics between the two sides became more explicit, Ilichev, chairman of the ideological department of the Party Secretariat wrote that the great leap forward 'was a policy divorced from real, objective possibilities, built on the desire to solve grandiose tasks faster and to "teach" others the newly invented methods of building socialism and communism. It was then that the slogan was proclaimed of the "people's communes", which formed the basis of the attempt to leap over the natural stages of socialist construction in the countryside, tested by the experience of other socialist countries' (*Kommunist*, 11/1964). If the Chinese road were accepted by other socialist parties then the primacy of the Soviet Union in the ideological field would have gone. Indeed, the Soviet Union, though possessing military force, could be depicted as a society which was ideologically backward in the construction of socialism. If it was ideologically backward then the reason for this was that bourgeois mentality and relations had not been extinguished or had reappeared. The Soviet leaders had reneged on Marxism–Leninism. From the Chinese point of view this explained the whole détente policy of the Soviets.

It is possible that the Soviets might have tolerated even this. Khrushchev, according to his testimony, suggested to Mao at the time of the 1957 Moscow conference, that there should be a division of labour in the world communist movement. The Chinese sphere should be Asia without India, Pakistan and Indonesia, and Africa (Khrushchev, 1974: p. 254). Whether Khrushchev ever made such a grossly un-Marxist suggestion may be doubted. Even if he had, the Chinese would certainly have had none of it. They had identified themselves with the Afro-Asian world at Bandung in 1955.

The Soviets could not tolerate direct Chinese intervention in their relations with capitalist powers. The Quemoy and Matsu crisis was the first of such instances where the Chinese tried to involve the Soviets in confrontation with the USA. They bombarded these two offshore islands. When Khrushchev had been in Beijing shortly before, the Chinese did not even tell him that this was what they intended to do. Khrushchev was expected to support the Chinese position, which he did, but only after the crisis had passed the danger point and the risks of American intervention decreased. A year later, after Khrushchev's return from the USA, he set out for Beijing. He went there to explain the Soviet policy of détente and found the Chinese fighting the Indians.

'No doubt now remains that one of the reasons for the attack by the Chinese leaders on the policy of the world communist movement was the lessening of international tension, which took place in 1959, when there was a definite relaxation in the cold war between the Soviet Union and the USA, especially after Comrade Khrushchev's trip to the USA. It cannot be considered accidental that at that actual period the Chinese leaders got themselves in an armed clash on the Indian–Chinese border, and this, besides creating an acute situation in that part of the world, was ultimately aimed at torpedoing the relaxation of international tension which had taken place' (*Pravda*, 21 Sep 1963).

Chinese anger is of course understandable. A Soviet understanding with the USA would have decreased the value of a Chinese alliance for the Soviets. After the missile crisis there was no longer any possibility of a détente in Sino-Soviet relations while Khrushchev and Mao Zedong remained to lead their countries. But Khrushchev's days were numbered, and his fall coincided with the first Chinese nuclear explosion.

Just as a revision of Stalinist policies after 1953 was caused by Stalin's internal rather than his external policies so the fall of Khrushchev was brought about by internal reforms which were not to the liking of his colleagues. Yet, foreign policy played a part. Khrushchev's adventurism and hare-brained schemes had resulted in Soviet retreats and no one in Moscow was willing to tolerate that. In any case, there was probably the fear that Khrushchev might, in his search for peaceful co-existence and détente, be prepared to abandon the ideologically essential conflict between capitalism and socialism. Certainly some of his statements would lead to such an interpretation. When in America in 1959 he had said that one could understand the existence of strained relations between countries that had 'real antagonisms for example, such as territorial disputes or economic claims'. It was one of the features of the cold war however that it involved countries that had 'no direct antagonisms of that kind' (Khrushchev, 1960: p. 198). To deny that there were no real antagonisms with the major capitalist powers was heresy indeed.

The new Party secretary, Brezhnev, found his power circumscribed by his colleagues within the Presidium, by men like Kosygin, Podgorny, Mikoyan and Suslov. Whatever may have been the power conflicts between them, however, they showed every intention of following the foreign policy laid down in the post-Stalin years. Yet differences made themselves felt. The Chinese had shown their personal abhorrence of Khrushchev and his removal was an opportunity for fence mending. This was the purpose of Zhou Enlai's visit to Moscow in November 1964 and Kosygin's visit to Beijing in February 1965. But as neither side was prepared to make any meaningful concessions the polemics broke out again when the consultative meeting of Communist Parties, scheduled to be held in December 1964, met in Moscow in March 1965. After that the situation rapidly deteriorated and resulted in major fighting in 1969 and possibly even an intention to take out China's nuclear capacity by a pre-emptive strike. Moreover the situation of the two communist powers changed radically in the Brezhnev era. The Soviets intervened frequently in the affairs of southern Asia. Although in 1965 they acted as peacemakers in the Indo-Pakistani conflict their friendship treaty with India in 1971 was followed by the dismemberment of Pakistan. Equally the treaty signed with Vietnam in 1978 was followed by the liquidation of the Khmer Rouge in Kampuchea. The invasion of Afghanistan was the first time Soviet armed forces had spread communism beyond the borders of the USSR since 1945. These moves extended Soviet influence at the expense of the old enemy, the USA, but also the new enemy, China. It was natural that this increased activity should result in a new constellation of forces. Kissinger went to Beijing in July 1971, to be followed by Nixon in February 1972. There was danger here for the Soviets, but the USA attachment to détente prevented them from exploiting fully this opportunity.

Ideologically the new regime was more conservative and more orthodox than the one it had replaced. It showed a greater readiness to listen to the military and this in turn enhanced its conservative character. Under such influences the aggressiveness in Asia, Africa and Latin America of the Khrushchev regime was enhanced. Moreover it had at its disposal military and logistic capabilities which Khrushchev did not have. It continued to support Nasser and his successor Sadat until the break in relations in 1972. Indeed, after the Six Days' War it provided air cover for Egypt and the Suez Canal. Also, it was responsible for one important innovation: the use of Cuban troops in various parts of Africa and in particular in Angola and Ethiopia to bolster up Marxist regimes. In return Cuba – and Vietnam too – became members of CMEA and the recipients of aid. In 1970 the Soviets began to build a nuclear submarine base at Cienfugos in Cuba, only to dismantle it under US pressure. But the Soviets were cautious. Another suppliant, Allende, went to Moscow to ask, so it was reported, for 500 million dollars of hard currency loans. All he got was a credit for 30 million dollars. For the Soviets Chile was too far away and too exposed; in any case Allende would not accept a Soviet military presence in Chile.

In the middle 1970s the international situation changed to the disadvantage of the West. Earlier the Brezhnev leadership had supported détente. In August 1968, the month of the Czechoslovak invasion, the Soviets agreed to SALT negotiations. The talks began in October 1969 and the SALT treaty together with an agreement on basic principles of relations was signed by Nixon in Moscow in May 1972. In June 1973 in Washington Brezhnev signed an agreement on the prevention of nuclear war. But the high-water mark had been reached. Four factors brought about a radical change in Soviet policy and the gradual retreat from détente. The oil-price increase following the Yom Kippur War had brought about a major crisis in the Western economic system. Second, US aggressiveness was paralysed in the later stages of the Vietnam War, by Watergate and by Nixon's resignation in August 1974. Third, in April 1975 the Vietnamese overran South Vietnam, certain that the Americans would do nothing. Finally the Export–Import Bank Act of December 1974 banning the use of any moneys to be loaned to the Soviets for energy development and production made them question the value of détente. It would be wrong to suppose that the Soviets wished to abandon détente. Their relations with the USA and their dependence on America was as great as ever. It was only that under the umbrella of détente their arsenal of nuclear and conventional weapons permitted them to challenge the USA more frequently and in more places.

11 Defence and Security

CHRISTOPH BLUTH

11.1   THE SHIFT IN SOVIET STRATEGIC THOUGHT AFTER THE DEATH OF STALIN

The Soviet Union came into being as a revolutionary state whose ideology was based on values and concepts fundamentally hostile to Western capitalist systems; its ultimate goal was the destruction of the imperialist powers and the world-wide establishment of socialism. Lenin declared that war was inevitable, since ultimately capitalism and socialism could not coexist. While on the one hand war was seen as intrinsic to imperialism, on the other hand revolutionary wars to spread socialism were by no means ruled out. The Allied intervention against the revolutionary regime, the punitive *cordon sanitaire* of Versailles and 'capitalist encirclements' as well as the post-war policies of containment and 'roll-back' created the perception of a very hostile international environment, thus strengthening the notion of the basic contradictions between capitalism and socialism and the perspective of the inevitability of war due to the aggressive nature of imperialism.

Stalin's understanding of the nature and role of war does not seem to have been affected by the advent of nuclear weapons. In 1942 he spoke of the 'permanently operating factors' which he saw as being decisive in war. As H. S. Dinerstein writes:

> Stalin's position was that was was a massive social phenomenon in which two or more societies were pitted against one another. In this contest all the strength and weakness of the societies came into play. It was not a gladiatorial contest in which the superior skill of one man, or the accident of, say, a man stumbling over a stone, could determine the outcome.

194

Since war is a social phenomenon, the laws of society were applicable to it. In the special context of warfare, what were known as the 'permanently operating factors' would determine the outcome. These factors were 'the stability of the rear, the morale of the army, the quantity and quality of divisions, the armament of the army, the organizational ability of the army commanders'. (Dinerstein, 1962: p. 6).

This remained the framework of the strategic discussion in the Soviet Union until the death of Stalin. Although Stalin obviously recognised that atomic bombs were important, since a great effort was made to break the American atomic monopoly, it was denied that nuclear weapons would by themselves suffice to produce victory, and their significance was played down. This may be due in part to the limited stockpile of atomic weapons in existence at the time, and also the Western lead in this area. It is important to note, however, that the existence of nuclear weapons did not significantly affect the Soviet understanding of the nature and role of war or its strategy during the Stalin era.

Stalin's death in 1953 had a profound effect on all aspects of Soviet politics. The immediate result was a power vacuum in which all the various Soviet institutions and vested interests increased in importance and attempted to assert themselves. The result was a major controversy about economic and military policies, accompanied by intense power struggles. Stalin's successor as Prime Minister, Georgy Malenkov, pursued a strategy of increasing the power of governmental and managerial institutions, to the detriment of the bureaucracy of the Communist Party (Garthoff, 1966: p. 48; Medvedev and Medvedev, 1977 ch. 1). He attempted to shift resources from heavy industry to consumer-goods industries and agriculture. The military budget was reduced in 1953 and 1954.

The shift in the allocation of resources and the ensuing power struggle was accompanied by a shift in thought about war and defence resulting in a vigorous debate about these issues. In September 1953 Major-General Talensky published an article in the journal *Voennaya Mysl* which criticised the prevailing understanding, particularly the application of the principle of 'permanently operating factors', and hinted at the possible effect of nuclear weapons on the conduct of war (*Voennaya Mysl*, 9/1953). This initiated a debate on Soviet military doctrine reaching into the highest levels of the Soviet military and government. Malenkov himself defended the view that nuclear weapons had a very radical impact on the nature of war and the military posture that should be adopted by the Soviet Union. He declared that a thermonuclear war would mean 'the destruction of world civilisation' (*Pravda*, 13 Mar 1954). It was no longer to be taken for granted that socialist countries would prevail in a war with capitalist countries. A nuclear war would result in the destruction of both capitalist and socialist nations. Hence Malenkov advocated a minimum deterrent to prevent aggression by capitalist nations and vigorously denounced the Cold War.

The Malenkov faction was opposed by Khrushchev and Bulganin, in alliance with military interests. In the light of Khrushchev's later policies it appears likely that his alliance with those who emphasised military preparedness and rearmament as opposed to minimum deterrence was largely politically motivated. Horelick and Rush conclude their analysis of this power struggle in this way: 'The post-Stalin debate in military circles on the revision of Soviet military doctrine, centering on the role of strategic surprise in nuclear war, coincided with the struggle between Malenkov and his presidium opponents and reached its culminating point precisely at the time of Malenkov's defeat' (Horelick and Rush, 1966: p. 22). In February 1955 Malenkov resigned as Prime Minister and the military budget was raised by 12 per cent.

11.2 THE DEVELOPMENT OF STRATEGIC POWER UNDER KHRUSHCHEV

At the time of Stalin's death in 1953 the USSR had a limited stockpile of atomic bombs and only obsolescent bombers of limited range to deliver them (the TU–4) (their range was insufficient for two-way missions to the USA). However, research and development of atomic weapons and delivery systems was in progress. In August 1953 the USSR exploded a thermonuclear device. Among the new developments were a new twin-turbojet medium-range bomber (the Badger) and two modern types of heavy bomber with intercontinental range (the four turbo-jet Bison and the multi-turboprop Bison) (Horelick and Rush, 1966: p. 17). In 1957 the USSR surprised the world by the launch of the Sputnik (on 4 Oct), thus demonstrating that it possessed the technology to develop intercontinental ballistic missiles (ICBM). In the same year ICBM development claims were made. In the period from November 1958 to October 1959 a number of public statements were designed, it seems, to create the impression that the Soviet Union was rapidly proceeding with the production of

ICBMs – Khrushchev and Defence Minister Malinovsky claimed to have achieved nuclear parity with the USA, and in early 1960 the capability was claimed to wipe any country that dared attack the USSR off the map by using rockets carrying atomic and thermo-nuclear warheads (Horelick and Rush, 1966: p. 59).

In reality, however, there was no such capability. A decision had obviously been made not to deploy the first-generation ICBM (SS–6) in more than token numbers. By 1960 the Soviet Union had deployed a total of four ICBMs and 145 heavy bombers of inter-continental range (see Table 11.1). Nevertheless there was some degree of uncertainty in the West regarding Soviet capabilities, given the lack of technical means at the time for aerial reconnaissance. President John F. Kennedy promised to redress the alleged 'missile gap' with respect to the Soviet Union in his election campaign. Although reliable data about Soviet rocket capabilities were not available until the advent of spy satellites in 1961, the overflight of the Soviet Union by U–2 spy-planes which became dramatically public when one of them was shot down made the Soviet leadership aware of the fact that the game might now be up. Although the Soviet Union did not admit to its lack of rocket facilities, in public pronouncements the emphasis was shifted from stressing Soviet capabilities to warnings about the mutually disastrous consequences of war. Horelick and Rush comment: 'The retreat in Soviet strategic claims that was evident after the U–2 incident continued and became even more pronounced in the winter of 1961' (Horelick and Rush, 1966: p. 82). The myth of the missile gap finally collapsed after September 1961 when Joseph Alsop, until then a strong critic of 'understated' estimates of Soviet missile strength, published an article confirming that the USSR was now believed to have no more than a handful of ICBMs. Indeed it seems that by 1960 the USSR had deployed a total of four SS–6, together with 145 heavy bombers of intercontinental range (the latter being much more susceptible, of course, to defensive measures (Berman and Baker, 1982: p. 42) (see Table 11.1).

The development of Soviet military power, in particular the capability to deliver nuclear strikes, was far more impressive in the European region (see Table 11.7). In 1955 the Soviet Union had 1296 bombers for use in a regional theatre, 25 battlefield nuclear missiles and a total estimated stockpile of 324 warheads (implying that many of the bombers would be used with conventional weapons). By 1960 a total of 200 medium-range land-based missiles had been deployed (SS–3 and SS–4), thus providing a considerably enhanced nuclear capability against Western Europe. In addition the number of battle-field nuclear missiles had been doubled (although this hardly consti-tuted a large-scale deployment) and nuclear submarines were carrying 36 medium-range sea-based missiles. There had been no increase in the number of medium-range bombers, but the stockpile of warheads had jumped to 1328 (of which 294 were designated for intercontinental delivery and 1034 for regional deployment). The deployment of medium-range missiles continued and by the time Khrushchev left office there were 705 such missiles deployed, while the number of bombers had been reduced to 880 and the number of medium-range sea-based missiles had grown to 105.

Second- and third-generation missiles with intercontinental range, the SS-7, SS-8, SS-9, SS-11 and SS-13 were already in development in the late 1950s. The deployment of SS-7 and SS-8 missiles did not get under way until 1962, but by the time Khrushchev left office the number of ICBMs deployed had risen to 224. The third-generation missiles were not deployed before 1965.

Development of an anti-ballistic missile system was apparently initiated in 1957 (Ghebhardt, 1975: p. 14). In 1958 the air-defence command was reorganised in anticipation of ABM deployment. The command split into the PSO (*protivo-samoletnaya oborona*) and the PRO (*protivo-raketnaya oborona*). In line with the general exagger-ation of Soviet strategic capabilities Khrushchev made some bold claims about Soviet ABM capabilities in 1961 and 1962. In 1962 the SAM–5 missile, code-named Griffon, was deployed around Lenin-grad. A second-generation ABM intended for deployment around Moscow, code-named Galosh by NATO, was shown on Red Square three weeks after the fall of Khrushchev, on 7 November 1964. The Soviet Union did not develop a nationwide ABM system, but accepted a restriction to 200 launchers (later reduced to 100) in the ABM Treaty of 1972.

11.3   KHRUSHCHEV'S ASCENDANCY 1955–60

Khrushchev's rise to power was based on an alliance with military interests, and the period from February 1955 to October 1957 'may best be understood in terms of an alliance between Khrushchev and Zhukov' (Garthoff, 1966: p. 49) whom Khrushchev rehabilitated and made Minister of Defence. Although Khrushchev came to power by opposing Malenkov's policies, it became evident in the course of the two following years that his own priorities were tending in the same direction, namely investment in consumer-goods industries and agriculture. In foreign policy Khrushchev did much to play down the danger of war; 1955 was seen as a year in which the international situation improved greatly. During the XX CPSU Congress in February 1956 Khrushchev went so far as to deny explicitly Lenin's concept of the inevitability of war (Garthoff, 1966: p. 96). His denunciation of Stalin in a secret session during the same congress also indicated the changes that were taking place (Wolfe, 1957). The new military technology of missiles and thermonuclear weapons clearly influenced Khrushchev's view of a proper military posture for the Soviet Union. His memoirs, for example, provide evidence of his fascination with missile technology and his conviction of its importance (Khrushchev, 1974: p. 22). The emphasis he placed on missiles and nuclear weapons led to conflicts with Zhukov, but for some time the Khrushchev–Zhukov axis remained intact. Zukov's support was crucial when Malenkov, Molotov and Kaganovich attempted to depose Khrushchev in June 1957. However, by October conflicts with Zhukov with regard to the political control of the military and the perception of a 'personality cult' led to his removal from office and the appointment of Malinovsky (Garthoff, 1966: pp. 52–4; Gosztony, 1980: pp. 340 ff.).

Despite Khrushchev's emphasis on peaceful coexistence and the dangers of war the Soviet Union pursued an apparently quite aggressive foreign policy. During the Suez crisis in November 1956 the Soviets 'rattled their rockets', and the USA let it be known that any missile attack on Britain or France would meet with US retaliation.

It seems that this was the first attempt by the Soviet leadership to use nuclear weapons to political advantage. It was based on bluff and did not succeed in its objective.

In October 1957 the Soviet Union claimed that Turkey was planning a military attack on Syria and threatened unspecified countermeasures. Although there was internal unrest in Syria such an attack was evidently never planned in the first place. A similar situation arose in 1958 in Iraq when there was a military coup, and Lebanon and Jordan asked for and received direct military aid (including marines and troops) from the USA and Britain. The Soviet Union threatened vague countermeasures against any intervention in Iraq, which again had not been planned. In the same year Khrushchev announced support for Chinese attacks on the islands of Quemoy and Matsu, and said that any attack on China would mean war with the USSR. His support did not, however, translate into tangible assistance, and he left it suitably unclear what would constitute an attack on China. The Chinese failed in their objectives.

One of the most notable foreign-policy ventures was the Berlin Crisis that began in 1958. As the launch of the Sputnik and Soviet claims in the field of ICBM development had created the impression in the West of a Soviet lead in ICBMs, Khrushchev attempted to convert his imaginary strategic superiority to political advantage. From 1958 to 1961 Khrushchev put pressure on the Western allies with a series of ultimata with the apparent objective of removing any Western presence from West Berlin. Although the Soviet Union had a clear local military superiority, and for some time there was a degree of uncertainty with regard to the global strategic balance,the Western allies refused to yield and despite various threats Khrushchev was never prepared to risk an actual military confrontation (Slusser, 1973).

Internally Khrushchev was in a strong position in 1959 (Linden, 1966). He thus was able to promote his policies further. In December 1959 the Strategic Rocket Forces were established as a separate service responsible for regional and intercontinental missile forces. The SRF were declared to be the pre-eminent service in wartime (instead of the Ground Forces). There was also a shift from strategic bomber to missile production (Berman and Baker, 1982: p. 46). In January 1960, during a speech before the Supreme Soviet, Khrushchev declared the primary importance of nuclear weapons and missiles. He emphasised that many of the traditional armed forces were becoming obsolete, that the initial phase of a nuclear war would probably be decisive and that such a war would be of short duration. However, he was confident that the Soviet Union would be able to survive such a war, even if it was attacked first, particularly if it took advantage of its size to camouflage and disperse its weapons. He also believed that the 'imperialist camp' was deterred by the strength of Soviet military forces and then announced a reduction in manpower in the Soviet armed forces from 3.6 million to 2.4 million men. He emphasised that nuclear firepower would more than make up for the reduction in manpower (*Pravda*, 15 Jan 1960).

There were several different strands that made up this policy. The first was clearly a new understanding of the nature of war in the nuclear age. Domestic priorities, however, were also an important factor. There was a manpower shortage in agriculture, and Khrushchev wanted again to shift resources from the military to agriculture and consumer-goods industry. His approach was bound to lead to resentment and conflict with the military. Thus Marshal Konev, for example, was removed from his post of Commander-in-Chief of Warsaw Pact Forces after disagreements with Khrushchev about his one-sided reliance on rocket forces. In April 1960 Marshal V. D. Sokolovsky had a row with Khrushchev about the manpower reductions with Sokolovsky demanding more resources for the modernisation of the air and ground forces. As a result Sokolovsky was asked to resign. At the beginning of 1960 Khrushchev was powerful enough to deal with any dissent and force his policies through.

The military must have been quite alarmed at Khrushchev's policy, not only because their own institutional power was to some extent threatened, but also because Khrushchev was basing Soviet foreign and military policies so completely on a Soviet ICBM capability which to a large extent did not exist. Why did Soviet leaders allow such a margin of superiority to develop in favour of the USA with regard to intercontinental delivery vehicles?

It seems fairly clear that although the SS–6 was used in large numbers for the Soviet space programme, there were considerable technical difficulties associated with its deployment as an ICBM. It used a highly unstable propellant which could not be stored, and furthermore needed ground-stations for guidance (Berman and Baker, 1982: p. 49). A second generation of ICBM was already being developed, but although Khrushchev was using nuclear weapons to argue for reduced military allocations, he may at the same time not have been prepared to invest enough to create rapidly a credible strategic strike force.

There are indications in some of Khrushchev's public statements that he was fairly convinced that there was no danger of an attack from the USA in the forseeable future (Horelick and Rush, 1966). One reason for this confidence may have been the growth of Soviet regional power in Europe, thus holding Western Europe hostage against American attack. In 1960 the USSR had 1296 bombers and 200 missiles deployed in Europe (plus 48 battlefield nuclear missiles). The resources of the SRF were apparently deliberately concentrated on building up military capabilities in Europe (one reason being most likely the state of missile technology) (Wolfe, 1970: pp. 152–4). None the less it is quite extraordinary that such an adventurous foreign policy was being pursued on the basis of strategic bluff. Horelick and Rush point out the dangers inherent in this approach: the bluff must never be called. While the West could discover the truth about Soviet capabilities (and did) the USSR could not easily risk finding out how far the West could be pushed.

Furthermore many aspects of Soviet foreign policy during the Khrushchev period starkly contradicted Khrushchev's emphasis on peaceful coexistence and détente. While some of these contradictions may have owed their origin to Khrushchev himself, it is also clear that he was not always the master of events and was at times driven to certain policies as the result of his power struggles with the military and the supporters of different economic and foreign policies.

11.4 THE POWER STRUGGLE IN THE KREMLIN 1960–4

There is no doubt that in response to Khrushchev's speech in January 1960 his opponents began to gather their forces. It was not merely the military, but, as John Dornberg put it, 'a conglomerate coalition of guardians of Communist orthodoxy, members of the military establishment and cold warriors' (Dornberg, 1974: p. 149). Among the most powerful hard-liners who had already at times forced a hardening of the stance towards the West were Mikhail Suslov and Frol Kozlov. The rival faction in the Soviet leadership argued strongly in favour of developing Soviet military strength and was opposed to this new view of a more permanent peaceful coexistence. Instead the Soviet Union should use its military strength to pursue a more aggressive strategy against capitalism and bring about its collapse. This, of course, was also the argument of the Chinese, and Edward Crankshaw has noted that 'from 1960 onwards it was quite impossible to understand Khrushchev's foreign policy, and a good deal of his domestic policy too, except in the light of his life and death struggle with China'. (Crankshaw, 1966; p. 274). It seems that the attitude to China was also a major point of contention within the Soviet leadership and that Kozlov supported the Chinese in some of their arguments with Khrushchev, particularly with regard to the posture *vis-à-vis* the West (Slusser, 1973: p. 214).

The first opening for the Kozlov faction came in May 1960 when the U–2 spy-plane of Gary Powers was shot down over Sverdlovsk. As a result Khrushchev's missile bluff was now clearly in danger of being exposed and the credibility of his military and foreign policies undermined. Furthermore the incident was a blow against Khrushchev's policy of rapprochement with the West, in particular since Eisenhower claimed personal responsibility for the overflights. At a Central Committee meeting three days after the U–2 incident the Party Secretariat was drastically reduced in size and Frol Kozlov was put in *de facto* control over it. Three men who were in no sense Khrushchev protégés were promoted to full membership in the Party Presidium: Dmitri Polyansky, Nikolai Podgorny and Aleksei Kosygin, the last being also appointed First Deputy Prime Minister (Dornberg, 1974: p. 160).

Possibly as a result of the growing strength of the Kozlov–Suslov faction Khrushchev subsequently pursued a more aggressive foreign policy, which was initiated by the break-up of the Paris Summit and a renewal of demands for a solution to the Berlin situation. The ups and downs of the Berlin crisis during the following year defy a rational account and it seems a likely explanation that they were a manifestation of a deep power struggle in the Soviet leadership. In the light of the worsening international situation Khrushchev was obliged to renege on some of his objectives; the manpower cut in the armed services had to be postponed and in 1961 and 1962 there was an increase in military expenditure (see Table 11.6). Later in 1961 Khrushchev was compelled to announce the resumption of nuclear tests, thus breaking a moratorium that had been observed by both the USSR and the US. The Berlin crisis seemed to reach its culmination when Khrushchev caught the West by surprise in permitting the building of the wall on 13 August to stem the tide of refugees from East Germany. The resulting stabilisation of the GDR was an essential prerequisite for the abatement of the Berlin crisis and the eventual regularisation of the status of West Berlin.

The climax of Khrushchev's power struggle with Kozlov seems to have been the XX Party Congress of the CPSU in October 1961, when Khrushchev managed to reassert his authority, albeit with some definite concessions to the Kozlov faction (Slusser, 1973: ch. 9).

Some analysts believe that 1961 marked a significant turning-point in Soviet strategic arms policy after the failure of the policy of strategic bluff, and in response to the international tension and the military build-up of the Kennedy administration. Thus Michael MccGwire argues that Marshal Malinovsky's speech at the XXII Party Congress 'clearly indicated a return to the traditional military values' (MccGwire, 1981: p. 216). He believes that this was a 'blow to Khrushchev's policies and vindicated those who argued that professional military opinion should prevail in matters of national defence'. In MccGwire's view this reversion to earlier views was a response to the defence policy decisions by the Kennedy administration, the perception of an increased threat and a greater likelihood of war. However, although Malinovsky's speech would confirm this impression at first glance, this would constitute a rather superficial interpretation of events at the XXII Party Congress, which took place in the midst of intense conflict. Thomas Wolfe interprets Malinovsky's speech as an attempt to compromise between the various factions (Wolfe, 1974: pp. 33 ff.). Roman Kolkowicz suggests that in the early 1960s the 'Stalingrad Group' of top military officials with which Khrushchev had close links (Kolkowicz, 1967: pp. 224–55) divided into two factions. The group which included Marshals Malinovsky and Grechko 'viewed their obligations to the military establishment as paramount to others' (Kolkowicz, 1967: p. 239), whereas Moskalenko and others were primarily loyal to Khrushchev. Whatever factional interests Malinvosky may have represented it is probably the best interpretation that the message from the XXII Party Congress was not very clear and represented some sort of compromise to pacify everyone. It was at the XXII Party Congress after all, when it was revealed that peaceful coexistence with capitalism was the general and permanent line, that war was not only not inevitable, but also not desirable or permissible to advance socialism, that communism in the USSR could be built while capitalism still existed in the world and that a peaceful transition to socialism was to be expected in capitalist countries (Garthoff, 1966: p. 96; Slusser, 1973: ch. 9; *XXII Sezd Kommunisticheskoi Partii Sovetskogo Soyuza*, 1962).

It is therefore far from clear to what extent Khrushchev was forced to change direction. There was obviously a doctrinal debate going on with regard to such questions as the size of the armed forces, the nature of the initial period of a war, the likely duration of a war, the role of strategic nuclear forces as opposed to ground forces, the likelihood of escalation of small wars, the likelihood of war with the West and the proper role of the military in the formulation of defence policy and strategy (Wolfe, 1964: pp. 33 ff.). The debate between Khrushchev and the supporters of a more traditional approach was reflected in the important work *Voennaya Strategiya*, edited by Marshal Sokolovsky and first published in 1962. While it agreed with many of Khrushchev's statements about nuclear war, by emphasising the importance of strategic rocket forces and the decisive importance of the initial period of the war, it also stressed the role of ground forces, declaring that nuclear war would be conducted by mass armies, and left the possibility open that the war might also be protracted (Sokolovsky, 1962; Wolfe, 1964; ch. IV; Holloway, 1983: pp. 40–3). The second edition which was published in 1963 was thoroughly reworked and reflected a number of interesting developments, but as far as the debate about strategic doctrine is concerned, it represented the same sort of balance as the first edition (Wolfe, 1964: ch. IV; Holloway, 1983: pp. 40–3).

Khrushchev's basic dilemma, however, remained: in view of the domestic priorities of agriculture, chemical and consumer-goods industries, how could he reduce investments in heavy metal industries and military expenditures, given his lack of foreign-policy successes and the inadequacy of Soviet strategic power which had become much more obvious? The USA had already acquired such a lead in strategic capabilities that it seemed impossible for the Soviet Union to catch up gradually. This forms the background to Khrushchev's decision in 1962 to install medium-range missiles in Cuba. The idea was to install the missiles in secret and present the world with a *fait accompli* that would be difficult to challenge. But the plan went wrong in that the Americans discovered what was going on far too soon and instituted a naval blockade around Cuba. They also threatened further military action if the missiles were not removed, the clear implication being that the USA was willing to risk an escalation even to the level of all-out nuclear war. The result was a humiliating defeat for the Soviet Union and the withdrawal of the missiles from Cuba. The attempt to achieve a sudden change in the strategic balance in favour of the Soviet Union had failed (Abel, 1966).

The Cuban missile crisis represented above all a deep personal defeat for Khrushchev, and there is some evidence that in its aftermath the conflict between him and the military reached a high point in early 1963. In March the long-standing effort by Khrushchev's opponents to reverse his policies of decentralisation reached their climax at a time when Khrushchev must have been politically weak. This becomes apparent from the drastic organisational changes that were announced on 13 March which involved nothing less than 'a mass promotion of all the top officials in the defence industry, the heavy industry lobby and other 'steel-eaters' against whom Khrushchev had been fighting ever since 1960' (Tatu, 1969: p. 329). The central element of the announcement of 13 March concerned the creation of a Supreme *Sovnarkhoz* at the apex of the administrative structure, to eliminate the disputes and rivalries among Gosplan, the federal *Sovnarkhoz* and the many other federal agencies created by Khrushchev's reforms in 1957. It is clear that Khrushchev was diametrically opposed to the idea of a Supreme *Sovnarkhoz* and the decision of 13 March constituted therefore a significant political defeat. What is significant for our study is the remarkable fact that the person entrusted with the management of the Supreme *Sovnarkhoz* was none other than D. F. Ustinov, who was thus promoted to First Deputy Chairman of the Council of Ministers. In this way what Veron V. Aspaturian has called 'the emerging military–industrial apparatus coaliton' (*Journal of International Affairs*, 26/1, (1972), pp. 1–28) gained important influence in the state administration. The driving force behind these changes was no doubt Frol Kozlov.

As a consequence of Kozlov's illness (he suffered a stroke in April 1963) Khrushchev made a substantial political recovery, and although he did not reverse the changes made in March, he managed to reassert some of his control over the system. He made a speech in which he upbraided the armament producers and particularly Ustinov (Tatu, 1969: pp. 343 ff.) warning them that it was out of the question that 'the Soviet Union will now only make missiles' (*Pravda*, 26 Apr 1963).

These controversies are significant because at that time the third generation of ICBMs was reaching its final stage of development. It appears that as the defence industry and the proponents of a build-up in the Soviet force posture gained influence in early 1963, this also involved plans to invest more in the production of missiles – hence Khrushchev's comments. No doubt resources were made available for the production of prototypes and the reconstruction of silos, given that the first test-flight of the SS–9 was reported in July 1964 (Freedman, 1977: p. 107) and by the end of 1964 42 hardened silos for the SS–9 had been discovered by US intelligence. It may be that Khrushchev's political comeback reimposed some limitations on the plans for missile production, and the deployment programme which emerged in 1964 was therefore comparatively modest.

In 1963 Khrushchev also began to reassert visibly his priorities on the military. Marshal M. V. Zakharov was dismissed as Chief of the General Staff for demanding a more balanced development of all forces. Marshal Biryuzov, who took his place, reiterated the old Khrushchev line of the decisive role of nuclear weapons (having been Commander-in-Chief of the SRF). Thus there was a reduction of military manpower by 300 000 men, and on 13 December 1963 Khrushchev announced further personnel reductions and a reduced military budget for 1964. In 1964 the Ground Forces were even abolished as a separate service with its own high command structure, and instead were to be administered by the General Staff. The year 1963 also saw the successful negotiation of a partial test-ban treaty with the USA, which became possible as a part of the general relaxation of tension after both sides had been faced with the stark reality of being at the brink of nuclear war during the Cuban missile crisis.

The inherent contradictions in Khrushchev's policies and the antagonism he provoked finally led to his downfall in 1964. As a result of his foreign policy failures, of which the Cuban missile crisis in particular had exposed various shortcomings in Soviet capabilities, most of all in regard of nuclear strategic forces and the navy, and his determined attempts to shift resources from the military and heavy industry to other sectors of the economy, the military mounted a vigorous campaign against Khrushchev (see, for example, Sokolovsky and Cherednichenko in *Krasnaya Zvezda*, 28 Aug 1964). The military supported the opposition to Khrushchev which was in part motivated by the failure of his agricultural programmes. Khrushchev was ousted in October 1964.

11.5   CONCLUSION: THE EVOLUTION OF THE SOVIET FORCE POSTURE IN THE 1960s

The new leadership took over in the Kremlin in 1964 having rejected many central aspects of Khrushchev's foreign, military and economic policies. His foreign policy was considered to have been a failure. His bombastic and adventurous style, followed by inevitable and at times humiliating retreats, such as at Suez, Berlin and most of all Cuba, was rejected as a dangerous form of gambling where Khrushchev had frequently overreached himself, seeking objectives he did not have the means to obtain (Dornberg, 1974: ch. XII; Medvedev and Medvedev, 1977: ch. 15). This analysis had a direct bearing on strategic-arms policy, since Khrushchev's failure to translate Soviet military might into political gain could at least in part be attributed to Soviet strategic inferiority. These views were apparently reinforced by an increase in international tension with the escalation of the US involvement in Vietnam and the intervention in the Dominican Republic. It appeared to the Kremlin that the USA was exploiting its strategic superiority in the pursuit of a more adventurous foreign policy than would otherwise be the case (see, for example, Suslov's speech in Sofia, quoted in *Pravda*, 5 June 1965). Thus Leonid I. Brezhnev and others endorsed the already growing conviction that the Soviet Union should increase its strategic effort to catch up with the USA.

With the advent of the Brezhnev regime the constant dispute about the nature of the Soviet force posture and the share of the resources allocated to heavy industry and the military was at least partially resolved in favour of heavy industry and an all-round build-up of conventional and nuclear strategic forces. There was a general reorganisation of the defence establishment, with D. F. Ustinov remaining the dominating figure in the defence industries. The year 1965 also saw the creation of the Ministry of General Machine-building exclusively concerned with the production of ballistic missiles, another strong indication of the new emphasis placed on increasing strategic strength by the deployment of ICBMs in large numbers. One must also note the increase in the importance of the General Staff. Immediately after Khrushchev's fall Marshal Biryuzov was killed in an aircraft accident and Marshal M. V. Zakharov was reinstated in his old post. This was a significant move, since Zakharov was clearly allied with Khrushchev's military critics. In the subsequent internal debates about ABM deployment, Zakharov turned out to be a significant supporter of the build-up of Soviet ICBM forces as opposed to missile defence (Ghebhardt, 1975: p. 86; Erickson, 1971: pp. 9–11). The first third-generation missile to become available for deployment was the SS–9. In the late 1960s there was much speculation about the SS–9 as a possible counterforce weapon, given its enormous throw-weight (it originally carried a 20-megaton warhead) but it seems unlikely that it was originally designed for this role. Given Khrushchev's penchant for multi-megaton weapons, it promised to be an effective successor to the SS–7. The testing of warheads for the SS–9 and SS–11 missiles most probably took place under the auspices of the Ministry of Medium Machine-building in 1961–2 (Berman and Baker, 1982: p. 80). The decision to make funds available for the construction of prototypes with the view to at least a limited deployment of the SS–9 was most likely made in early 1963. The choice of the SS–9 may have been influenced at this point by the simple fact that it was the most advanced third-generation ICBM available. Khrushchev apparently had some interest in the fractional orbital bombardment system

(FOBS), which was the kind of spectacular weapon that fitted in well with his boastful announcements about Soviet military capabilities designed to support his foreign policy ventures. Development of the system began during his time, and it was based on the SS–9 – possibly another reason why the SS–9 found support.

When the decision was made (after Khrushchev's fall) to go for strategic parity with the USA, the SS–9 became an important component of the Soviet strategic arsenal. The main role in countering the large number of American Minuteman missiles was given, however, to the SS–11. The main reason for this must be that the SS–9 was a very large missile, not so easily deployed in large number, whereas the SS–11 was more comparable to the Minuteman in size and payload.

The original intention behind the development of the SS–11 was apparently that it should be used against nuclear-armed carrier-based aircraft (Berman and Baker, 1982: p. 121). The first test-flight of the SS–11 did not take place until after Khrushchev's fall. There must therefore have been a complete change in the mission objectives of the SS–11 some time in 1965. Thomas Wolfe, taking into account the time needed for launching-site construction, concludes that the production and deployment decisions with regard to the SS–11 were taken shortly after the advent of the new regime (Wolfe, 1970: p. 432). The SS–11 was then deployed in very large numbers, reaching 720 in 1970, whereas the SS–9 was deployed at a constant rate of 49 missiles per year, levelling off at a total of about 280 missiles.

This analysis indicates how institutional interests, growing threat perceptions in a hostile environment and the evolution of Soviet military strategy all combined to produce the Soviet force posture which emerged in the late 1960s.

TABLE 11.1   *Development of Soviet ICBM Deployment 1960–70*

Year	SS–6	SS–7/8	SS–9	SS–11	SS–13	Total
1960	4	–	–	–	–	4
1961	4	46	–	–	–	50
1962	4	71	–	–	–	75
1963	4	87	–	–	–	91
1964	4	196	–	–	–	200
1965	4	220	–	–	–	220
1966	4	220	72	48	–	344
1967	–	220	114	236	–	570
1968	–	220	156	520	–	896
1969	–	220	198	644	15	1077
1970	–	220	240	720	40	1220

TABLE 11.2   *Development of Soviet SLBM Deployment 1960–70*

Year	SS–N–4/SS–N–5	SS–N–6	Total
1960	36	–	36
1961	36+	–	36+
1962	36+	–	36+
1963	117	–	117
1964	117	–	117
1965	117	–	117
1966	117	–	117
1967	117	–	117
1968	117	32	149
1969	117	128	245
1970	117	224	341

TABLE 11.3   *Soviet Deployment of Bombers with Intercontinental Range 1960–70*

Year	TU–20 Bear	MYA–4 Bison	Total
1960	60	100	160
1961	70	120	190
1962	70	120	190
1963	70	120	190
1964	70	120	190
1965	80	120	200
1966	90	110	200
1967	90	110	200
1968	90	110	200
1969	90	110	200
1970	100	90	190

TABLE 11.4   *Megatonnage Deliverable by Soviet ICBMs 1960–70*

Year	ICBM	SLBM	Total
1960	20	126	146
1961	158	126 +	284 +
1962	233	126 +	359 +
1963	281	468	749
1964	866	468	1334
1965	1010	468	1478
1966	2495.6	468	2963.6
1967	3494.2	468	3962.2
1968	4604	490.4	5094.4
1969	5570.8	557.6	6128.4
1970	6498	624.8	7122.8

TABLE 11.5 *Estimated Throw Weight of Soviet ICBMs 1960–70 (in pounds)*

Year	Throw Weight Total
1960	32 000
1961	193 000
1962	280 500
1963	336 500
1964	718 000
1965	802 000
1966	1 594 000
1967	2 264 000
1968	3 110 000
1969	3 731 000
1970	4 290 000

TABLE 11.6 *USSR Military Budget 1960–70*

Year	Defence Budget (in billion roubles)	Defence Budget (per cent of total budget)
1960	9.3	12.7
1961	11.6	15.2
1962	12.6	13.9
1963	13.9	15.9
1964	13.3	14.4
1960	12.8	12.6
1966	13.4	12.7
1967	14.5	13.2
1968	16.7	13.5
1969	17.7	13.2
1970	17.9	12.4

TABLE 11.7 *Soviet Regional Power 1960–70*

LANDBASED MISSILES

Year	SS–3	SS–4	SS–5	SS–11	SS–12	SS–14	Total
1960	48	200	0	0	0	0	248
1965	28	608	97	0	0	0	733
1970	0	508	90	290	54	29	971

BOMBERS

Year	TU–4	TU–16	TU–22	Total
1960	296	1000	0	1296
1965	0	775	105	880
1970	0	550	174	724

TABLE 11.8 *Total Soviet Military Manpower 1960–70*

1960	3 623 000
1961	3 000 000
1962	3 600 000
1963	3 300 000
1964	3 300 000
1965	3 150 000
1966	3 220 000
1967	3 220 000
1968	3 220 000
1969	3 300 000
1970	3 305 000

Tables 11.1–11.8 have been carefully reconstructed from the following sources: Robert P. Berman, *Soviet Air Power in Transition* (Washington, DC, Brookings Institution 1978; Robert P. Berman, and John C. Baker (1982); Lawrence Freedman, (1977); International Institute for Strategic Studies, *The Military Balance*; all editions from 1960–1 to 1970–1; C. G. Jacobson, *Soviet Strategy Soviet Foreign Policy* (Glasgow, Maclehose, 1972); Robert S. McNamara, 'Statement of Secretary of Defense Robert S. McNamara before a Joint Session of the Senate Armed Services Committee and the Senate Subcommittee on Department of Defense Appropriations on

the Fiscal Year 1966–70 Defense Program and the 1966 Defense Budget' (declassified) (Washington, D.C., U.S. Department of Defense, 1965); Mark E. Miller, *Soviet Strategic Power and Doctrine: The Quest for Superiority* (New York, Advanced International Institute, 1982); Scientific American, *Progress in Arms Control?* (San Francisco, Freeman, 1979); Stockholm International Peace Research Institute, 1976, *Armaments and Disarmament in the Nuclear Age* (Cambridge, Mass., MIT Press, 1976); Edward L. Warner, *The Military in Contemporary Soviet Politics: An Institutional Analysis* (New York, Praeger, 1977).

12 Encounters with Khrushchev

FRANK K. ROBERTS

I have read with great interest the many scholarly studies in this volume on Khrushchev and his times and, as someone who worked closely with Khrushchev, having previously worked with Stalin and Molotov at the end of the war, I am grateful for this opportunity to complete the picture with some personal touches. I was recently given a similar opportunity to add my personal contribution to a University of Wales series of studies on the foreign policy of the Labour government from 1945 to 1951, mainly therefore on Ernest Bevin's record as Foreign Secretary in the immediate post-war years. While Somerset and the TUC on the one hand, and the borderlands between Russia and the Ukraine and Stalin's Communist Party on the other, provided very different backgrounds, and while I would not want to carry the comparison too far, either in terms of political morality or of far-sighted wisdom, there was something these two men had in common, a deep earthy humanity and sense of humour, an intense curiosity in events and people, a sort of peasant cunning most valuable for political infighting at home and abroad, knowledge based on self-education stemming, as Bevin once put it to King George VI, from the hedgerows of experience, and last but not least a capacity to learn and move with the times. At all events, as Ambassador I found Nikita Khrushchev as stimulating and exciting in an adversarial relationship as I had found Ernest Bevin as a Chief, when I was his Private Secretary. I recall Bevin telling me once that he did not recognise in himself – as Foreign Secretary, bearing his heavy responsibilities with care – the rumbustious, explosive and often bullying and quarrelsome trade-union leader of his youth. I am sure that Khrushchev must often have compared his role as a responsible international leader and the introducer of major and by Soviet standards liberal improvements in the lot of the Soviet population with his early days as a young favourite of Stalin, building the Moscow Metro and then disciplining the Ukraine by rough-and-ready Stalinist methods. Another thing the two men had in common was great self-confidence and what Bevin called a 'strong ego'. Bevin once described himself as 'a turn-up in a million'; Khrushchev was equally exceptional in communist Russia.

Of course, the conditions in which Khrushchev worked were entirely different. In the early years after the Revolution there had been many Soviet leaders rich in personality and temperament. They had all disappeared in Stalin's purges, to be replaced by the colourless apparatchiks he terrorised. In his memoirs, and even in his secret speech denouncing Stalin's methods, Khrushchev admitted that he himself had followed the pattern of obedience required for survival at Stalin's court, and, as he typically put it, had danced the *gopak* when ordered to do so. But he had somehow retained an ebullient personality of his own quite distinct from the dull prevailing norm. Perhaps he owed this – and maybe his very survival as well – to his absence from Moscow as Gauleiter of the Ukraine for long years before, during and after the war. This may also have encouraged his obvious self-reliance, so different from the obsequious drabness of other members of Stalin's ruling circle, even including men of greater seniority or importance than Khrushchev, such as Beria, Malenkov and Molotov, who had been a colleague of Lenin and Stalin in 1917.

Khrushchev's long absence from Moscow had another important effect. Being out of sight he was also safely out of mind as a potential successor to Stalin in the immediate post-war years. When I was first in Moscow in 1939 and later in 1941, at Yalta in February 1945 and immediately after that Minister in Moscow until the autumn of 1947 or again in Moscow as British representative in the Berlin blocade negotiations in the summer of 1948, I do not recall seeing Khrushchev at any of the many Kremlin dinners and receptions hosted by Stalin and attended by other members of the Politburo. Zhdanov on the one hand, and the strange double act of Malenkov and Beria on the other, appeared to be the main contenders for the succession until Zhdanov's death in 1948. Nor do I recall ever hearing Khrushchev's name so much as mentioned in this context. So his rise to supreme power in the two years after Stalin's death at the expense of better-educated and apparently better-equipped rivals came as a surprise and had much in common with Stalin's own rise to the top after

Lenin's death. Behind his bluff and genial manner he was a good organiser and a cunning intriguer with strong roots in the Communist Party institutions which, unlike Malenkov then and Kosygin later, he regarded as the true source of political power. With all his innovations and brainwaves, he always regarded himself first and foremost as a loyal Party man.

My first direct contact with Khrushchev came when I was Ambassador in Yugoslavia at the time he made his expedition to Canossa in 1955 to persuade Tito to forgive and forget the breach made by Stalin in 1948. His behaviour then was typical of Khrushchev's approach to so many of the problems he thought he could solve. He started with a brainwave, calling for rapid action alien to the normal thought processes of his more plodding colleagues and running serious risks of failure and even humiliation, but which, if successful, could bring big dividends and realise important policy objectives. His impulsive handling of the situation was clumsy and counter-productive, but he then retrieved from the apparent wreck enough of his original purpose to justify the enterprise. On his arrival in Belgrade he had made a speech at the airport inviting the erring Yugoslav comrades back into the Communist Party fold, to which Tito had not even deigned to reply; Tito was prepared only for inter-state and not inter-party relations to be resumed. At the subsequent reception in the White Palace it was fascinating to observe the surprised disdain with which the elegant Yugoslav leaders and their ladies in Paris dresses resumed acquaintance after some years with Khrushchev and his colleagues in their bell-bottomed trousers and the disapproving amazement of the Soviet team at the 'capitalist' appearance of those who had once been their favourite and most zealous communist disciples. Yugoslav disdain was increased at Khrushchev's return reception, when he drank too much and had to be carried out between rows of diplomats and other guests on the arms of Tito and Ranković, with his feet sketching out the motions of walking without ever touching the ground. But the end result, although it fell short of the original objectives of luring Tito away from Western contacts and perhaps also from his new role as a leader of the non-aligned countries, but above all back into the Communist International Party structure, did ensure that Yugoslavia resumed inter-state relations and on many issues afterwards she leant to the Soviet side. This stood Khrushchev in good stead a year later at the time of the Hungarian uprising. The Yugoslav visit, coupled with the Austrian State Treaty, also persuaded the West that the Stalinist mould had been broken and that negotiation with Khrushchev could be worth while. On the negative side, as in so many of his subsequent initiatives, Khrushchev left his colleagues with an impression of risk-taking and unpredictability, coupled with some sense of national humiliation.

Khrushchev then turned to globe-trotting in a big way in complete contrast to Stalin, who as leader had never left the Soviet Union with the one exception of the Tehran Conference, which took place, however, in war-time occupied territory. Khrushchev was always an eager and a curious 'tourist', visiting London and other Western capitals in fairly rapid succession, resuming summitry at Geneva in 1955 and eventually penetrating, to his huge delight, into the USA itself with well publicised visits to Hollywood and studies of US maize production. Although hardly an easy guest and one with a prickly inferiority complex, he everywhere left the impression of a not unattractive and human personality with a quick wit and a good if rather broad sense of humour. These trips served not only to satisfy his great natural curiosity and to enable him to pick up for himself tips for improving living conditions at home, but also were part of a continuing process of self-education.

More important for Soviet foreign policy were Khrushchev's visits to Third World countries, where he had considerable initial success in drawing many of the biggest among them, India, Indonesia and Egypt, into a closer and more sympathetic relationship with the Soviet Union than anything ever attempted by Stalin. In all this he set out consciously to weaken Western influence as much as to increase that of the Soviet Union. India has probably provided the most enduring of these relationships, admittedly cemented later by common worries over China and on India's side by US support for Pakistan. But the most striking was that with Egypt under Nasser, where Khrushchev proudly took credit for the Aswan Dam and, with little or no justification, for frustrating the Suez adventure of France and Britain in 1956. Khrushchev moved on to court Nkrumah and the leaders of newly independent countries in West Africa. Three of them, Nkumrah himself, Sekou Touré of Guinea and Modiba Keita of Mali, were invited to Moscow in my time as Ambassador in the early 1960s and treated as honorary members of the communist family. Even more important in its consequences was Khrushchev's support for Castro's Cuba, although she was to become a rather independent, expensive and burdensome addition to the communist bloc. Vietnam was equally welcome, but also demanding and burdensome as a Soviet ally in Asia. Both, however, became militant Soviet surrogates in spreading communist influence, even by military intervention, without direct Soviet involvement. For Khrushchev each was something of a problem child, but always available for action against the Soviet Union's main adversaries, whether the USA or China.

This expansion of Soviet influence in the Third World, which owed so much to Khrushchev's personal initiatives, was carried out under the slogan of aiding 'national liberation movements' and on the principle that peaceful coexistence with the West did not extend to ideological neutrality nor geographically to areas beyond the defined limits of the NATO–Warsaw Pact confrontation. It was very much a development of Lenin's blueprint for ensuring the victory of communism over the 'capitalist' West by a route which was intended to lead to Paris via Shanghai, Calcutta and Cairo. It reflected Khrushchev's greatly increased self-confidence after the Soviet Union had launched the first man in space, Gagarin, in the Sputnik in 1961. I have never seen him more pleased with himself and with his country than at his reception of Gagarin at Moscow Airport and at the subsequent Kremlin reception. It was at this time that he coined the slogan that the Soviet Union should not only catch up with, but also overtake the USA following upon the misunderstood quip that the Soviet Union would see the US buried (not bury her itself). The Moscow wits were wiser when they commented that, while catching up was all right, there should be no overtaking, since this would only enable the Americans to see the patches on the seats of Russian trousers.

In all this hectic international activity there was the usual Khrushchev mixture of bright ideas, rash and uncoordinated execution, and attempts to achieve irreconcilable objectives. His not unsuccessful wooing of the West with the Austrian State Treaty (1955) and the reconciliation with Yugoslavia was put at risk by the ruthless repression of the Hungarians in Budapest. His policy of peaceful coexistence with the USA in the NATO area was called in question by his support of Cuba and by his actions throughout the Third World. Later he brought the world to what seemed to many the brink of nuclear war in the Cuba Missile Crisis of 1962 following on the Berlin Wall crisis of 1961, both of which I experienced in Moscow. And all his undoubted successes in the Third World were in effect nullified by the loss of China as the Soviet Union's main ally, a loss due very largely to Mao's disapproval of Khrushchev's character and policies. And yet this bull in a china shop, apparently oblivious of traditional Russian attitudes of care and caution, was in fact so well aware of the fundamental change in international relations created by the existence of nuclear weapons that he modified what had been a basic Marxist–Leninist doctrine on the inevitability of war in achieving the eventual destruction of capitalism and put his own new ideological precepts into practice in opposition to Mao's more traditional concept that although millions might perish in such a war, this could be accepted because the victory of communism would be the end result.

Khrushchev's fascination with international affairs and with the world outside the Soviet Union and the communist bloc did not distract him from the home front, on which he left an even greater mark. When I reached Moscow in the autumn of 1960 after twelve years' absence, Khrushchev had been dominant for five years, after effectively disposing first of Beria in 1953 and then of Malenkov as Prime Minister in 1955, and finally getting rid of him with Molotov and Kaganovich in 1957. Marshal Zhukov, to whom he owed this hard-won victory, fared no better and disappeared from power shortly afterwards. All these rivals, like Khrushchev himself in 1964, were however sent into a comfortable retirement and, with the solitary exception of Beria in 1953, there were no executions nor even imprisonments. Indeed at one time there were more former Prime Ministers living on their pensions in the Soviet Union than there were living former Prime Ministers in the UK. Khrushchev, in agreement with his colleagues, had decided to make this complete and welcome break with Stalinist practice. Khrushchev was determined that the Soviet people should also benefit. Stalin's prisoners were brought back in their millions from the Gulags of Siberia, more attention was given to housing, however rough and ready, and to increasing, however inadequately, the provision of consumer goods. He recognised that he was often sacrificing quality to quantity, but argued that this was inevitable in such a vast and urgent enterprise. The fear of KGB arrests with a knock on the door at night was removed, although the possibility was still there, and writers and other artists enjoyed relative freedom tempered from time to time by bursts of explosive criticism. Khrushchev's own views on the arts were orthodox and conservative, which made for 'stop–go' policies, but he tolerated and even supported Solzhenitsyn's writings and, with much back-tracking, allowed exhibitions of modern abstract art, far removed from Soviet realism. Above all, Stalin's harsh disipline in factories and other places of work was relaxed. And contact between Soviet citizens and foreigners, including even diplomats, became somewhat easier.

So it was to a very different and more agreeable Moscow life that I returned in 1960, as compared with that I had experienced under Stalin in the 1940s. Delegation after delegation of British and other Western 'experts' in all fields, including nuclear and other scientists, doctors and businessmen, came to Moscow, each such visit providing contacts with their Soviet opposite numbers who poured into the British and other embassies to a gratifying if at times embarrassing degree.

Khrushchev set the tone himself by attending parties and receptions continually, whether as host or guest, dragging his colleagues along with him like a *corps de ballet* behind the prima ballerina. On these occasions he singled out Western Ambassadors and foreign non-communists for special attention. He was also readily available for more serious discussions in his Kremlin office with diplomats and well-known foreign visitors. An Ambassador in Moscow saw much more of him than would be seen by diplomats of a Western head of government. These meetings were never dull, although they could on occasions be stormy. I will recall some of them to give the flavour of the man.

At one Kremlin reception I had been warned beforehand that he had just made a speech elsewhere rather insulting to the British and I intended to be very cold with him. He at once singled me out and in full view of the assembled guests was demonstratively friendly, saying that he often said things he should not and his remarks should not always be taken too seriously, going on to give me a bear-hug when I had asked him in the course of a long conversation whether bears were still to be found in central Russia and ending with several toasts in brandy, which he was at that time under strict doctor's orders not to drink. On another occasion I had arrived at his office with a message from Harold Macmillan, which I said I would just leave with him to consider and return later for his reply. He insisted, however, that I must stay, because no one ever saw him for less than an hour. If I left at once his staff would think our countries were going to war. He would not, however, even open the envelope until after I had left and meanwhile we might have a general conversation, for example on books we had each been reading. It emerged that he was in the middle of *War and Peace*, which he tried to reread every year and from which he quoted long passages, as I afterwards checked, with great accuracy. When it was my turn and I mentioned Turgenev's *Sportsman's Sketches*, he at once showed his familiarity with it. I have rarely passed a more surprising or a more agreeable hour.

But these meetings could be less agreeable. Just before the building of the Berlin Wall in 1961 (of which we in Moscow had no advance warning) he took me aside at a reception to inform me that a certain General who had 'put down the Budapest rising' in 1956 had been appointed to command the Soviet troops around Berlin. When I failed to react with what he considered appropriate concern, he suddenly warned me that he could destroy Britain with eight nuclear bombs. But when I retorted that while six should be enough for a relatively small island, twenty of his major cities could then be destroyed by British nuclear weapons, he calmed down and again sent for drinks with which to toast each other. Another occasion in 1961 before the Berlin Wall at the opening performance of our Royal Ballet at the Bolshoi Theatre, my wife and I were sent for to sup with him and several of his colleagues, not to talk about Margot Fonteyn and our dancers (who were not invited to this supper) but to impress upon me the importance of finding a solution to the crisis he had himself created over Berlin; he could not tolerate this bone in his throat any longer, but was offering us a way out in the substitution of a United Nations presence for that of the three Western powers.

I recall above all my farewell talk with Khrushchev just after he had climbed down in the Cuba Missile Crisis of 1962. I knew he was exhausted and expected that for once my time with him would be short. Exhausted he certainly was, but as he talked his batteries were recharged and he kept me for two hours to talk about Germany, which was to be my next post. He himself was then hoping to visit West Germany for the first time, having of course visited East Germany many times. There were none of the usual attacks upon German militarism and revanchism, but instead a most objective review of German virtues and failings, with the emphasis upon the virtues and upon how much Russians had learnt from Germans in the past.

Returning to the home front and to broader issues than my own personal encounters with Khrushchev, I often asked myself how he had come to adopt his relatively liberal policies. I think he must have been influenced by his own family, which included as a son-in-law the brilliant Adzhubei (then editor of *Izvestiya*). He saw that this third and well-educated generation of Soviet citizens had to be handled in a different way from the uneducated peasants, whom Stalin had brought from their villages into factories, and that coercion and repression were not the best way to achieve results. He must also have been influenced by what he saw abroad. He was not of course consistent in his 'liberalism' and the Orthodox Church suffered more under Khrushchev than it had under Stalin at all events since the Great Patriotic War, when Stalin had been clever enough to realise the value of Russian national traditions.

Khrushchev was as rash and impulsive in the way he educated his major internal policies as in his international actions, even when he was broadly right in his general approach, as over de-Stalinisation, agricultural reforms or military policies. His secret speech exposing Stalin was a high-risk operation, but one without which it would have been difficult, if not impossible, for him to transform the climate of Soviet society in the way he did. But he does not seem to have realised the extent to which he was undermining the very foundations of Communist Party authority at home and abroad, nor the threat this represented to his colleagues in the Politburo and the Central Committee and to the whole *nomenklatura*, who like himself, had been appointed by and worked without protest under Stalin. So he had to back-track to a considerable extent and never carried the message in the secret speech through to its logical conclusion. Nor perhaps was it ever his intention to do so. He remained himself an orthodox and unrestructured communist, changing few of the institutions and principles of Soviet society and concentrating instead upon trying to work the system more effectively and humanely. In this his approach does not seem to have differed much from that followed so far by the current 'reforming' leader, Gorbachev.

An even more serious problem, which can only be touched upon here, was Khrushchev's new approach to national defence. Realising as he did the increasing importance of nuclear weapons, in which the Soviet Union was at that time very much behind the USA, he drew the exaggerated conclusion that conventional arms, for example surface ships, were relatively useless and that less should be spent on them. Such policies involved him in trouble with large sections of the Soviet military establishment, a group which had not hitherto dominated the Soviet political set-up and least of all the Party, but which Soviet leaders since Khrushchev have found it prudent to live on good terms. Looking back upon our two years in Moscow under Khrushchev, from the autumn of 1960 to the autumn of 1962, I find myself recalling mainly the improvements in the living conditions of the Soviet people, at all events in Moscow and the greater cities, the much greater opportunities for contact with Russians from Khrushchev downwards, the interest in following Khrushchev's hectic activity at home and abroad, and other more agreeable features of diplomatic life in the Soviet Union as compared with my earlier service there in the mid-1940s. But this picture requires retouching, since these two years were also those of the two most serious crises in East–West relations since the Berlin blockade of 1948 and the Korean War of 1950, the Berlin Wall of 1961 and the Cuban Missile Crisis of 1962, and also those of the breach between the Soviet Union and China. And it was the same genial, human and 'liberal' reformer, Nikita Khrushchev, who was personally responsible for each of them, for the resulting dangerous international tension, more especially over the Cuban Missile Crisis and for the eventual loss of Soviet prestige and influence in each case.

The breach with China was also mainly his doing, although there was never much love lost between the Russians and the Chinese. As a diplomat in Moscow I only caught glimpses from time to time of the growing tension with China. The rare foreign travellers via Nakhodka or Vladivostok in the Far East brought back stories that the quarrel with China was a frequent topic of conversation there and the more numerous foreign visitors to Irkutsk, Tashkent or Alma Ata in central Asia heard it more frequently mentioned. But it was not until well into 1961 that I had direct evidence myself in the reaction of the Rector of Moscow University to a question I put to him about his Chinese students at an Embassy party for our own British students. He described them with a mixture of respect and alarm as so dedicated and hardworking with no time for drinking or other student pleasures that they reminded him of Russian students in the Revolutionary years and, as he concluded 'were we not dangerous then?' I had better, however, concentrate upon Khrushchev's handling of the Berlin and Cuban crises, in which I was more closely involved. They were each as typical of his methods as my first example of his visit to Yugoslavia in 1955 or for that matter of his handling of de-Stalinisation, agricultural reform or even the arts on the home front.

The second Berlin crisis was by Khrushchev's standards a long-drawn-out affair. It had begun in 1958, when I was still at NATO, with a mixture of threats against the Western air routes and would-be tempting offers of a new solution to the Berlin problem which would relieve the Western powers of their burdensome responsibilities, while offering a special position for Berlin and Berliners under UN auspices. Khrushchev understood that he would fail, as Stalin had in 1948, if he relied on threats alone. He resorted instead to tactics combining the carrot and the stick. He was rightly convinced that from his point of view and of course that of his satellite, the GDR, he must do something to stop the increasing flow to the West of East Germans with the best qualifications. He wrongly thought that the Western protecting powers would be glad to get themselves off their Berlim hook and that they might therefore be tempted to accept his alternative UN presence, more especially if they were also reminded from time to time that their air communications could be endangered or interrupted. Another of his threats was to tear up existing quadripartite agreements on Berlin and to sign a new Treaty with the GDR, giving it full sovereign rights throughout Berlin. Of the Western allies, de Gaulle refused to negotiate at all over Allied rights in Berlin and it was left to the US Ambassador, Tommy Thompson, who got on very well personally with Khrushchev, as did the West German Ambassador, Kroll, to conduct some very difficult negotiations. When Khrushchev finally realised in 1961 that he could not succeed by agreement with the Western allies and decided that it would be too dangerous to carry out his threat to transfer to the GDR existing Soviet rights and responsibilities under long-standing quadripartite agreements, he resorted to the Berlin Wall, in many ways a humiliating confession of the failure of communist society, but also the most effective way to stop the flow of East Germans to the West. So he achieved his original objective, not at all in the way he had intended, by a method which involved considerable risk and amounted to a public confession of the shortcomings of the communist way of life in Eastern Europe. On the positive side, he confirmed that the Western powers, over Berlin in 1961, as over Budapest in 1956, had no intention of moving against the Soviet Union within Soviet-controlled territory.

Cuba was an even better example of Khrushchev's rashness and readiness to run very serious risks, combined with skill in achieving important results even from another miscalculation and another humiliating climbdown. The origins of the Cuban crisis went back a year or two. The Russians had been surprised by Castro's successful take-over and at first did not know what to make of this self-confident and independent leader, who was not at that time even a Communist Party member. But after the unsuccessful US attempt to get rid of him in the Bay of Pigs fiasco of 1961 Khrushchev supported Cuba at considerable expense as a thorn in the US side and Castro became a fellow Communist. The development of this relationship also became closely involved with one of Khrushchev's main concerns, the Superpower nuclear balance, and with his personal assessment of Kennedy. At their first meeting in Vienna in 1961 and, having the Bay of Pigs in mind, he underrated him as a young man lacking experience. After the Berlin and Cuban crises had been surmounted his assessment changed and by the time of Kennedy's assassination, he admired and even regretted him. But the initial wrong assessment had encouraged him to take considerable risks in Berlin and later in Cuba.

Khrushchev's approach to the Cuba problem was double-pronged. On the one hand he wanted to deter the Americans from attempting a second and this time successful Bay of Pigs aggression against Castro, which would have shown up the Soviet Union's inability to protect its new Cuban satellite. On the other hand, he wanted to use the direct threat to the USA of Soviet nuclear weapons in Cuba as a means of removing US nuclear weapons then threatening the Soviet Union from Italy and Turkey. He certainly expected and indeed wanted the Americans to discover that Soviet missiles had been deployed in Cuba. Although I know of no direct evidence to confirm this, I think myself that he wanted the whole matter, missiles in Cuba, Turkey and Italy, to be taken to the UN, where he could have made another major appearance to argue the case for removing any such nuclear threat from the Soviet Union as well as from the USA. But any such scheme was frustrated by the unexpected US threat to use their superior naval power and local advantage to stop his ships at sea and insistence upon his missiles being removed unilaterally from Cuba without any compensating deal on US missiles in Europe. It was clear to me in Moscow that this US response had taken the Russians completely by surprise and exposed their naval weakness. Also, because of Penkovsky's revelations, we and the Americans knew how few missiles the Russians then had relative to those of the Americans and the Russians knew that we knew this. Khrushchev had never intended that his Cuban adventure should involve any risk of war. There was no hint in Moscow of preparing the Soviet population for any emergency. Indeed the first news of the crisis for the Soviet people was the publication of an exchange of messages between Bertrand Russell and Khrushchev on the Thursday of the last crisis week in which Khrushchev came out firmly for a peaceful solution. This was accompanied by news that at the height of the crisis he had taken his Politburo colleagues to a performance of *Boris Godunov* to hear an American singer in the title role at a time when Kennedy was closeted with his advisers in a series of 24-hour vigils. But even then he played with fire, possibly on the insistence of his colleagues, by following up his first message to Kennedy agreeing to remove the missiles with a second referring to his demands for the removal of US missiles from Italy and Turkey. In Moscow during that crisis week we were in a calm at the centre of the typhoon. It was abundantly clear that nuclear war would not erupt by Soviet intention, despite Khrushchev's entire responsibility for creating the scenario. The only and at one moment serious risk was that of a misunderstanding at the US end as a result of this second message, which the Kennedy brothers wisely decided to ignore, so leaving Khrushchev a way out of his self-created predicament. But then Khrushchev yet again saved much of his original purpose from the disaster, by obtaining from Washington an undertaking not to attack Cuba.

In his memoirs Khrushchev therefore claims, and with some justification, that the results of both the Berlin and Cuba crises were successes for his policy of safeguarding his East German and Cuba protégés. But in each case, and particularly over Cuba, he had come too near to disaster for the comfort of his more cautious colleagues in the Politburo. His rashness and unpredictability in these matters, as earlier at home over de-Stalinisation and agricultural reforms, and with the communist bloc over China, had strained their confidence too far. Within little more than a year they succeeded in replacing him by the much less brilliant but safer Brezhnev. It then became clear that, while Khrushchev had improved many of its practices, he had not basically changed the Soviet system, as it had been created by Lenin and remoulded by Stalin, and which still survives today under Gorbachev.

Looking back upon my contacts with Khrushchev there come to mind at once his inimitable conversational style, larded with Russian proverbs, personal experiences, funny if often dirty stories, sweeping assertions, improbable threats, sudden and usually calculated outbursts, alternating with considerable and disarming charm and down-to-earth *ad hominem* practical arguments, his constant and rather obvious searching for the effect he was making on his interlocutor, his insatiable curiosity about the world outside the communist countries and his realisation that in the nuclear age new methods of living and even working together had to be found between East and West, at all events until the time was ripe for plucking capitalist plums from the tree. But this did not prevent him from embarking upon more provocative policies than Stalin would ever have countenanced in the Third World, nor deter him from high-risk policies over Berlin and Cuba. He remained the captive of his upbringing and of his surroundings. Even in his memoirs, when recounting Stalin's crimes he also recorded his continuing admiration for Stalin as a statesman and the builder of Soviet communist society after Lenin's death.

Khrushchev often reminded me of the driver of an autocar too big and heavy for his skills, too often pressing his foot down on the accelerator around dangerous bends and too often having jerkily to apply the brakes. He lacked Stalin's basic caution, so much closer to Russian traditional policies, and embarked confidently upon adventurous courses with attractive options without seeing clearly where they might lead him. When the risks became too great, he had to beat hasty retreats, usually skilfully conducted, but finally trying too far the nerves and patience of his colleagues. Nor did he acquire the confident support of the Soviet population, despite all he had done to free them from Stalin's tyranny. They instinctively felt his behaviour was not that expected of a Russian leader. Worst of all he lost respect by showing himself 'uncultured' (*nekulturny*) – a terrible reproach – as for example, in the shoe-slapping episode at the UN. However, for me he remains a man who, despite mixed motives, often confused thinking, despite the fact that as a convinced communist his aims were in no sense well-disposed to the western democracies or to erring members of his own communist community, did bring some fresh air into Stalin's hot-house Soviet Union, did make life less dangerous and unpredictable and somewhat more comfortable for most people in the Soviet Union and did bring to the continuing East–West confrontation a more open and almost frank approach and above all the conviction that nuclear war must be avoided. Last but not least, from my point of view as a former Ambassador in Moscow, he was a most accessible, communicative, human and stimulating leader, however adversarial, with whom to do business.

Bibliography

Abel, Elie. *The Missile Crisis* (New York, Lippincott, 1966).

Amann, R. and J. M. Cooper (eds), *Industrial Innovation in the Soviet Union* (New Haven, Conn., and London, Yale University Press, 1982).

Anderson, J., 'A Historical-Geographical Perspective on Khrushchev's Corn Program', in J. F. Karcz (ed.), *Soviet and East European Agriculture* (Berkeley, Calif. University of California Press, 1967).

Ascherson, N. *The Polish August: What Happened in Poland* (Harmondsworth, Penguin Books, 1981).

Barabashev, G. V. and O. E. Kutafin. *Osnovy znaniy o Sovetskom gosudarstve i prave* (Moscow, 1977).

Baras, Victor. 'Beria's Fall and Ulbricht's Survival', *Soviet Studies*, 2 (1975).

Batkaev, R. A. and V. I. Markov. *Differentsiatsiya zarabotnoi platy v promyshlennosti v SSSR* (Moscow, 1964).

Belyaev, E. A. *KPSS i organitzatsiya nauki v SSSR* (Moscow, 1982).

Belyaev, E. A. and N. S. Pyshkova. *Formirovanie i razvitie seti nauchnykh uchrezhdenii SSSR* (Moscow, 1979).

Berman, Robert P. and John C. Baker. *Soviet Strategic Forces* (Washington, D.C., Brookings Institution, 1982).

Bialer, Seweryn. *Stalin's Successors: Leadership, Stability and Change in the Soviet Union* (Cambridge, Cambridge University Press, 1980).

Bialer, Seweryn (ed.), *The Domestic Context of Soviet Foreign Policy* (Boulder, Colo., Westview Press, 1981).

Borodina, S. D. and I. P. Fursov *Deyatelnost KPSS po povysheniyu blagosostoyaniya trudyashchikhsya v period razvitogo sotsializma* (Moscow, 1983).

Bradley, M. and M. G. Clark. 'Supervision and Efficiency in Socialised Agriculture', *Soviet Studies*, 1 (1972).

Breslauer, George W. 'Khrushchev Reconsidered', *Problems of Communism*, 5 (1976).

Breslauer, George W. *Khrushchev and Brezhnev as Leaders*: Building Authority in Soviet Politics (London, Allen & Unwin, 1982).

Brown, Archie and Michael Kaser (eds), *Soviet Policy for the 1980s* (London, Macmillan, 1982).

Brown, Emily Clark. *Soviet Trade Unions and Labor Relations* (Cambridge, Mass., Harvard University Press, 1966).

Brown, J. F. *The New Eastern Europe: The Khrushchev Era* (New York, Praeger, 1966).

Brown, J. F. *Bulgaria under Communist Rule* (New York, Praeger, 1970).

Brus, W. *Socialist Ownership and Political Systems* (London, Routledge & Kegan Paul, 1975).

Brzezinski, Z. K. *The Soviet Bloc: Unity and Conflict* (Cambridge, Mass., Harvard University Press, 1967).

Bulganin, N. A. *O zadachakh po dalneishemu podemu promyshlennosti, tekhnicheskomu progressu i uluchsheniyu organizatsii proizvodstva* (Moscow, 1955).

Butenko, A. P. *Sotsializm kak obshchestvennyi stroi* (Moscow, 1974).

Butler, W. E. *Soviet Law* (London, Butterworth, 1983).

Calvert, Peter. 'The Institutionalisation of the Mexican Revolution', *Journal of Inter-American Studies*, **4** (1969).

Chkhikvadze, V. M. *KPSS i Sovetskoe gosudarstvo i pravo* (Moscow, 1984).

Chotiner, Barbara Ann. 'Institutional Innovation under Khrushchev: The Case of the 1962 Reorganization of the Communist Party', *Soviet Union/Union Sovietique*, **2** (1982).

Churchward, L. G. 'To Divide or Not to Divide?', *Soviet Studies*, **1** (1965).

Churchward, L. G. *Contemporary Soviet Government*, 2nd ed. (London, Routledge & Kegan Paul, 1975).

Clark, M. G. 'Soviet Agricultural Policy', in H. Shaffer (ed.), *Soviet Agriculture* (New York, Praeger, 1977).

Clissold, Stephen (ed.), *Soviet Relations with Latin America 1918–1968* (London, Oxford University Press, 1970).

Clissold, Stephen (ed.), *Yugoslavia and the Soviet Union 1939–73* (London, Oxford University Press, 1975).

Cohen, Stephen F., Alexander Rabinowitch and Robert Sharlet (eds), *The Soviet Union since Stalin* (London, Macmillan, 1980).

Collard, D., *et al.*, *Income Distribution: The Limits of Redistribution* (Bristol, Scientechnica, 1980).

Crankshaw, Edward. *Khrushchev* (London, Collins, 1966).

Davies, R. W. 'The Reappraisal of Industry', *Soviet Studies*, **1** (1956).

Dinerstein, H. S. *War and the Soviet Union* (New York, Praeger, 1962).

Dornberg, John. *Brezhnev: The Masks of Power* (London, Deutsch, 1974),

Dunham, Vera. *In Stalin's Time* (Cambridge, Cambridge University Press, 1979).

XX Sezd Kommunisticheskoi Partii Sovetskogo Soyuza Stenograficheskii otchet, 2 vols (Moscow, 1956).

XXII Sezd Kommunisticheskoi Partii Sovetskogo Soyuza Stenograficheskii otchet, 3 vols (Moscow, 1962).

Erickson, John. *Soviet Military Power* (London, RUSI, 1971).

Fainsod, Merle. 'Khrushchevism', in M. M. Drachkovitch (ed.), *Marxism in the Modern World* (Stanford, Calif. Stanford University Press, 1965a).

Fainsod, Merle. 'Khrushchevism in Retrospect', *Problems of Communism*, **1** (1965b).

Fakiolas, R. 'Problems of Labour Mobility in the USSR', *Soviet Studies*, **3** (1962).

Fehér, F. 'Kadarism as Applied Khrushchevism', in R. F. Miller and F.

Fehér (eds), *Khrushchev and the Communist World* (London, Croom Helm, 1984a).

Fehér, F. 'The Social Character of Khrushchevism: A Transition or a New Phase?', in R. F. Miller and F. Fehér (eds), *Khrushchev and the Communist World* (London, Croom Helm, 1984b).

Fehér, F. and A. Heller. *Hungary 1956 Revisited: The Message of a Revolution – A Quarter of a Century Later* (London, Allen & Unwin, 1983)

Fehér, F., A. Heller and G. Márkus. *Dictatorship over Needs* (Oxford, Basil Blackwell, 1983).

Feshbach, Murray. 'Manpower in the USSR: A Survey of Recent Trends and Prospects', in *New Directions in the Soviet Economy*, part III (Washington, D.C., US. Congress, 1966).

Filtzer, Donald A. *Soviet Workers and Stalinist Industrialization: The Formation of Modern Soviet Production Relations 1928–1941* (London, Pluto, 1986).

Fischer-Galati, S. *The New Rumania from People's Democracy to Socialist Republic* (Cambridge, Mass., MIT Press, 1967).

Frankland, Mark. *Khrushchev* (Harmondsworth, Penguin Books, 1966).

Freedman, Lawrence. *U.S. Intelligence and the Soviet Strategic Threat* (London, Macmillan, 1977).

Friedgut, Theodore H. *Political Participation in the USSR* (Princeton, N.J., Princeton University Press, 1979).

Fry, M. G. and C. Rice. 'The Hungarian Crisis of 1956: the Soviet Decision', *Studies in Comparative Communism*, **1–2** (1983).

Garthoff, Raymond L. *Soviet Military Policy* (London, Faber & Faber, 1966).

Ghebhardt, Alexander O. 'Implications of Organizational and Bureaucratic Policy Models for Soviet ABM Decisionmaking' (unpublished Ph.D. dissertation, Columbia University, 1975).

Gilison, Jerome M. 'Khrushchev, Brezhnev, and Constitutional Reform', *Problems of Communism*, **5** (1972).

Gill, Graeme. 'Institutionalization and Revolution: Rules and the Soviet Political System', *Soviet Studies*, **2** (1985).

Gitelman, Z. 'The Diffusion of Political Innovation: From Eastern Europe to the Soviet Union', in R. Szpolruk (ed.), *The Influence of Eastern Europe and the Soviet West on the USSR* (New York, Praeger, 1975).

Gitelman, Z. 'The Politics of Socialist Restoration in Hungary and Czechoslovakia', *Comparative Politics*, **2** (1981).

Gliksman, Jerzy. 'Recent Trends in Soviet Labor Legislation', *Problems of Communism*, **4** (1956).

Golan, G. *The Czechoslovak Reform Movement: Communism in Crisis 1962–1968* (Cambridge, Cambridge University Press, 1971).

Goldman, M. I. *USSR in Crisis* (New York, Praeger, 1983).

Gosztony, Peter. *Die Rote Armee* (Munich, Fritz Molden, 1980).

Gosztony, Peter. 'Albania's Enver Hoxha and the Revolution', in B. K. Király, B. Lotze and N. F. Dreisziger (eds), *The First War between Socialist States: The Hungarian Revolution of 1956 and its Impact* (New York, Brooklyn College Press, 1984).

Granin, D. A. *Iskateli* (Leningrad, 1969).

Gustafson, Thane. *Reform in Soviet Politics Lessons of Recent Policies on Land and Water* (Cambridge, Cambridge University Press, 1981).

Hahn, W. G. *The Politics of Soviet Agriculture 1960–1970* (Baltimore, Md, Johns Hopkins University Press, 1972).

Hauslohner, Peter. 'Managing the Soviet Labor Market: Politics and Policies under Brezhnev' (unpublished Ph.D. dissertation, University of Michigan, 1984).

Hegel's Philosophy of Right, translated with notes by T. M. Knox (London, Oxford University Press, 1967).

Heikal, M. *The Sphinx and the Commissar* (New York, Harper & Row, 1978).

Hill, Ronald J. 'Participation in the Central Committee Plenums in Moldavia', *Soviet Studies*, 2 (1969).

Hill, Ronald J. *Soviet Political Elites: The Case of Tiraspol* (London, Martin Robertson, 1977).

Hill, Ronald J. *Soviet Politics, Political Science and Reform* (Oxford, Martin Robertson, 1980).

Hill, Ronald J. 'The "All-People's State" and "Devoloped Socialism" ', in Neil Harding (ed.), *The State in Socialist Society* (London, Macmillan, 1984).

Holloway, David. 'Foreign and Defence Policy', in Archie Brown and Michael Kaser (eds), *The Soviet Union since the Fall of Khrushchev* (New York, The Free Press, 1975).

Holloway, David, *The Soviet Union and the Arms Race* (New Haven, Conn., Yale University Press, 1983).

Horelick, Arnold L. and Myron Rush. *Strategic Power and Soviet Foreign Policy* (Chicago, University of Chicago Press, 1966).

Hough, Jerry F. *The Soviet Union and Social Science Theory* (Cambridge, Mass., Harvard University Press, 1977).

Hough, Jerry F. and Merle Fainsod. *How the Soviet Union is Governed* (Cambridge, Mass., Harvard University Press, 1979).

Hoxha, Enver. *The Khrushchevists: Memoirs* (Tirana, 1980).

Huntington, Samuel P. *Political Order in Changing Societies* (New Haven, Conn., Yale University Press, 1968).

Hutchins, R. L. *Soviet–East European Relations*: *Consolidation and Conflict 1968–1980* (Madison, Wisc., University of Wisconsin Press, 1983).

Jackson, M. R. 'Soviet Project and Design Organisations: A Study of Technological Decision-Making in a Command Economy' (unpublished Ph.D. dissertation, University of California, Berkeley, 1967).

Johnson, R. A. 'The Warsaw Pact: Soviet Military Policy in Eastern Europe', in S. M. Terry (ed.), *Soviet Policy in Eastern Europe* (New Haven, Conn., Yale University Press, 1984).

Jones, C. D. *Soviet Influence in Eastern Europe: Political Autonomy and the Warsaw Pact* (New York, Praeger, 1981).

Jones, C. D. 'National Armies and National Sovereignty', in David Holloway and J. M. O. Sharp (eds), *The Warsaw Pact*: *Alliance in Transition?* (London, Macmillan, 1984).

Jowitt, K. *Revolutionary Breakthroughs and National Development: The Case of Romania* (Berkeley, Calif., University of California Press, 1971).

Jowitt, K. 'Inclusion of Mobilization in European Communist Regimes', *World Politics*, **1** (1975).

Juviler, Peter H. *Revolutionary Law and Order: Politics and Social Change in the USSR* (New York, The Free Press, 1976).

Kanet, Roger. 'The Rise and Fall of the "All People's State": Recent Changes in Soviet Theory of the State', *Soviet Studies*, **1** (1968).

Kapitsa, P. L. *Teoriya, eksperiment, praktika* (Moscow, 1966).

Kapitsa, P. L. *Teoriya, eksperiment, praktika*, 3rd ed. (Moscow, 1984).

Karcz, J. F. 'Soviet Agricultural Policy 1953–1962', in J. F. Karcz, *The Economics of Communist Agriculture* (Bloomington, Ind., University of Indiana Press, 1979a).

Karcz, J. F. 'The New Soviet Agricultural Program', in J. F. Karcz, *The Economics of Communist Agriculture* (Bloomington, Ind., University of Indiana Press, 1979b).

Karcz, J. F. 'Seven Years on the Farm: Retrospect and Prospects', in J. F. Karcz, *The Economics of Communist Agriculture* (Bloomington, Ind., University of Indiana Press, 1979c).

Khrushchev, N. S. *Mir bez oruzhiya – Mir bez voin*, vol. 2 (Moscow, 1960).

Khrushchev, N. S. *O vneshnei Politike Sovetskogo Soyza*, vol. 2 (Moscow, 1961a).

Khrushchev, N. S. *Kommunizm: Mir i Schaste Narodov*, vol. 1 (Moscow, 1961b)

Khrushchev, N. S. *Predotvratit Voiny, Otstoyat Mir* (Moscow, 1963).

Khrushchev, N. S. *Khrushchev Remembers*, ed. Strobe Talbott (New York, Bantam Books, 1971).

Khrushchev, N. S. *Khrushchev Remembers: The Last Testament*, ed. Strobe Talbott (London, Deutsch, 1974).

Kirsch, Leonard J. *Soviet Wages: Changes in Structure and Administration since 1956* (Cambridge, Mass., MIT Press, 1972).

Kolkowicz, Roman. *The Soviet Military and the Communist Party* (Princeton, N.J., Princeton University Press, 1967).

Korbonski, A. 'The Revolution and East Central Europe', in B. K. Király, B. Lotze and N. F. Dreisziger (eds), *The First War between Socialist States: The Hungarian Revolution and its Impact* (New York, Brooklyn College Press, 1984a).

Korbonski, A. 'Soviet Policy toward Poland', in S. M. Terry (ed.), *Soviet Policy in Eastern Europe* (New Haven, Conn. Yale University Press, 1984b).

Kovrig, B. *Communism in Hungary: From Kun to Kádár* (Stanford, Calif., Hoover Institution Press, 1979).

KPSS o kulture, proveshchenii i nauke(Moscow, 1963).

KPSS v rezolyutsiyakh i resheniyakh sezdov, konferentsii i plenumov TsK, vol. 8 (Moscow, 1972).

Kusin, V. V. 'Dissent in Czechoslovakia', in J. Lefwich (ed.), *Dissent in Eastern Europe* (New York, Praeger, 1983).

Laird, Roy D. 'The Politics of Soviet Agriculture', in Roy D. Laird (ed.), *Soviet Agricultural and Peasant Affairs* (Kansas, University of Kansas Press, 1964).

Laird, Roy D. 'Khrushchev's Administrative Reforms in Agriculture: An

Appraisal', in J. F. Karcz (ed.), *Soviet and East European Agriculture* (Berkeley, Calif., University of California Press, 1967).

Lantsev, M. S. *Sotsialnoe obespechenie v SSSR* (Moscow, 1976).

Larrabee, F. S. 'Soviet Crisis Management in Eastern Europe', in David Holloway and J. M. O. Sharp (eds,) *The Warsaw Pact: Alliance in Transition?* (London, Macmillan, 1984).

Lendvai, Paul. *Eagles in Cobwebs: Nationalism and Communism in the Balkans* (London, Macdonald, 1969).

Lenin, V. I. *Collected Works*, 45 vols (Moscow, 1960–70).

Levesque, J. *The USSR and the Cuban Revolution* (New York, Praeger, 1978).

Liehm, A. J. 'The Intellectuals and the New Social Contract', *Telos*, **23** (1975).

Linden, Carl A. *Khrushchev and the Soviet Leadership* (Baltimore, Md, Johns Hopkins University Press, 1966).

Lowenhardt, J. *Decision Making in Soviet Politics* (London, Macmillan, 1982).

Lowenthal, Richard. 'Development vs. Utopia in Communist Policy', in C. Johnson (ed.), *Change in Communist Systems* (Stanford, Calif., Stanford University Press, 1970).

McAuley, Alastair. *Economic Welfare in the Soviet Union* (Madison, Wisc., Wisconsin University Press, 1979).

McAuley, Alastair. 'Social Policy', in Archie Brown and Michael Kaser (eds), *Soviet Policy for the 1980s* (London, Macmillan, 1982).

McAuley, Mary. *Labour Disputes in Soviet Russia 1957–1965* (London, Oxford University Press, 1969).

McAuley, Mary, *Politics and the Soviet Union* (Harmondsworth, 1977).

McCauley, Martin. *Khrushchev and the Development of Soviet Agriculture: The Virgin Lands Programme* (London, Macmillan, 1976).

McCauley, Martin *Marxism–Leninism in the German Democratic Republic: The Socialist Unity Party (SED)* (London, Macmillan, 1979).

MccGwire, Michael. 'The Rationale for the Development of Soviet Seapower', in John Baylis and Gerald Segal (eds), *Soviet Strategy* (London, Croom Helm, 1981).

Mackintosh, Malcolm. 'The Warsaw Treaty Organization: A History', in David Holloway and J. M. O. Sharp (eds), *The Warsaw Pact: Alliance in Transition?* (London, Macmillan, 1984).

Maevskii, S. A. *Gosudarstvennoe rukovodstvo teckhnicheskim progressom promyshlennosti v SSSR* (Moscow, 1962).

Marer, P. 'The Political Economy of Soviet Relations with Eastern Europe', in S. M. Terry (ed.), *Soviet Policy in Eastern Europe* (New Haven, Conn., Yale University Press, 1984).

Marx, Karl and Friedrich Engels. *Werke* (MEW) (Berlin, DDR, 1969–71).

Matthews, Mervyn. *Soviet Education* (London, Allen & Unwin, 1982).

Medvedev, Roy A. *Khrushchev* (Oxford, Basil Blackwell, 1982).

Medvedev, Roy A. and Zhores A. Medvedev. *Khrushchev: The Years in Power* (New York, Columbia University Press 1977).

Medvedev, Zhores A. *National Frontiers and International Scientific Co-operation* (Nottingham, 1975).

Medvedev, Zhores A. *Soviet Science* (Oxford, Oxford University Press, 1979).

Michnik, A. 'The New Evolutionism', *Survey*, **3–4** (1976).

Mićunović, V. *Moscow Diary* (New York, Doubleday, 1980).

Miller, John H. 'The Communist Party: Trends and Problems', in Archie Brown and Michael Kaser (eds), *Soviet Policy for the 1980s* (London, Macmillan, 1982).

Miller, R. F. and F. Fehér (eds), *Khrushchev and the Communist World* (London, Croom Helm, 1984).

Mlynář, Z. *Nightfrost in Prague: The End of Human Socialism* (New York, Karz, 1980).

Mlynář, Z. *Relative Stabilization of the Soviet System in the 1970s* (Cologne, Research Project Crises in Soviet–type Systems, 2) (1983).

Mlynář, Z. 'Khrushchev's Policies as a Forerunner in the Prague Spring', in R. F. Miller and F. Fehér (eds), *Khrushchev and the Communist World* (London, Croom Helm, 1984).

Montias, John Michael. *Economic Development in Communist Rumania* (Cambridge, Mass, Harvard University Press (1967).

Nagy, Imre. *On Communism: In Defence of the New Course* (New York, Praeger, 1957).

Narodnoe Khozyaistvo SSSR v 1961 godu (Moscow, 1962).

Narodnoe Khozyaistvo SSSR v 1964 godu (Moscow, 1965).

Narodnoe Khozyaistvo SSSR v 1967 godu (Moscow, 1968).

Narodnoe Khozyaistvo SSSR v 1922–1982 (Moscow, 1982).

Nekrich, A. M. 'The Socio-political Effects of Khrushchev: His Impact on Soviet Intellectual Life', in R. F. Miller and F. Fehér (eds), *Khrushchev and the Communist World* (London, Croom Helm, 1984).

Nemchenko, V. S. (ed.), *Sotsialno-ekonomicheskie voprosy organizatsii truda* (Moscow, 1974).

Noulting, L. *The Planning of Research, Development and Innovation in the USSR*, Foreign Economic Report 14 (Washington, D.C., G.P.O., 1978).

Nove, Alec. 'Incentives for Peasants and Administrators', in Roy D. Laird (ed.), *Soviet Agricultural and Peasant Affairs* (Kansas, University of Kansas Press, 1964).

Pálóczi-Horváth, G. *Khrushchev: The Road to Power* (London, Secker & Warburg, 1960).

Parrott, Bruce. *Politics and Technology in the Soviet Union* (Cambridge, Mass., MIT Press, 1983).

Pethybridge, Roger. *A Key to Soviet Politics: The Crisis of the 'Anti-Party' Group* (London, Allen & Unwin, 1962).

Plenum tsentralnogo komiteta kommunisticheskoi partii Sovetskogo Soyuza, 24–29 iyunya 1959 (Moscow, 1960).

Plenum tsentralnogo komiteta kommunisticheskoi partii Sovetskogo Soyuza, 19–23 noyabrya 1962 (Moscow, 1963).

Plenum tsentralnogo komiteta kommunisticheskoi partii Sovetskogo Soyuza, 9–13 dekabrya 1963 (Moscow, 1964).

Postanovleniya tsentralnogo komiteta KPSS i Soveta ministrov SSSR po voprosam promyshlennosti i stroitelstva (Moscow, 1956).

Problemy sovershenstvovaniya upravleniya nauchno-tekhnicheskim progressom (Moscow, 1975).

Rabkina, N. E. and N. M. Rimashevskaya. 'Raspredelitelnye otnosheniya i sotsialnoe razvitie', *EKO*, **5** (1978).

Radványi, Janoš. *Hungary and the Superpowers* (Stanford, Calif., Stanford University Press, 1972).

Radványi, Janoš. 'Introduction: The Hungarian Revolution and the Superpowers', in B. K. Király, B. Lotze and N. F. Dreisziger (eds), *The First War between Socialist States: The Hungarian Revolution of 1956 and its Impact* (New York, Brooklyn College Press, 1984).

Remington, R. A. *The Warsaw Pact: Cast Studies in Communist Conflict Resolution* (Cambridge, Mass., MIT Press, 1971).

Resheniya partii i pravitelstva po khozyaistvennym voprosam, vol. 5 (Moscow, 1968).

Rigby, T. H. 'The Soviet Leadership: Towards a Self-Stabilizing Oligarchy?', *Soviet Studies*, **4** (1970).

Rigby, T. H. 'A Conceptual Approach to Authority, Power and Policy in the Soviet Union', in T. H. Rigby, A. Brown and P. Reddaway (eds), *Authority, Power and Policy in the Soviet Union* (New York, St Martin's Press, 1980).

Royal Institution of International Affairs. *Documents on International Affairs, 1955* (Oxford, Oxford University Press, 1958).

Rupnik, J. 'Dissent in Poland, 1968–78: The End of Revisionism and the Rebirth of Civil Soviety', in R. F. Tökés (ed.), *Opposition in Eastern Europe* (London, Macmillan, 1979).

Rupnik, J. 'The Restoration of the Party-State in Czechoslovakia in 1968', in Leslie Holmes (ed.), *The Withering Away of the State? Party and State under Communism* (London, Sage, 1981).

Salisbury, Harrison E. *Khrushchev's* Mein Kampf, *with Background by Harrison E. Salisbury* (New York, Bantam Books, 1961).

Sarkisyan, G. S. and N. P. Kuznetsova. *Potrebnosti i dokhod semi* (Moscow, 1967).

Schapiro, Leonard (ed.), *The USSR and the Future: An Analysis of the New Program of the CPSU* (New York, Praeger, 1963).

Schöpflin, G. 'Opposition and Para-opposition Critical Currents in Hungary 1968–78', in R. L. Tökés (ed.), *Opposition in Eastern Europe* (London, Macmillan, 1979).

Schöpflin, G. 'The Political Structure of Eastern Europe as a Factor in Intra-bloc Relations', in Karen Dawisha and Philip Henson (eds.), *Soviet–East European Dilemmas: Coercion, Competition and Consent* (London, Heinemann, 1981).

Schöpflin, G. *Hungary between Prosperity and Crisis* (London, Institute for the Study of Conflict, 136, 1982).

Schöpflin, G. 'Leadership Options and the Hungarian Revolution', in B. K. Király, B. Lotze and N. F. Dreisziger (eds), *The First War between Socialist States: The Hungarian Revolution of 1956 and its Impact* (New York, Brooklyn College Press, 1984).

Schwarz, Solomon. *Labor in the Soviet Union* (New York, Praeger, 1952).

Selskoe Khozyaistvo SSSR (Moscow, 1960).

Service, R. J. 'The Road to the Twentieth Party Congress: An Analysis of the Events Surrounding the Central Committee Plenum of July 1953', *Soviet Studies*, 2 (1981).

Shafir, Michael. *Romania: Politics, Economics and Society Stagnation and Simulated Change* (London, Frances Pinter, 1985).

Siegalbaum, Lewis. 'Soviet Norm Determination in Theory and Practice', 1917–1941', *Soviet Studies*, 1 (1984).

Skilling, H. G. *Czechoslovakia's Interrupted Revolution* (Princeton, N.J., Princeton University Press, 1976).

Skilling, H. G. and V. Prečan (eds), 'Parallel Politics Essays in Czech and Slovak Samizdat', *International Journal of Politics*, XI (1981).

Slusser, Robert. *The Berlin Crisis of 1961* (Baltimore, Md, Johns Hopkins University Press, 1973).

Smith, G. A. E. 'The Industrial Problems of Soviet Agriculture', *Critique*, 14 (1981).

Sokolovsky, V. D. (ed.), *Voennaya Strategiya* (Moscow 1962).

Stent, A. E. 'Soviet Policy toward the German Democratic Republic', in S. M. Terry (ed.), *Soviet Policy in Eastern Europe* (New Haven, Conn., Yale University Press 1984).

Stepanyan, Ts. A. and A. S. Frish (eds), *Razvitoi sotsializm i aktualnye problemy nauchnogo kommunizma* (Moscow, 1979).

Strauss, Erich. *Soviet Agriculture in Perspective* (London, Allen & Unwin, 1969).

Swearer, H. R. 'Agricultural Administration under Khrushchev', in Roy D. Laird (ed.), *Soviet Agricultural and Peasant Affairs* (Kansas, Kansas University Press, 1964).

Tatu, M. *Power in the Kremlin from Khrushchev to Kosygin* (New York, Viking Press, 1968).

Terry, S. M. 'Theories of Social Development in Soviet–East European Relations', in S. M. Terry (ed.), *Soviet Policy in Eastern Europe* (New Haven, Conn. Yale University Press, 1984).

Tismaneanu, V. 'Ceausescu's Socialism', *Problems of Communism*, 1 (1985).

Touraine, A., *et al. Solidarity: Poland 1980–81* (Cambridge, Cambridge University Press, 1983).

Triska, J. F. (ed.). *Soviet Communism: Programs and Rules Lenin–Khrushchev 1961–1952–1919* (San Francisco, Calif., Chandler, 1962).

Ustavy Akademii nauk SSSR 1724–1974 (Moscow, 1974).

Vajda, M. *The State and Socialism: Political Essays* (London, Allison & Busby, 1981).

Valenta, Jiri. *Soviet Intervention in Czechoslovakia 1968: Anatomy of a Decision* (Baltimore, Md, Johns Hopkins University Press, 1979).

Valenta, Jiri. 'Soviet Decision Making and the Hungarian Revolution', in B. K. Király, B. Lotze and N. F. Dreisziger (eds), *The First War between Socialist States: The Hungarian Revolution of 1956 and its Impact* (New York, Brooklyn College Press, 1984a).

Valenta, Jiri. 'Soviet Policy Toward Hungary and Czechoslovakia', in S. M. Terry (ed.), *Soviet Policy in Eastern Europe* (New Haven, Conn., Yale University Press, 1984b).

Vali, F. *Rift and Revolt in Hungary: Nationalism versus Communism* (Cambridge, Mass., Harvard University Press, 1961).

van den Berg, G. P. *Organisation und Arbeitsweise der sowjetischen Regierung* (Baden-Baden, Nomos, 1984).

Vneocherednoi XXI sezd Kommunisticheskoi Partii Sovetskogo Soyuza: Stenograficheskii otchet, 2 vols (Moscow, 1959).

Volgyes, I. ' "Never Again '56!" Cooptation, Privatization and Terror in Hungarian Society since the Revolution', in B. K. Király, B. Lotze and N. F. Dreisziger (eds), *The First War between Socialist States: The Hungarian Revolution of 1956 and its Impact* (New York, Brooklyn College Press, 1984).

Volin, L. *A Century of Russian Agriculture* (Cambridge, Mass., Harvard University Press, 1970).

Vsesoyuznoe soveshchanie nauchnykh rabotnikov v Kremle 12–14 iyunya 1961 g. Stenogrammy, materialy (Moscow, 1961).

Vucinich, A. *Empire of Knowledge: The Academy of Sciences of the USSR* (Berkeley, Calif., University of California Press, 1984).

Wädekin, K.-E. *The Private Sector in Soviet Agriculture* (Berkeley, Calif. University of California Press, 1973).

Winning the Cold War: The US Ideological Offensive (Washington, D.C., G.P.O., 1965).

Wolfe, Thomas W. *Soviet Strategy at the Crossroads* (Cambridge, Mass., Harvard University Press, 1964).

Wolfe, Thomas W. *Soviet Power and Europe 1945–70* (Baltimore, Md, Johns Hopkins University Press, 1970).

Yanowitch, Murray. *Work in the Soviet Union* (New York, M. E. Sharpe, 1985).

Zaleski, E., *et al. Science Policy in the USSR* (Paris, 1969).

Zinner, Paul (ed.) *National Communism and Popular Revolt in Eastern Europe: A Selection of Documents on Events in Poland and Hungary* (New York, Columbia University Press, 1957).

Zinner, Paul *Revolution in Hungary* (New York, Columbia University Press, 1962).

Index